COLLECTOR'S ENCYCLOPEDIA OF

# Cookie JARS

### BOOK II

## Fred Roerig
## and
## Joyce Herndon Roerig

COLLECTOR BOOKS
*A Division of Schroeder Publishing Co., Inc.*

The current values in this book should be used only as a guide. They are not intended to set prices, which vary from one section of the country to another. Auction prices as well as dealer prices vary greatly and are affected by condition as well as demand. Neither the Authors nor the Publisher assumes responsibility for any losses that might be incurred as a result of consulting this guide.

# Searching for a Publisher?

We are always looking for knowledgeable people considered to be experts within their fields. If you feel that there is a real need for a book on your collectible subject and have a large comprehensive collection, contact us.

COLLECTOR BOOKS
P.O. Box 3009
Paducah, Kentucky 42002-3009

Cover design: Beth Summers
Book design: Pamela Shumaker
Cover photo: Bill Bone, Walterboro, S.C.

Printed by IMAGE GRAPHICS, INC., Paducah, Kentucky

# Dedication

When we published our first cookie jar book, we hoped it would be a success. What better proof of that than a beautiful little boy with an endearing smile and a sparkle in his eyes as he flips through it, page after page, time and time again, giving special attention to the cookie jars most easily recognized by a two-year-old. The page containing the California Originals Sesame Street characters is well-worn with Scotch tape supporting the tears. The damage came from loving use, not malicious mischief at the hands of a toddler.

Our grandson has been a joyous and refreshing inspiration in our never-ending odyssey of collecting. So, it is with much love that we dedicate this second book to Herndon Joseph Roerig.

Ma and Poppy

# Acknowledgments

It is hard to capsulize gratitude. The response to Book II has been overwhelming. We simply have so many photos, and offers of photos, some are being held for Book III. It is amazing how much incentive and encouragement is gained from positive comments. As an added indicator, we have chosen to identify the jars contributed by other collectors and dealers. The last name of the contributor is the final notation in the descriptive text after marks, etc. This should eliminate the guesswork of trying to figure out who owns which jar. Any jar without a contributor's name is from our own personal collection. The index of contributing consultants, collectors, and dealers lists the full names and addresses of the participants.

Much of the factual documentation would not be available without the help of pottery giants such as Don Winton of Twin Winton; Bruce Levin of Treasure Craft; William Bailey of California Originals; William Lenaburg of Sierra Vista and Hondo Ceramics; Charles and Mary Allen of The American Bisque Company, Harold Roman of Roman Ceramics, Cumberland Ware, and California Originals; and Melinda Shaw Avery of Metlox. Each and every one has generously given of his/her time, helping to record their personal contributions to American pottery. Myths surrounding Starnes, Sierra Vista, and Maurice Ceramics have been removed, and additional jars have been identified, thanks to the California potters. We hope that seeing more facts available to collectors will help encourage others to contribute for future volumes.

Paula Herndon Polk, English teacher extraordinaire and my patient friend, deserves a "gold" star for her stamina. I think she had the hardest job – it's hard to teach an old dog new tricks! Thanks to Apple Computers, Inc. for inventing user-friendly computers (the rule above also applies here). Thanks to Harvey Duke, Jack Chipman, Pam Curran, Duane and Janice Vanderbilt, and Jim and Bev Mangus for your willingness to share each and every time you come across documentation that you feel could be important to cookie jar collectors.

A special thank-you goes to the Collector Books family: Bill and Meredith Schroeder, Billy Schroeder, Lisa Stroup, Pamela Shumaker, plus all of the "behind the scenes" employees that make it possible to extend our cookie jar passion through **the** publishing house, Collector Books, a division of Schroeder Publishing.

# Introduction

Since the release of *The Collector's Encyclopedia of Cookie Jars, Book I* in December of 1990, we have witnessed amazing growth in the popularity of cookie jars as a collectible and investment. Many of the jars we love, but have taken for granted, have become, to our amazement highly, coveted. As prices rise, the stage is set for both negative and positive effects. Positive growth encompasses talented artisans putting their ideas into tangible form. Most of these originals are being produced as limited editions. Major corporations have seen the light; cookie jars sell, thus, an influx of new commercial jars is hitting the market. What educated general collector can pass up a licensed Disney jar, such as *Bull Dog Cafe*? They did. It was discontinued after one year's production, immediately setting the procrastinators in search of the jar before it became public knowledge that the jar was discontinued. We probably will not see the ceiling on new jar prices in our lifetime, but, in our opinion, any Walt Disney jar is, or will become, collectible. For that matter, any licensed character should become collectible in varying degrees. The English-distributed *Homer Simpson* jar was brought into the United States in a limited quantity before being discontinued. Production numbers are not always a contributing factor in the value of cookie jars. The *Woody Woodpecker* head, produced in Taiwan and marked "© 1967 Walter Lantz" and which sold circa 1988 through the Home Shopper's Network for eighteen dollars, was most surely produced in large numbers. In many instances copyright dates are mistaken for production dates and can be a confusing factor in placing value.

A major negative factor is the prominent role reproductions are beginning to play. The average collector will never be able to own every cookie jar example he/she desires, encouraging a few to capitalize on the market. There is nothing wrong with a well-executed reproduction, if it is marked, priced fairly, and accurately represented. There will always be reproductions, and rumors of reproductions. As prices rise, so does the temptation to "cash in." At least eleven of the original Brush cookie jar molds that were sold at auction when Brush was dispersed have surfaced. The molds of which we are aware are *Old Shoe, Donkey and Cart, Panda, Humpty Dumpty with Beanie and Bow Tie, Granny, Elephant (AKA Ice Cream Cone Elephant), Chick and Nest, Puppy Police, Sitting Pig, Covered Wagon*, and, of course, the *Hillbilly Frog*. The jars re-issued from these molds are larger than the original Brush jars and employ the perfect medium for an authentically sized reproduction, or a ready cash crop. Experience is the best teacher in detecting new from old. No matter how astute the modern potter, one will never be able to effectively duplicate the old hues and finish. Why should he/she want to? One manufacturer of reproductions stresses that his product is the same size as the original. Again, why? A reproduction is just that, a reproduction. Why distort the image by "stretching" it in order to say his/her product is the same size as the original?

It is our intention to pass our knowledge along to cookie jar enthusiasts. We have no intention of glorifying any company or individual's product. We strive to accurately document the history of cookie jars, lightening the load for tomorrow's authors and researchers.

# Hints to Collectors

Consider your options. Cookie jars are rapidly becoming a limited commodity. Pottery can chip, crack, and break, but not stretch, to fill voids in collections. Each collection is unique in its own right. No matter how small, there is, undoubtedly, at least one jar any seasoned collector could cry for. Price is a major factor to consider. We would love to have a Lincoln Continental but we drive a Ford. This most certainly does not kill our dream or stop us from collecting. One-half or more of the collecting fun is in the chase. We all have cringed at the price of certain jars we felt we had to have. Our biggest extravagance to date is the Metlox *Scrub Woman*. We paid a high, but fair, price considering today's market. We have waited many years to own her, long before we knew she was Metlox.

The scale was balanced with *Swee' Pea*. We longed for this little fellow no less than ten years before receiving a call from a friend telling us he was going up for auction in South Carolina. Unbelievably, we survived a tense week between the call and the auction. We dreaded the trip for fear every attendee would be after "our" jar. The result, good things come to those who wait. You must make the decision what you can and will pay for a jar. What is the privilege of ownership worth to you?

Be careful of reputed one-of-a-kind jars. This is an easy statement to make, but not so easy to substantiate. While working with Regal China on the creation of *Cookie Jarrin's Little Angel* we learned that the original or "waste" mold can produce five to six pieces before losing sharp detail. It is our understanding it was common practice among potteries to pour at least five jars for color samples, etc., before making production decisions. It is possible that only one jar survived the ages, but we do not know that for sure.

Be careful of assuming anything or taking for granted that something is just because.... For years, we, as collectors, assumed the illusive *Dem Cookies Mammy* said "Shor am good" on the back side of the jar. Two "Dem Cookies Sho Got Dat Vitamin A" have recently surfaced, one yellow with under-glaze decoration and one in plain aqua glaze. The feeling among seasoned McCoy collectors is that this is the original *Dem Cookies Mammy*. Two examples have surfaced. Are there more?

To err is human, to forgive divine. We omitted the "©, Walt Disney, Productions" mark found just above *Thumper's* tail. There is some minor confusion whether Thumper is *Thumper*, or just a "wannabe." He is a licensed Disney product believed to have been produced by American Pottery. On the other hand, the Terrace Ceramics version is called *Chipmunk* and is not a Disney product. That is the beauty of encyclopedias and general price guides; volumes can be added along. No cookie jar book will ever be complete, nor will any text on a limited subject contain everything produced from the first to the last. Each and every collector has something to add; we are all just beginning to learn.

Reproductions, re-issues, and commemoratives are not new. Re-issues of Abingdon jars are everywhere. Just because they have the Abingdon serial number impressed into the jar does not make them Abingdon. It is a known fact that Hager and Pidgeon each purchased some of the Abingdon molds. We were fortunate in finding a *Hobby Horse* with the "Pidgeon Vitrified China" label still intact. This alone will not make each and every jar found without the Abingdon stamp a Pidgeon. It is too easy to assume. As long as there is money to be made, these facsimiles are not going to go away. The most important factor continues to be proper identification.

A relatively new option to collectors is restoration. The wonderful old jars cannot be replaced, but they can be restored. Again, we have rights. The wrong comes into play when a restored item is sold as not having been restored. There is nothing wrong with restoration in itself.

Tasteful re-painting is another option. As prices rise, so does temptation. Legitimate re-painting does not include altering the original. The American Bisque "star" jars are excellent examples. These jars were never issued as black-skinned jars, no matter what the facial features might suggest. Some that have been skillfully airbrushed to provide authenticity are surfacing. Shawnee jars with new gold and decals applied to old jars have been appearing. Be careful where you buy; choose reputable markets and dealers willing to stand behind their word. Avoid auctions that are not buyer friendly. If they refuse to tell you the origin of a large collection or refuse inspection before the sale, be wary.

To sum it up, consider all of your options. There is nothing wrong with buying a reproduction, a re-issue, or commemorative jar if it is *your* choice. There is nothing wrong with restoring or repainting jars, if you *knowingly* make that choice. Do not believe *everything* you read or everything you hear. Be leery of the over-used term *one-of-a-kind*. You be the judge; make your own choices. Buy what you like; enjoy all aspects of collecting. Try net-working, making friends all across the country; you will never regret forming a *true* friendship. It you discover something factual, such as a label on a previously unidentified jar, share your knowledge where it will count. If you follow these few guidelines, you will never tire of this wonderful hobby. It can only enrich your life.

# A Little Company

The charm and wit so evident in the work of Michael Buonaiuto and Shelley Tincher Buonaiuto have attracted collectors from all over the United States. Not surprisingly, their cookie jars, which demonstrate so much heart and expression, come from their experiences in life rather than from Shelley's formal training as an etcher and painter or Michael's as an architect and sculptor, and the places they have known since leaving art school at the University of Massachusetts.

A few years after leaving art school, they joined a group in Warwick, New York known as the "Chardavogne Barn" that followed the teachings of Gurdjieff, a Greek Caucasian spiritual master. The twelve years spent at the "Barn" proved to be a major influence on their lives. It was at the Barn in 1971 that Shelley first began working in clay making Crèche figures for the group store. In time she began drawing upon ideas from the life around them. Living close to two dairy farms, Shelley became interested in cows and realized their shape would make a wonderful butter dish. The cow butter dish was to become her first earthenware piece.

While at the Barn they met Edmund, a neighboring farmer who became their beloved friend. Because Edmund always carried a cookie in his pocket, he was the inspiration for the *Edmund* cookie jar.

Contributing his skill as a sculptor and his knowledge of casting and molding Michael joined Shelley at work in the pottery in 1975. Today, collaborating on their earthenware pieces, Shelley creates the masters, and Michael is reponsible for the molding and casting. Michael and Shelley guide the painting of their employees, and encourage them to use their own imaginations.

Original ideas for the often humorous, whimsical, and/or stylized pieces coming from a wide range of experiences, people, and places belong to both Michael and Shelley.

According to Michael Buonaiuto, after leaving New York they spent seven months traveling with their children through South America before settling in Sante Fe. Friends have told them their experiences in South America have influenced their work. Ideas for pieces may come originally from a specific person or place, but they see the personality of the final piece as being more universal.

The *Two Lovers* (Italian couple) cookie jar, for instance, is not of two specific lovers, but a stylized expression of all lovers. They feel that is why this piece is appealing to so many different people.

Whatever draws the collector to Michael and Shelley's work – the humor, their stylized, sculptural forms, the bright lively colors, or their whimsical and often loving expression of the universal human heart – their work, in the words of one collector, "fills the soul."

**Row 1:**  *Pegapuss*, a winged feline, 13" long. "A Little Co 1992 ©."  $110.00+
 *Small Pig*, 7½" high. "A Little Co. 1992 ©."  $90.00+

**Row 2:**  *Medium Pig*, 9" at highest point. Supnick. "A Little Co 1992 ©."  $100.00+
 *Large Pig*, 10" high. "A Little Co 1992."  $110.00+

**Row 1:**   *David,* "A Little Co. © 1992." David, a friend of the Buonaiutos in New York, is an accomplished photographer, professor, and a generally jovial fellow. Photos taken of David in his children's swimming pool became the foundation for a series of sculptural studies. The resulting image comes across as a modern day Hotei, or Buddha, with facial features that adapt equally well to white or black skin tones. The t-shirt is available with your choice of a stock logo or one of your own design. *David* is a very large jar standing 19" tall which leaves ample room for cookies.                                                                $160.00+

   *Edmund,* "A Little Co. ©1992," 19" tall.                                        $140.00+

**Row 2:**   *Italian Couple*, "A Little Co. 1991©," 12" tall. Supnick.                 $140.00+

   *Blanket Couple*, "A Little Co.© 87," 12" tall. Supnick.                       $130.00+

The measurements given on the jars created by A Little Company are strictly a close approximation. The measuring of cookie jars is not an exact science. No two jars are exactly the same size even when produced by the same company.

**Row 1:**    *Smile*, "A Little Co 1991©." Supnick.                                                $120.00+

*Earth Goddess*, "A Little Co 1991©." Beads and a wrap-around skirt were additions suggested by Leonard Davis, a New York clothing designer and collector of Black Americana.    $120.00+

*Diva*, "A Little Co 1991 ©." Since the appearance of *Diva* in the October 1990 edition of *Good Housekeeping*, Michael and Shelley have received numerous requests from collectors of Black Americana requesting that *Diva* be painted as an African-American.    $120.00+

**Row 2:**    *Fats*, a 1992 limited edition. The left shoulder rises, just slightly, as if in search of that elusive note. Standing 3" tall, he is wearing a fired gold ring and cufflinks, in addition to the gold accents highlighting the piano. Two hundred and fifty signed, numbered, and dated pieces are being produced. "A Little Co 1992 ©, #12 of 250."    $160.00+

*Stella*, the mate to *Fats*, is a limited edition of 250. Returning to the 1940's, this thick-walled earthenware jar is 15" tall. She wears a fired gold bracelet, earrings, and a flower. The silver microphone and cord have also been kiln-fired. "A Little Co 1992 © #12 of 250."    $160.00+

Shelley says "I never knew any of the women who inspired the original *Black Mammy* cookie jar, and the African-Americans I know are teachers, artists, musicians, parents, and friends. I want to respond to a multi-cultural and multi-racial world focusing upon the charm and dignity of individuals and sometimes the warmth of people in relationships."

**Row 1:**  *Grandma with Child*, 13" tall and designed to work as either a black or
white figure. A limited edition of 100 was introduced in 1992.          $140.00+

*Bride*, discontinued, "A Little Co © 87."          $120.00+

*Woman with Scarf*, 11" tall with the lid opening in the middle of the scarf.
She is available only with African-American skin tones. This limited edition
of 100 was introduced in 1992. "A Little Co, 11 of 100, 1992 ©."          $120.00+

**Row 2:**  *Sugar Blues*, inspired by the Blues Shelley listened to while working.
Hoping to catch something of a person who deeply understands the
emotional source of the Blues, and who is able to transcend it with his
music, Shelley researched the traditional dress and took particular care
with expression. Bits of gold set off the bi-colored guitar and one tooth.
*Sugar Blues*, 15½" high, is a limited edition of 150 pieces which was introduced to collectors and music lovers in 1992. "A Little Co 1992 © 18/150."          $160.00+

*The Secret* is 11" high and designed to be either two white women, two
black women, or a black and a white together, in a limited edition of 150.
"A Little Co 1992 © 11/150."          $160.00+

The measurements of all cookie jars, including the ones from A Little Company, are an approximation
and are never exact. Cookie jars originate from molds rather than being stamped out or cloned.

# Abingdon
## with
### "The clear ring of fine china"

For extensive coverage of Abingdon cookie jars, consult Book I. Page seven shows one example of a decorated *Hippo* and a *Pumpkin* made from an Abingdon mold but not produced at Abingdon.

**Row 3:**  *Hippo*, has impressed "549" on the lid and base, as well as "Abingdon
U.S.A." stamped in block form under the glaze. Snyder.          $250.00+

*Pumpkin*, "674" with "Abingdon U.S.A." under glaze.          $325.00+

*Hippo Bar Jar*, "549" impressed into the lid and on the bottom of the
base. The "Abingdon U.S.A." stamp confirms the authenticity of this jar.          $350.00+

The Black Americana version of Abingdon's Little Old Lady #471 can be found as a reproduction. Hope-
fully, all are marked and properly identified as reproductions.

# Advertising

Today more and more companies have begun to see the value of using cookie jars as an advertising medium to enhance their product. Cookie jar collectors and advertising buffs seek each and every example from dog bones to real estate to add to their expanding collections. Since the release of Book I, many different and exciting examples have surfaced – some old, some new, and some from our neighboring country, Canada.

**Row 1:**    *Milk Bone Dog Biscuits*, "Roman, Made in Thailand," paper label.    $50.00-60.00

*Pepperidge Farm Ginger Man*, "Pepperidge Farm® Old Fashioned Ginger Man Cookies–Pepperidge Farm cookies contain no artificial flavor or preservatives" on one side. "Pepperidge Farm® Old Fashioned Chocolate Chip Cookies – Pepperidge Farm cookies contain no artificial flavor or preservatives" on opposite side.    $35.00-45.00

*Colonial Home*, "Williamsburg Real Estate © 1980 Licensee Enesco Imports - Made in Japan."    $40.00-50.00

**Row 2:**    *Famous Amos*, "Treasure Craft © Made in USA." Braly.    $40.00-50.00

*Chip it*, the Canadian chocolate chip. "RD Nabisco Brands LTD 1983, ENR Nabisco Brands LTEE 1983." Braly.    $60.00-80.00

*Campbell's Kid* "© 1990 Campbell Soup Company - Campbell's red and white label and The Campbell Kids are trademarks of the Campbell Soup Co. used under license by Westwood International" on box. "Made in Taiwan" paper label.    $25.00-35.00

**Row 3:**    *Little Debbie Snack Cakes*, glass canister.    $20.00-25.00

*Mr. Peanut*, range-size salt or pepper shaker licensed and distributed by Benjamin & Medwin of New York, New York. "© 1990 PLS, Made in Taiwan" on paper label.    Set, $20.00-25.00

*Mr. Peanut* cookie jar, also from Benjamin & Medwin. "© 1990 PLC, Made in Taiwan." on paper label.    $50.00-60.00

*Delicious Cookies* milk can. "Delicious Cookies, Made in Taiwan ROC " on paper label.    Set, $30.00-40.00

**Below:** *Mr. Peanut* catalog sheet from Benjamin & Medwin. All items are discontinued.

| | | |
|---|---|---|
| Item #95003 - Tool Holder | $20.00-25.00 |
| Item #95001 - Cookie Jar | $50.00-60.00 |
| Item #95002 - Bank | $20.00-25.00 |
| Item #95006 - Napkin Holder | $20.00-25.00 |
| Item #95035 - Peanut Bowl | $15.00-20.00 |
| Item #95005 - Spoon Rest | $15.00-18.00 |
| Item #95004 - Range Size Salt & Pepper | $20.00-25.00 |
| Item #95022 - Magnet | $3.00-5.00 |

**Row 1:** *Avon Panda Bear,* with heart-shaped decal permanently fired onto one
paw giving new dimension to McCoy's *Upside-down Panda.* "210 USA."    $75.00-85.00

*Big Boy Hamburger* shaker was designed, modeled, and produced by
Kathy Wolfe in 1991 for Elias Brothers' Big Boy Restaurant in a limited
edition of 1000 pairs.    Set, $25.00-35.00

*Big Boy* cookie jar offered by Elias Brothers of Warren, MI, as a limited
edition of 250 pieces in 1992. Just as soon as word leaked this jar was
available, the entire edition sold. The cookie jar is also a Wolfe original.    $250.00+

*Big Boy* shaker, the mate to the *Big Boy Hamburger* on the left.    Set, $25.00-35.00

*Mohawk Indian* reproduction. Book I features the original jar which was
produced by American Bisque. "G, 1 of 200." Snyder.    $150.00-155.00

**Row 2:** *Edy's Grand Ice Cream,* unmarked. Snyder.    $40.00-50.00

*Eddie Bauer Bear,* paper label, "MADE IN JAPAN FOR Eddie Bauer (in
script)®." Stamped "OUTDOOR•OUTFITTER SINCE 1920. Eddie Bauer (in
script) Made in Japan" on paper label. Wooldridge.    $45.00-55.00

*Dreyer's Grand Ice Cream,* unmarked. Snyder.    $40.00-50.00

**Row 3:** *Romper Room* "DO-BEE, E-2200" stamped on bottom. "Laurel Sales Cleveland,
OH. Romper Room© DO-BEE, Made in Japan," on paper label. Snyder.    $175.00-200.00

*Century 21,* "©Century 21 Real Estate Corp. 1978, Made in USA," incised
into the bottom of the base. This is the newer version. Notice the words
"Real Estate" are no longer included on the sign. 1978 is the copyright
date, not the production date. Snyder.    $250.00+

*Pepperidge Farm Distinctive Milano Cookies,* "No 1 in a Series 400-P" incised
into the bottom of the base. Snyder.    $75.00-85.00

**Below:** *Rondec T Pinocchio,* "Rondec T" across back. Rondec is a manufacturer of children's medications. Early in the 1960's they introduced a trial run of vitamins
labeled Rondec "T" that was not well received and soon discontinued.    $55.00-65.00

*Grandma's Cookies,* with "Monmouth, Ill USA" impressed within the maple
leaf logo of Monmouth Pottery.    $40.00-50.00

*M & M Cookie Jar,* "©M & M Mars Inc. 1982" on the lower back of the base.
Produced by Haeger.    $55.00-65.00

**Row 1:** *Harley-Davidson Gas Tank* cookie jar, made in Taiwan.      $75.00-95.00

*Harley-Davidson Gas Pump* creamer, "© 1990 Harley-Davidson, Inc."
stamped onto bottom.      Set, $30.00-40.00

*Harley-Davidson Gas Tank* covered sugar. "© 1990 Harley-Davidson,
Inc." stamped onto bottom.      Set, $30.00-40.00

*RSO Bull* bearing the logo of the RSO recording company. The gift tag
hanging from the collar says "RSO" on one side and "Season's Greetings
1978 from the RSO Family" on the other. RSO is short for the Robert
Stigwood Organization. Mr. Stigwood managed, among others, the Bee
Gees and Andy Gibb. He worked for Atlantic Records until 1976 when
he left to start his own company and record distribution network for
the BeeGees. RSO is most famous for the theme music in *Sergeant Pepper's
Lonely Hearts Club Band* and *Saturday Night Fever*.      $200.00-250.00

**Row 2:** *Harley Hog* bank, stamped "Reproduction of a 1935 Model Year Gas Tank
Design." Snyder.      $35.00-45.00

*Harley Hog* bank, unmarked Haeger. Snyder.      $15.00-20.00

*Harley Hog* bank, unmarked. Snyder.      $25.00-30.00

*Harley Hog* cookie jar, "© 1984 HD." McCoy.      $300.00+

**Row 3:** *President's Choice Cookies*, from Canada, unmarked.      $50.00-65.00

*Shedd's Spread Butter Tub*, unmarked.      $30.00-35.00

*Aramis* ¾ LBS., "Aramis, Made in USA."      $15.00-20.00

*Florida Bear*, though unmarked, we feel certain it must be an import. All states
should have a cookie jar as a representation (i.e., New York, the Statue of Liberty).      $35.00-45.00

**Below:** *Elmer the Borden Bull* covered sugar by F & F Mold and Die Works of Dayton,
Ohio. "F & F."      Sugar and Creamer Set, $50.00-75.00

*Famous Amos* cookie bank, "Treasure Craft, Made in USA." Braly.      $20.00-30.00

*Famous Amos* cookie jar, "Treasure Craft © Made in USA." Snyder.      $40.00-50.00

*Elsie the Borden Cow* creamer by F & F Mold and Die Works, Dayton, Ohio,
"F & F."      Sugar and Creamer Set, $50.00-75.00

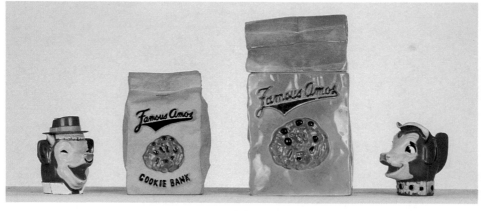

**Row 1:**   *Stag Beer* bean pot or snack container. "West Bend USA."   $15.00-20.00

*Mrs. Fields* cookie sack produced for the Salt Lake City, Utah-based bakery. This earthenware container for cookies is so realistic we almost passed it by while strolling through a Charleston mall. "Made in Taiwan" paper label.   $25.00-35.00

*Tony the Tiger* plastic container. As Tony would say, "It's g-r-r-r-eat!" "© Kellogg Co. 1968."   $65.00-75.00

**Row 2:**   *Maurice Lenell Cookies,* unmarked.   $30.00-40.00

*Entenmann's Chef*, "Made in USA." To date we are unable to identify this wonderful jar.   $400.00+

*Keith* jar, also fondly known as the *Little Keith* jar is a limited edition of 250 in the likeness of C. Keith Lytle, of Antioch, CA. Keith, dba Cookie Jar Antiques, joined forces with his friend and business associate, antique show promoter Don Wirfs. The jar was molded and designed by an unknown Oklahoma City, OK, artist and decorated by ceramist Carol Gifford. "Carol Gifford original, Made exclusively for Cookie Jar Antiques and Don Wirfs and Associates 1990. CG 3/250" incised into base.   150.00+

**Row 3:**   *Frookie Cookies*, "R W Frookie®" on back. Made in Taiwan.   $35.00-45.00

*Liv-R-Snaps®* dog, one of three different, yet similar, jars produced for Alpo. "USA." On back of collar, "LIV-R-SNAPS®."   $50.00-60.00

*Black Label* bean pot or snack jar. "West Bend USA."   $15.00-20.00

*Alpo* dog. "USA ALPO DAN THE DOG."   $50.00-60.00

**Below:**   *Alpo* dog, "USA ALPO DAN THE DOG."   $50.00-60.00

*Liv-R-Snaps* dog. "USA" on bottom. "LIV-R-SNAPS®" on back of collar.   $50.00-60.00

*Liv-R-Snaps* dog. "B & B – PA USA" on glazed bottom of base. "LIV-R-SNAPS®" on the back of the collar.   $50.00-60.00

A subscriber of *Exclusively Shawnee*, March 1992, contributed to readers that the *ALPO* dog with the totally flat unglazed bottom is considered a McCoy. We have attempted numerous times to contact major corporations in regard to production of these limited items. Very little cooperation has ever been received.

Benjamin & Medwin is a New York-based importer and distributor that offered all the licensed items featured on this page.

**Row 1:**  *Pillsbury Dough Boy and Girl* salt and pepper shakers, small.                          $10.00-12.00

*Pillsbury Dough Boy* bank. "© 1988 The Pillsbury Company."                          $18.00-20.00

*Funfetti Dough Boy* shaker, "© 1992 TPC, Made in Taiwan" on paper label. Snyder.                          $15.00-20.00

*Pillsbury Dough Boy* cookie jar. "© 1988 The Pillsbury Company."                          $35.00-45.00

*Funfetti Cupcake* shaker, "© 1992 TPC, Made in Taiwan" on paper label. Snyder.                          $15.00-20.00

*Pillsbury Dough Boy and Girl* shakers, range size. "© 1988 TPC."                          $15.00-20.00

**Row 2:**  *Funfetti* utensil holder, "© 1992 The Pillsbury Company." Snyder.                          $18.00-20.00

*Funfetti* spoon rest, "© 1992, The Pillsbury Company." "Made in Taiwan" on paper label. Snyder.                          $12.00-15.00

*Funfetti* cookie jar, "© 1992, The Pillsbury Company," "Made in Taiwan " paper label. Snyder.                          $35.00-45.00

*Pillsbury Dough Boy* utensil holder, "© 1988 The Pillsbury Company."                          $18.00-20.00

*Funfetti* napkin holder, "© 1992, TPC, Made in Taiwan," paper label. Snyder.                          $15.00-20.00

**Row 3:**  *Blue Bonnet Sue* bank "© 1989 Nabisco."                          $18.00-20.00

*Ernie the Keebler Elf* cookie jar. "© 1989 Keebler Company."                          $35.00-45.00

*Blue Bonnet Sue* cookie jar. "© 1989 Nabisco."                          $35.00-45.00

*Blue Bonnet Sue* tub butter holder. "© 1989 Nabisco."                          $18.00-20.00

**Below:**  *Chip*, "Chip by F & F - Wally Amos ®, © 1991 Christine Harris Amos." "F & F Korea" on paper label.                          $55.00-65.00

*Snausages Barking Dog®,* "© 1991 THE QUAKER OATS COMPANY, MANUFACTURED IN CHINA."                          $50.00-60.00

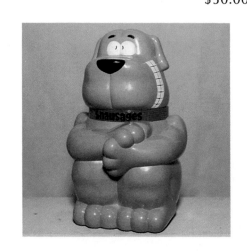

The *Jazz'e Junque* cookie jar below is a replica of the Chicago, IL, based business modeled and produced by Kathy Wolfe of West Bloomfield, MI. Limited to 100 pieces, this jar was offered to collectors in 1993.

Jazz'e Junque's proprietor Mercedes DiRenzo established Chicago's first cookie jar shop in 1989. She has worked tirelessly to promote cookie jars through any and all mediums, including appearances on the *Oprah Winfrey* show, *Wild Chicago*, Channel 2 and Channel 5 news in Chicago. She is featured in the 1993 summer edition of *Home Decorating Ideas*, numerous newspapers, and *North Shore* magazine.

Mercedes has rented cookie jars to *Nickelodeon*, a children's cable station. She sold Twentieth Century Fox the *Toy Soldier* visible in the kitchen scene of *Home Alone*. Columbia Studios rented fruits, vegetables, chefs, and pig cookie jars for the restaurant scene in *Ground Hog Day*, starring Bill Murray.

"JAZZ'E JUNQUE, Chicago's 1st Cookie Jar Shop" stamped on unglazed bottom. "KW, 3/100, 1993." $195.00-205.00

Front

Back

24

Actual scenes from *Ground Hog Day.*

*Little Green Sprout Catalog Sheet*

80001 – Little Green Sprout, tool holder.................................................................$15.00-20.00
80002 – Little Green Sprout, napkin holder..............................................................$10.00-15.00
80003 – Little Green Sprout, spoon rest .................................................................$8.00-12.00
80004 – Little Green Sprout, salt & pepper shakers..................................................$10.00-15.00
80005 – Little Green Sprout, scouring pad holder.....................................................$15.00-20.00
80010 – Little Green Sprout, magnet (set of 2) ........................................................$4.00-6.00
80007 – Little Green Sprout, scrubber set ...............................................................$15.00-20.00
80008 – Little Green Sprout, cookie jar ...................................................................$40.00-45.00
80009 – Little Green Sprout, planter.......................................................................$15.00-20.00

*Nabisco Blue Bonnet Sue Catalog Sheet*

92001 – Nabisco Blue Bonnet Sue, cookie jar.......................................................................$40.00-45.00
92002 – Nabisco Blue Bonnet Sue, bank...............................................................................$10.00-15.00
92003 – Nabisco Blue Bonnet Sue, tool holder.....................................................................$10.00-15.00
92005 – Nabisco Blue Bonnet Sue, spoon rest .....................................................................$8.00-12.00
92008 – Nabisco Blue Bonnet Sue, range set........................................................................$15.00-20.00
92017 – Nabisco Blue Bonnet Sue, scouring pad holder ......................................................$10.00-15.00
92022 – Nabisco Blue Bonnet Sue, magnet set......................................................................$4.00-6.00
92035 – Nabisco Blue Bonnet Sue, dinner bell......................................................................$10.00-12.00
92036 – Nabisco Blue Bonnet Sue, margarine holder............................................................$15.00-20.00

*Ernie the Keebler Elf Catalog Sheet*

93001 – Ernie the Keebler Elf, cookie jar.................................................................$40.00-45.00
93002 – Ernie the Keebler Elf, bank.........................................................................$10.00-15.00
93003 – Ernie the Keebler Elf, tool holder................................................................$10.00-15.00
93004 – Ernie the Keebler Elf, salt & pepper shakers................................................$10.00-15.00
93005 – Ernie the Keebler Elf, spoon rest ................................................................$8.00-12.00
93006 – Ernie the Keebler Elf, napkin holder.............................................................$10.00-15.00
93008 – Ernie the Keebler Elf, range set...................................................................$15.00-20.00
93029 – Ernie the Keebler Elf, planter......................................................................$15.00-20.00

*Pillsbury Dough Boy Catalog Sheet*

90008 – Pillsbury Dough Boy, range set................................................................$15.00-20.00
90009 – Pillsbury Dough Boy, towel holder boy ...................................................$10.00-15.00
90010 – Pillsbury Dough Boy, towel holder girl ....................................................$10.00-15.00
90011 – Pillsbury Dough Boy, soap dish boy ........................................................$10.00-12.00
90012 – Pillsbury Dough Boy, soap dish girl .........................................................$10.00-12.00
90014 – Pillsbury Dough Boy, cream & sugar .......................................................$15.00-20.00
90017 – Pillsbury Dough Boy, scouring pad holder ..............................................$10.00-15.00
90022 – Pillsbury Dough Boy, magnets (set) ............................................................$4.00-6.00
90026 – Pillsbury Dough Boy, scrubber set ..........................................................$15.00-20.00

# American Bisque

The American Bisque Company of Williamstown, WV, the all-around pottery company, was headed by A.N. Allen and active for approximately 60 years. American Bisque produced many top-dollar cookie jars which are eagerly sought by collectors today. New discoveries continue to surface–Will every jar American Bisque produced ever be found and accurately identified? A.N. Allen died in 1990 at the age of eighty-one years. His in-depth knowledge and expertise will no longer be available as a guide. Charles Allen, the son of A.N. Allen, states his father realized too late that he had been part of an important event, the creation of Americana.

| | | |
|---|---|---|
| **Row 1:** | *Churn*, a color variant of the *Churn* featured in Book I. "USA" Snyder. | $20.00-25.00 |
| | *Acorn* corner jar, marked "USA." Supnick. | $100.00-125.00 |
| | *Oaken Bucket with Dipper*, "USA." Snyder. | $65.00-75.00 |
| **Row 2:** | *Kittens and Yarn,* the larger version. Supnick. | $90.00-110.00 |
| | *Liberty Bell*, "USA." Snyder. | $100.00-125.00 |
| | *Kittens and Yarn* pitcher to match the cookie jar. Other accessories include a planter and salt and pepper shakers. Supnick. | $50.00-60.00 |
| **Row 3:** | *Rooster*, "USA." Snyder. | $50.00-60.00 |
| | *School Bus* for "After School Cookies." Snyder. | $50.00-75.00 |
| | Rooster,"USA." Snyder. | $50.00-60.00 |
| **Below:** | *Spoon Rest* cookie jar, unmarked. Though this jar has not been positively identified, there are several indicators leaning towards American Bisque. The lettering in "Cookies" is laid out similarly to the *Recipe* jar (see Book I). This jar also has wedges though they are shallower and shaped slightly differently. | $55.00-60.00 |
| | *Snowman* bank, unmarked. | $20.00-30.00 |

**Row 1:**    *Rudolph*, "© RLM" for Robert L. May, the creator of the children's classic, *Rudolph the Red-Nosed Reindeer*.    $350.00+

*Ribbon-Handled Ring Jar*, unmarked. Similar, yet dressier than the *Ring* jar featured in Book I. Snyder.    $35.00-40.00

*Yarn Doll* with gold trim, unmarked. Snyder.    $175.00+

**Row 2:**    *French Poodle* in burgundy, "USA."    $95.00-100.00

*Sears Strawberry* shaker, unmarked. Okamoto.    $12.00-15.00

*Sears Strawberry* cookie jar, "Sears Exclusively USA." Okamoto.    $30.00-40.00

*Sears Strawberry* shaker, unmarked. Okamoto.    $12.00-15.00

*Coach Lamp*, "USA." Wooldridge.    $100.00-125.00

**Row 3:**    *Kitten and Beehive*, "USA."    $35.00-45.00

*Mug of Hot Chocolate*, "USA." Burnette.    $50.00-60.00

*Oaken Bucket with Dipper*, "USA."    $50.00-65.00

**Below:**    *Herman and Katnip*, stamped "Harvey Famous Cartoons ©1960. USA" on bottom of the base. To date we can document the ownership of three of these jars in collections. We feel sure that more will surface. Wallick.    $2,000.00+

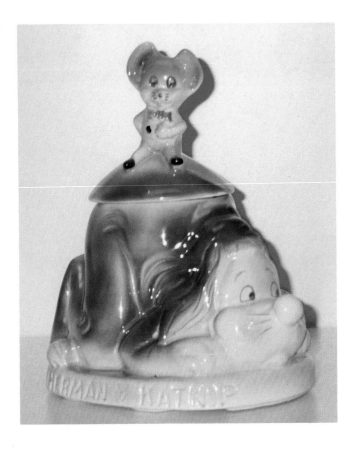

**Row 1:**    *Popeye* bank, "USA."                                                                                    $300.00+

*Corner Chiffonier*, "USA." Supnick.                                                   $125.00-150.00

*Clown* planter. Though not a typical coloration for ABC, it does
have wedges.                                                                                                $10.00-12.00

*Cat* bank, unmarked. Wooldridge.                                                        $15.00-18.00

**Row 2:**    *Fruit Box* with tray lid, "USA 602." Wooldridge.                          $100.00-125.00

*Sadiron,* "USA."                                                                                       $50.00-60.00

*Row 3:*    *Paddy Pig* bank, "Paddy Pig © ABCO 1958 USA." Donated to our
collection by Fred's younger brother, Mike of Dubuque, IA.                $20.00-25.00

*Toothache Dog,* "USA."                                                                          $350.00+

*Donald Duck* look-a-like, unmarked. Not Disney, which places a ceiling on
the value. Snyder.                                                                                $150.00-175.00

**Below:**    Five examples from the *Pippin* line, A.N. Allen's first attempt at modeling after taking over the
reins of American Bisque Company in the early 1940's.

Left: *Pippin* salt and pepper shakers, unmarked.                             $10.00-12.00

Center: *Pippin* covered container, unmarked.                                   $20.00-30.00

Right: *Pippin* covered sugar and creamer, unmarked.                      $15.00-18.00

**Row 1:**  *Baby Huey*, "USA." Rose Snyder.   $1,500.00+

*Casper* bank, "USA."   $350.00+

*Swee' Pea*, "USA."   $2,000.00+

**Row 2:**  *Fire Chief*, "USA." Snyder.   $100.00-125.00

*Pirate*, "USA." Snyder.   $100.00-125.00

*Captain*, "USA." Snyder.   $100.00-125.00

**Row 3:**  *Saddle without Blackboard.* "USA."   $250.00-300.00

*Yarn Doll* bank, "USA." Wooldridge.   $15.00-20.00

*Hen with Chick*, missing decorative cold paint. "USA."   $100.00-125.00

*Saddle* lamp. "USA." Prestwood.   $100.00-125.00

# Animals & Company

Allan Walter and Jenny Lind began Animals & Company in March of 1982. Both studio potters with a total of twenty-five years of experience in clay between them had a philosophy of making each design special with regard not only to the "look," but also to the care and consideration that was crafted into each piece. They felt nothing in the marketplace came close to capturing their liveliness and humor.

In order to maintain their unique character, considerable time was spent on minute detail. Molds were made so that every detail appears as on the original model. Sometimes an elaborate mold required as many as 5–6 parts for the body and another 2–3 part mold for the lid and added appendages. The slip is porcelain and was fired to approximately 2150° Farenheit. All painting was done in the greenware stage, then fired, glazed, and re-fired with a lead-free transparent glaze. Animals & Company was still based in Santa Fe, NM in 1992. When Joyce tried to call in 1993, there was no longer a telephone listing.

**Below:**  *Man with Chicken*, "© 1989 Animals & Co 11SG5 192 USA." Supnick.   $250.00+

*Lady with Cat*, "© 1990 Animals & Co 26 - MP 92." Supnick.   $250.00+

*Animals & Company catalog sheets from 1990 and 1991 follow on page 38 and page 39.*

4180

5010          5018

4015  4010

Large, 4192 Medium 4191

4040

4810, 4820

4193

4210

4105

4075, 4076

4066

4166

4214

4901

4510

4080

4104, 4102, 4100

4160

4051, 4059, 4057, 4056

4130

4064

4190          4800          4750          4700

4120

4650

4150      4165      4083      4212      4061      4063

4149      4146      4195      4196      4157

4110

4145

Animals & Co.
(505) 471-5339

4790

4170

4070

Route 14 Box 226
La Cienega
Santa Fe
New Mexico 87505

# Appleman

Glenn Appleman was born in New York City in 1949. He graduated from the City University of New York in 1971 with a Fine Arts degree. In 1970 he began creating unique sculptures by hand, and soon changed over to the potter's wheel. Within six months he became adept at throwing cups, bowls, and vases. His big break came the day he decided to make sculptures from thrown forms, which created numerous round, bulbous pieces. His style was born.

Funny sculptures would not pay bills, so it became a necessity to make an endless series of pitchers that looked like pelicans, bird casseroles, pussy cat toothbrush holders, rhinoceroses, and whatnot. With his trusty Volkswagon and folding table, he began selling at street fairs.

All Appleman cars were created solely by Glenn Appleman and manufactured in one of three locations: Thirty-three Bleecker Street in New York from March of 1977 through January of 1978; Five Great Jones Street in New York City from February of 1978 until August of 1982; and 527 40th Street in Union City, NJ, from September of 1982 until August of 1987. Numerous accommodations of special orders for color combinations and other unusual decorations not generally available were requested throughout the manufacturing period. Thus, a number of genuine Applemans may not fit exactly into the familiar criteria.

The inspiration for the cookie cars came directly from Glenn's childhood. From 1950 to 1959, the most important cultural event to Glenn was the yearly unveiling and subsequent appearance around the neighborhood of the fabulous new car models. It was as if the car designers were out to appeal directly to this boy from the Bronx. Everything was chrome, fins, and two-tone pastels with no restraint or boring clean lines. It might have been America's love affair with the automobile that kept Appleman in business from 1978 to 1987, but it was his love for cars that made his cookie jars beautiful.

The *Humperbump Sedan*, created in 1978, was not modeled after a particular car. Produced at both the New York and the New Jersey Locations, it was available in red, white, brown, black, and green. Blue *Humperbumps* are very rare. The *Humperbump* was discontinued in 1984. — $650.00+

The *Humperbump Police Car*, created in 1978, features a little red light on the lid, as do all the police cars. Originally, it was made in green and white with a decal facsimile of the NYC police on the door. Later, it became available in black and white with a gold police decal. — $700.00+

The *Sid's Taxi*, created in 1978, has a yellow-orange body, a white taxi dome light, and a black decal on the the door. Some have especially decorative decals which might say "Night Owl Service" or "Serving Greater New York." This is the most popular model. — $700.00+

The *Packard Sedan*, created in 1979, was taken largely from a 1939 *Packard Coupe* seen in a car museum near Asbury Park, NJ. It was made in very small numbers in New York and New Jersey from 1979 to 1983 in the same colors as the *Humperbump*. It is considered scarce. — $850.00

The *Packard Convertible*, the same as the *Sedan* with the exception of production numbers, was made through 1985. The basic colors used are the same colors as were used for the *Humperbump*. Convertibles are fancier and require more work, so they will hold their value in spite of the higher production numbers. — $750.00+

The yellow-orange *Skyway Cab*, created in 1979, has a white dome light and a black and white soaring airplane decal which decorates the doors and sides. Fewer were made than *Sid's Taxi*. The *Skyway* was discontinued in 1985. — $800.00

# Glenn Appleman

is America's best-known ceramic sculptor. His automotive artworks adorn the collections of celebrities and connoisseurs the world over.

Born in New York City in 1949, he earned his degree in Fine Art at the City University of New York in 1971. He then established his own studio and began producing distinctive sculpture encompassing subjects ranging from Mao Tse Tung and Richard Nixon to armadillos and gorillas.

His work has been praised by Thomas Hoving, and been featured in *Architectural Digest* and in *American Crafts: A Sourcebook for the Home*, and in numerous other publications, in films and on television.

His sculptures are included in the private collections of **Sophia Loren, Bill Cosby, Sylvester Stallone, Bruce Springsteen, Dustin Hoffman, Reggie Jackson, Dolly Parton, Liberace,** and many other discriminating art and automobile lovers.

Our Signed Original Ceramic Sculptures are Hand-Made in the U.S.A. Each individually-crafted piece takes seven days or more to complete.

GREENWARE TRIMMING

BISQUEWARE SANDING

HAND-GLAZING COLORS

LUSTRE-GLAZING DETAILS

All sculptures have removable lids, are finished with food-safe glazes and may be used as containers. None are models or replicas of actual automobiles. Inquiries invited through your dealer regarding customization, private editions, and one-of-a-kind commissioned works.

© 1986 APPLEMAN AUTOWORKS, INC.

The *Packard Police* car was created in 1979, in black and white or blue and white with a gold police decal on the doors and a red light on the roof. It was discontinued in 1985. $700.00+

The *Buick Sedan was* created in 1980, in red, white, black, brown, or green. The *Buick* is a combination of the Buick Roadmaster model for the years 1950 through 1953. Because of the massive grill, each car had approximately two dollars worth of luster applied. $700.00+

The *Buick Convertible was* created in 1981, in the same colors as the *Sedan.* It was discontinued in 1987. $750.00+

*Ten Cats on a Red Buick* has the *Buick Convertible* copyright date, but it was actually created in 1984. Between thirty and fifty of them were made. $1,700.00

*Dewey Defeats Truman* was created from a black *Buick Convertible* in 1982 for a public television auction. In 1985 about eight more were made. $1,700.00

The *Phantazoom,* created in 1981, gave Glenn a good reason to start using pastels on his cars. Based on several cars with big fins from the late fifties, *Phantazooms* are mostly two-tone with a pink body and a gray inset. Other color combinations exist, but in far fewer numbers. A pink and gray is the combination most commonly found. Other combinations will demand slightly higher prices. $700.00

The *Limited Edition* Rolls Royce was created in 1983. One thousand numbered pieces, each accompanied with a certificate of authenticity, were produced. This was, by far, the most intricate and laborious piece created by Appleman Autoworks. The first 150 were completed before licensing, and have a different hood ornament. The remaining 850 have a replica of a Rolls Royce statuette. The *Limited Edition* was made in combinations of black and crimson, black and pearl gray, black and yellow, maroon and cream, and brown and tan. $1,100.00+

The *Mercedes Benz*, created in 1985, was modeled after a 1965 220SE convertible in black, royal blue, ivory, pearl gray, chocolate brown, or crimson red. It is the only car available with different lids depicting the opened or closed convertible top. Special luster was applied to the windshield to effect an iridescent blue-black. $900.00

The *Corvette* was styled after the 1959 model and was created in 1985. It is a personal favorite of Appleman, because it successfully marries the cartoon look of his pieces with the actual beauty of a stunning automobile. It is two-toned, with either a red body and a white scoop, a white body with a red scoop, or the much rarer black body with the white scoop. It is the only car with a sculpted interior and has the same luster on the windshield as the *Mercedes.* $1,000.00+

Appleman cars are earthenware with low fire glazes and a platinum luster on the bumpers, hub caps, grillwork, and trim. All production ended in August of 1987 with the exception of the re-issue of fifty *Sid's Taxis* made in his home studio and offered through *Cookie Jarrin'*, **The** *Cookie Jar Newsletter.*

Copyright dates appear to be hand-drawn on the bottom of most of the cars. They denote the year of the design's creation, not when the individual piece was made. Above the copyright is a hand-scrawled "Appleman" in script. Below the copyright is a hand-drawn picture of an apple with an arrow coming out of it. This means Appleman. This is how most pieces were signed prior to 1978. Only sporadically was a copyright mark used. Pieces made from 1985 have a glazed decal on the bottom of the car which says, "HAND MADE in the USA, Glenn Appleman, Appleman Autoworks, Inc. ALL RIGHTS RESERVED." The Appleman Autoworks logo appears alongside.

Occasionally, different initials will be found on jars, such as "JT," which hold special significance. John Timony, who joined Appleman Autoworks just as it was moving to New Jersey in 1982, became an important member who was instrumental in creating order out of chaos and of setting a new standard of excellence for manufacturing. Glenn Appleman states, "An Appleman piece with the initials 'J T' on it means it was a piece about which I never worried, including a shipment to Saks Fifth Avenue, or to the vice president of Rolls Royce of America, or to Reggie Jackson. During my most productive years he was my best producer and a good friend." John's last year at the firm was 1985.

Appleman artworks adorn the collections of celebrities and connoisseurs the world over. His work has been featured in *Architectural Digest* and in *American Crafts: A Sourcebook for the Home*, and in numerous other publications, in films, and on television. His distinctive sculptures encompass subjects ranging from Mao Tse Tung and Richard Nixon to armadillos and gorillas.

His sculptures are included in the private collections of Sophia Loren, Bill Cosby, Sylvester Stallone, Bruce Springsteen, Dustin Hoffman, Reggie Jackson, Dolly Parton, the late Liberace, and many other discriminating art and automobile lovers.

*Top: Sid's Taxi, limited edition. Snyder.*
*Bottom: Skyway Cab.*

MOOSEHEAD BEER

STROH'S BEER

VITO'S VEGGIES With Driver

GOTHAM TRUCKING

GREAT AMERICAN TRUCKS Deco Delights in Several Styles

DEWEY DEFEATS TRUMAN Give 'Em Hell Harry's Historic Triumph

THE MERCEDES-BENZ
Choose Convertible Top Down or Raised
Signed and Numbered

THE CORVETTE
Brimming With the Style and Spirit of America!
Signed and Numbered

THE "LIMITED EDITION"
Spectacular! Signed and Numbered Edition of Just 1000 Pieces.
Produced under license from Rolls-Royce Motors Limited.

# Benjamin & Medwin

Benjamin & Medwin Inc., the New York City based importer/distributor, proudly supports the conservation efforts of the World Wildlife Fund. They are sponsoring a Nature Series and are donating a portion of the profits back to the Wildlife Fund.

**Below:** *Snowy Owl* salt and pepper shakers, "Panda Logo®: World Wildlife Fund© 1992, D.P.I., Made in Taiwan" paper label. Snyder.    Set, $10.00-12.00

*Snowy Owl* cookie jar, "Panda device and WWF are registered  trademarks of World Wildlife Fund. Design: © 1992 Determined Production, Inc., Made in Taiwan," on paper label. Snyder.    $40.00-45.00

*Giant Panda* salt and pepper shaker, "Panda Logo®: World Wildlife Fund© 1992, D.P.I., Made in Taiwan" paper label. Snyder.    Set, $10.00-12.00

*Giant Panda* cookie jar, "Panda device and WWF are registered, trademarks of World Wildlife Fund. Design: © 1992 Determined Productions, Inc., Made in Taiwan" on paper label. Snyder.    $40.00-50.00

*Giant Panda* salt and pepper shaker, Panda Logo®: World Wildlife Fund © 1992, D.P.I., Made in Taiwan" paper label. Mate on left. Snyder.    Set, $10.00-12.00

*Emperor Penguin* cookie jar, "Panda device and WWF are registered trademarks of World Wildlife Fund. Design; © 1992 Determined Productions, Inc., Made in Taiwan," all on paper label. Snyder.    $40.00-45.00

*Emperor Penguin* salt and pepper shakers, "Panda Logo®: World Wildlife Fund© 1992, D.P.I., Made in Taiwan" on paper label. Snyder.    Set, $10.00-12.00

*Benjamin & Medwin catalog sheet on next page.*

46

# WORLD WILDLIFE FUND CERAMICS

## BENJAMIN & MEDWIN
© 1992

230 Fifth Avenue   New York, N.Y. 10001   (212) 686-0060
FAX (212) 213-4895   DUNS No. 198-9136

WWF

96001
96003
96006
96005
96022
96004

96101
96103
96106
96104
96105
96122

96201
96203
96206
96204
96205
96222

# Black Americana

Black Americana continues to be among the most "collectible" of all cookie jars. Escalating prices are hampering the average collectors trying to add older jars to their collections, but with so many new originals, look-a-likes, and reproductions entering the marketplace there is something available in all price ranges enabling everyone to actively collect. After all, old was once new. There is no sure indicator of which jars will "click" and become tomorrow's valued collectible. There is a broad range of prices on new jars. Bear in mind most of the time you get what you pay for. Import jars, mostly from the Far East, are usually very inexpensive, mirroring the quality. While mass produced, we wonder how many will survive out of the hands of collectors for the new collectors of tomorrow.

**Row 1:**    *Crawling Clown*, unmarked with red clay body.                      $150.00-200.00

                 *Chef* shaker, unmarked Taiwan.                          Set, $12.00-15.00

                 *Chef* utensil holder, "Made in Taiwan" paper label.            $15.00-20.00

                 *Chef* shaker, mate on left.

                 *Chef* bank, unmarked Taiwan.                          $15.00-20.00

                 *Chef* cookie jar, "Made in Taiwan" paper label.             $25.00-30.00

                 *Chef* measuring spoon holder, unmarked Taiwan.        $8.00-10.00

**Row 2:**    *Barrel Mammy*, "Made in Taiwan" paper label. Introduced in 1992.     $30.00-40.00

                 *Cream of Wheat Chef* shaker, unmarked. Braly.           Set, $40.00-50.00

                 *Barrel Chef*, "Made in Taiwan" paper label. New for 1992.

                 *Cream of Wheat Chef* shaker, unmarked. Braly.           Set, $40.00-50.00

                 *Barrel Mammy*, "Made in Taiwan" paper label. Also new in 1992.    $30.00-40.00

**Row 3:**    *Rosie*, a Christy mold produced in conjunction with Proctor Pottery located in the Low Country of South Carolina. This jar is technically not a reproduction, though smaller than and bearing great similarity to the original *Mosaic Tile Mammy*. "Rosie, Hand Painted, Made in U.S.A." Mincks.        $80.00-90.00

                 *Dottie*, a reproduction of the *Gilner Mammy*. Unlike the original, *Dottie* has underglaze colors that will not wash off and is decorated differently so new cannot be mistaken for old. "Proctor Pottery, Hand Painted, Made in U.S.A." Berry.                                              $95.00-105.00

                 *Sara,* Mann look-a-like. "Sara, Hand Painted, Made in U.S.A." Braly.    $90.00-100.00

# Erwin Pottery

Erwin Potttery is an outgrowth of a forced retirement. Negatha Peterson, a 16-year veteran of Southern Potteries design department, was in their employ when they closed in 1957. She chose to continue her career and opened her own pottery that she called Erwin Pottery, located in Erwin, TN. Erwin Pottery wares are backstamped "Erwin Pottery" and signed by Negatha, the sole decorator.

Erwin Pottery's *Mammy* came from an Acme mold she bought from Acme Craftware of Wellsville, OH at their closing. Negatha decorates today with many of the same designs she used while in Southern's employ.

**Row 1:**  *Christmas Tree Mammy* shaker, signed "NP" on apron.                  Pair, $20.00-25.00

*Christmas Tree Mammy* cookie jar, "Erwin Pottery, Handpainted Erwin, Tenn."        $100.00+

*Christmas Tree Mammy* shaker, mate at the left of cookie jar.

*McCoy Mammy* reproduction, "Proctor Pottery, Made in USA."          $55.00-65.00

*Ham 'n' Eggs Mammy* shaker, "NP" on apron.                  Pair, $20.00-25.00

*Ham 'n' Eggs Mammy* cookie jar, "Erwin Pottery, Handpainted Erwin, Tenn."        $100.00+

*Ham 'n' Eggs Mammy* shaker, mate on the left of cookie jar. "NP" on apron.

**Row 2:**  *Halloween Mammy* shaker, "NP" on apron.                  Pair, $200.00-25.00

*Halloween Mammy* cookie jar. "Erwin Pottery, Handpainted Erwin, Tenn."        $100.00+

*Halloween Mammy* shaker mate. "NP" on corner of apron.

*Tri-Star Mammy*, designed by Linda Kulhanek. Unmarked.          $100.00-125.00

*Thanksgiving Turkey Mammy* shaker, "NP" on apron.                  Pair, $20.00-25.00

*Thanksgiving Turkey Mammy* cookie jar, "Erwin Pottery, Handpainted, Erwin, Tenn."          $100.00+

*Thanksgiving Turkey* shaker mate. "NP" on corner of apron.

**Row 3:**  *Wonder Boy*, "Arnell's XI The Wonder Boy <u>Black</u> by Marge."          $125.00+

*Sara*, Mann look-a-like, "Sara (in script), HAND PAINTED, MADE IN U.S.A."          $90.00-100.00

*Dinah* or Crackpot's *Old Southern Mammy*, previously called the *Fall Creek Mammy* in Book I. "Dinah (in script), HAND PAINTED, MADE IN U.S.A."          $85.00-95.00

**Row 1:**  *Basket-Handle Mammy* biscuit jar, "Japan."  $750.00-850.00

*Basket-Handle Mammy* cookie jar, "Japan." Though featured in Book I, we felt it was important to demonstrate the size difference between the biscuit jar and cookie jar.  $1,000.00-1,200.00

*Googly-Eyed Man*, the mate to the *Googly-Eyed Mammy* at the bottom of page 62, Book I. This base was being used as a planter and was purchased complete with plant. Though the lid is missing, it is still quite worthy of photography. This jar, as well as his mate, is available in two sizes, cookie and biscuit. "Japan." Very Rare. Grace.  $1,000.00+

**Row 2:**  *Gone With the Wind Mammy*, the first edition. Licensed and distributed by Hamilton Gifts, a division of Enesco. "GONE WITH THE WIND, H4115, Distributed by The Heirloom Tradition®, A division of Hamilton Gifts, © 1939 Selsnick Ren. 1967 MGM© 1990 Turner Entertainment Co., All Rights Reserved, Made in Taiwan." on paper label.  $300.00

*Brayton Mammy*, "Brayton California USA," inscribed into base.  $900.00-1,100.00

*Mandy* planter by Brayton, "1A."  $125.00-150.00

**Row 3:**  *Topsy*, "Metlox, Calif. USA."  $550.00-650.00

*Mosaic Tile Mammy*, unmarked. Rare color.  $1,100.00+

*Topsy*, "Metlox, Calif. USA."  $350.00-400.00

**Below:**  *Manny and Fanny*, "LIMITED EDITION 1993 © S A Corl (in script). " This jar is a turnabout, an original design by Shirley Corl.  $225.00+

*The Bell Captain*, in a heart "MC/ME, © 92, U.S.A." The Bell Captain stands 10" tall, is hand painted, and glazed in four, food-safe colors. This jar is not a reproduction or a recreation, but a new jar made entirely in the U.S. for Gerald Meyer of Simi Valley, California.  $75.00-80.00

**Row 1:** *Napping Della and Pet*, produced in a limited edition of fifty from a retired commercial mold. "S Corl 13/50 1991."                    $125.00+

*Victorian Santa*, an original limited edition of seventy-five. "Limited
Edition © 1991 – S Corl 5/75."                                 $165.00+

*Mosaic Tile* reproduction by Shirley Corl. "6/50 S Corl."     $195.00+

**Row 2:** *Brayton Mammy* reproduction by Shirley Corl. "6/50 S Corl."     $100.00-125.00

*Brayton Mammy* shaker by Shirley Corl. "35/50 S Corl 1992."   Set, $20.00-25.00

*Mammy* clock, designed by Charles E. Murphy and believed to have been produced at the Red Wing Pottery in Red Wing, MN. Clockworks by Lanshire.   $250.00+

*Brayton Mammy* shaker, mate to above.                         Set, $20.00-25.00

*Butler* decanter, "Made in Japan" stamp. Grace.               $225.00+

**Row 3:** *Wash Tub Mammy*, "Made in Taiwan" paper label. Introduced in 1992, this jar
is not a reproduction, though we feel sure the idea was "borrowed" from the
Metlox *Scrub Woman*. The lid to the *Scrub Woman* is enclosed with only a vent
hole in the bottom. The lid to the import is open with a ring of unglazed
pottery, or "dry foot." There are less noticeable differences such as a
straighter stance, foamier bubbles, more distinct bust line, etc. An additional
difference to look for is the cold paint used on the new version. The paint alone
is not a foolproof guide; it could be altered.                 $25.00-35.00

*Brayton Mammy* reproduction, "91 USA."                        $100.00-125.00

*McCoy Mammy* reproduction, "Proctor Pottery, Made in USA."    $55.00-65.00

**Below:** *Abingdon Mammy*, stamped "Abingdon USA." To date, this is the only known example. It is believed

that this 21" tall jar was produced as a display piece to promote cookie jars. One example is not enough to establish
accurate value. Walker.

**Row 1:**    *Boy with Watermelon* planter, unmarked.       $50.00-60.00

           *Corn Kids* shaker, unmarked.       Set, $125.00-150.00

           *Cookie*, an original by Kathy Wolfe. Limited edition of one hundred. "16/100."       $90.00-110.00

           *Mammy* thimble. "Taiwan" on paper label.       $3.00-5.00

           *Brayton Mammy* reproduction by Kathy Wolfe. "KW."       $90.00-110.00

           *Corn Kids* shaker, unmarked. Mate at left.       $Set, $125.00-150.00

           *Girl with Corn* planter, unmarked.       $50.00-60.00

**Row 2:**    *Man* mug, red clay with brown glaze. "USA."       $15.00-20.00

           *Valentine Girl* shaker, "Japan."       Set, $100.00-125.00

           *Bernadine*, distributed by the N.S. Gustin Co. of Los Angeles, CA. Artist signed, "T.F."       $65.00-75.00

           *Valentine Boy* shaker, mate to girl on left, "Japan."       Set, $100.00-125.00

           *Basket Babies*, "Japan."       Set, $100.00-125.00

**Row 3:**    *Gone with the Wind Mammy* teapot, second edition. Licensed and Distributed by Hamilton Gifts, a division of Enesco."GONE WITH THE WIND, H4115, Distributed by the Heirloom Tradition®, a division of Hamilton Gifts, © 1939 Selznick Ren. 1967 MGM © 1990 Turner Entertainment Co., All Rights Reserved, Made in Taiwan," on paper label.       $80.00+

           *Uncle Mose* shaker, "Taiwan" paper label.       Set, $10.00-12.00

           *Gone with the Wind Mammy* cookie jar, second edition.       $100.00-125.00

           *Mixing Bowl Mammy* shaker, "Taiwan" paper label. Mate on left.       Set, $10.00-12.00

           *Jazz Singer,* "Clay Art Jazz Series © Clay Art, San Francisco, Made in Phillipines."       $50.00-75.00

**Below:**    *Rio Rita* shaker distributed by Fitz and Floyd.       Set, $40.00-50.00

           *Calypso Dancer* candle holder, mate to Rio Rita candle holder. Distributed by Fitz and Floyd.       Pair, $50.00-60.00

           *Rio Rita* cookie jar designed by Vicky Balcou for Fitz and Floyd. Though the majority of the line was discontinued, the cookie jar was still available in 1993.       $125.00-150.00

           *Rio Rita* candle holder, mate to dancer on left.       Pair, $50.00-60.00

           *Calypso Dancer* shaker, mate to Rio Rita shaker on left.       Set, $40.00-50.00

# Memories of Mama®
# trademark of Treasures From the Heart

Diane Goodin is an artisan who creates from childhood memories. The faces she saw as a five-year-old inspire realism in the faces she paints today. She wishes to express in each piece a feeling of nostalgia and affection destined to fill your heart with love and treasured memories.

The Memories of Mama® collection began when Diane created her own version of the famous *Mosaic Tile* cookie jar that she now calls *Thelma* (originally referred to as the *Large Head Mammy* in Book I). Soon she did the same with the *McCoy Mammy,* which she now calls *Ora (Small Head Mammy* in Book I).

From her first two cookie jars, Diane began adding to the collection by creating other *Thelma* and *Ora* collectibles. The newest additions to the collection are Diane's own copyrighted original cookie jars, *Savannah and Lee Roy.*

Extraordinary lifelike detail is present in each piece of the Memories of Mama® collection. Each piece is hand-painted by Diane and sought after by serious collectors throughout the United States.

| | | |
|---|---|---|
| **Row 1:** | *Ora* jar cover, regular size, unmarked. | $25.00-30.00 |
| | *Ora* covered sugar, unmarked. | Creamer and sugar set, $40.00-50.00 |
| | *Thelma* jar cover, large mouth, unmarked. | $25.00-30.00 |
| | *Thelma* covered sugar, unmarked. | Creamer and sugar set, $40.00-50.00 |
| | *Thelma* lamp, "Memories of Mama, Tulsa, OK." Complete with shade. | $90.00-95.00 |
| | *Thelma* napkin holder, "Memories of Mama™, Tulsa, OK." | $30.00-40.00 |
| | *Thelma* jar cover, regular size, unmarked. | $25.00-30.00 |
| | *Ora* jar cover, wide mouth, unmarked. | $25.00-30.00 |
| **Row 2:** | *Thelma* creamer, "Memories of Mama, Tulsa, OK." | Set $40.00-50.00 |
| | *Thelma* utensil holder, "Memories of Mama ™." | $30.00-40.00 |
| | *Thelma* canister, tea #4. "Memories of Mama ™, Tulsa, OK." | $30.00-35.00 Set of four, $180.00-190.00 |
| | *Thelma* canister, coffee #3. "Memories of Mama™, Tulsa, OK." | $40.00-45.00 |
| | *Thelma* canister, sugar #2. "Memories of Mama™, Tulsa, OK." | $50.00-55.00 |
| | *Thelma* salt and pepper shakers. "Memories of Mama™." | Pair, $40.00-50.00 |
| | *Ora* salt and pepper shakers. "Memories of Mama™." | Pair, $40.00-50.00 |
| | *Thelma* canister, flour #1. "Memories of Mama™, Tulsa, OK." | $60.00-65.00 |
| | *Ora* creamer, "Memories of Mama™, Tulsa, OK." | Set, $40.00-50.00 |
| **Row 3:** | *Savannah,* "Memories of Mama™, Prototype #2." | $150.00+ |
| | *Lee Roy,* "Memories of Mama®, *Lee Roy* prototype 9/15/92 © 1992, Treasures from the Heart, Tulsa, OK." | $150.00+ |

# Rick Wisecarver Cookie Classics

The Black Americana examples featured on the following pages are merely a sampling of the talents of Rick Wisecarver of Roseville, OH. Additional examples are found in the Rick Wisecarver section, as well as the Black Americana section of Book I.

**Row 1:**    *Pappy Bust*, cookie jar aged version. "Wihoa's Cookie Classic© Rick Wisecarver #12© 90, Roseville, Ohio 43777."     $125.00-150.00

*Mammy and Pappy Bust* salt and pepper shakers. "©Rick Wisecarver Originals, R Sims, #1, 90."     Set, $35.00-45.00

*Mammy Bust* cookie jar. "Original by Rick Wisecarver Cookie Classic #1, R Sims."     $125.00-150.00

**Row 2:**    *Mammy Bust* cookie jar, aged version. "Original by Rick Wisecarver Cookie Classics, #12 R Sims."     $125.00-150.00

*Mammy and Pappy Bust* salt and pepper shakers, aged version.     $35.00-45.00

*Pappy Bust*, "Wihoa's Cookie Classic, ©Rick Wisecarver, ©90, Roseville, Ohio 43777."     $125.00-150.00

**Row 3:**    *Crooked Lady*, a documented one-of-a-kind cookie jar. An outstanding example of the creative abilities of Rick Wisecarver. "Hand Sculptured One-of-a-Kind, December 25, 1991, Rick Wisecarver, R Sims."     $250.00+

*Christmas Day*, "Wihoa's Cookie Classic by Rick Wisecarver, 1991® G-931-0999."     $125.00-150.00

*Little Red Riding Hood*, painted as a one-of-a-kind black jar. The *Red Riding Hood* design was produced in a limited edition production run.     $250.00+

**Below:**    *New Stove Mammy*, "Rick Wisecarver #68, '93, RS."     $175.00+

*Quilting Mammy*, "Wihoa's" on back of base. "© G 931-0999 DJO," on unglazed bottom on base. "Rick Wisecarver #79, 93' RS" on back of lid.     $160.00-175.00

*Quilting Mammy*, aged version. "No. 78-93, Rick Wisecarver, RS," on back of base. "© G 931-0999" and "DJO" on unglazed bottom of base.     $160.00-175.00

**Row 1:**  *Morning Aggravation*, "©® G 931-0999 Rick Wisecarver."                                             $125.00-150.00

*The Pickers*, Wihoa's Cookie Classic Original No-1-90 color test by Rick
Wisecarver, R. Sims."                                                                                            $175.00-225.00

**Row 2:**  *Santa*, "Wihoa's Cookie Classic by Rick Wisecarver." "1990," "Wisecarver"
on back of base. Discontinued.                                                                                   $200.00-250.00

*Sunday Dinner*, Wihoa's Cookie Classic by Rick Wisecarver. No 58 1991, R.S."    $125.00-150.00

*Banjo Man*, "© 90, Wihoa's Original Cookie Classic by Rick Wisecarver,
Roseville, OH 43777, R Sims" on unglazed bottom. "Rick Wisecarver Special"
on back.                                                                                                         $150.00-175.00

**Row 3:**  *Saturday Bath*, "Wihoa's Cookie Classic Original by Rick Wisecarver 1990
R Sims No 1 Roseville OH."                                                                                       $150.00-175.00

*Angel*, "Wihoa's Cookie Classic by Rick Wisecarver, No. 29-91, R.S." on back.
"©, ® G 931-0999" on unglazed bottom.                                                                            $125.00-150.00

*Christmas Churn Mammy*, "© 89, Wihoa's Original Cookie Classic by
Rick Wisecarver, Roseville, OH 43777, R Sims" inscribed into unglazed
bottom of base. "Rick Wisecarver Christmas 89" on side of skirt.                                                 $250.00+

# Adrian Pottery
# of Jefferson City, Missouri

Randy and Stephanie Adrian started their business early in 1992 with a figurine resembling the Shawnee Bulldog. Encouraged by the positive response, they used the money derived from sales to buy a kiln.

Their next creation was an original Mammy pie vent and a Chef pie vent introduced at a Kansas City, MO antique show in December of 1992. They innocently included in their display a *Cotton Pickin' Mammy*, which was their first attempt at cookie jars. Enough interest was generated to take orders. Ten were produced in addition to the original test jars, which brings total production to twelve. The *Cotton Pickin' Mammy* is no longer in production.

Additional items, other than cookie jar and pie vents produced by Adrian Pottery include a Mammy string holder, Mammy sugar, Mammy and Chef salt and pepper shakers, a Chef egg timer, Mammy sock darner, and Mammy bank.

*Castor Oil Mammy* or *Mammy & Child* cookie jar, limited to one hundred numbered pieces. "Adrian Pottery© USA 2/100."                                                    $45.00+

*Papa Clyde & Mammy Pearl*, introduced in 1993. "Cyde & Pearl, Adrian
Pottery © 93."                                                                                                   $75.00+

*Cotton Pickin' Mammy*, "Adrian Pottery USA."                                                                    $75.00+

# Someone's in the Kitchen
# by Department 56

Department 56 is an importer/distributor based in Eden Prairie, MN.

**Row 1:**  *Someone's in the Kitchen* napkin holder, "Someone's in the Kitchen© Hand-painted Japan © Department 56."  $20.00-25.00

*Someone's in the Kitchen* shaker, unmarked.  Pair, $18.00-22.00

*Someone's in the Kitchen* cookie jar, "Someone's in the Kitchen© Hand-painted Japan © Department 56." Discontinued.  $65.00-75.00

*Someone's in the Kitchen* teapot, "Someone's in the Kitchen© Handpainted Japan©Department 56."  $45.00-50.00

**Row 2:**  *Someone's in the Kitchen* butter dish, "Someone's in the Kitchen© Hand-painted Japan© Department 56."  $25.00-30.00

*Someone's in the Kitchen* planter/utensil holder, "Someone's in the Kitchen© Handpainted Japan© Department 56."  $25.00-30.00

*Someone's in the Kitchen* salt and pepper shaker, unmarked, mate on Row 1.  $18.00-22.00

*Someone's in the Kitchen* spoon rest, "Someone's in the Kitchen© Hand-painted Japan© Department 56."  $10.00-12.00

**Row 3:**  *Someone's in the Kitchen* cracker tray, "Someone's in the Kitchen © Hand-painted Japan © Department 56."  $22.00-25.00

*Someone's in the Kitchen* large platter, "Someone's in the Kitchen © Hand-painted Japan © Department 56."  $50.00-55.00

*Someone's in the Kitchen* muffin bowl, "Someone's in the Kitchen © Hand-painted Japan © Department 56."  $55.00-60.00

**Row 1:**    *Mammy* covered sugar, "Made in Taiwan" on paper label.          $7.00-10.00

             *Mammy* bank, "Made in Taiwan" on paper label.            $12.00-15.00

             *Mammy*, 7" wide across bottom of base. "ARTMK, © 1992"       $30.00-40.00

             *Mammy* nodder bank, "Made in Taiwan" on paper label.      $15.00-20.00

             *Mammy* creamer, mate to covered sugar at left. "Made in Taiwan" paper label.    $7.00-10.00

**Row 2:**    *Mammy*, small. "Made in Taiwan" paper label.            $15.00-25.00

             *Uncle Mose* cookie jar. "Made in Taiwan" paper label.       $35.00-45.00

             *Mammy* toothpick holder, unmarked. Taiwan.            $5.00-10.00

             *Mammy*, medium-size utensil holder. "Made in Taiwan."       $20.00-25.00

             *Mammy* bell, unmarked Taiwan.            $10.00-15.00

             *Mammy*, larger than large-size, 12" tall. The large-size Mammy in Book I
             is 10½" tall. "Made in Taiwan" paper label.            $20.00-25.00

             *Mammy* measuring spoon holder. "Made in Taiwan" paper label.      $10.00-15.00

**Row 3:**    *Mammy* teapot. "Made in Taiwan" paper label.            $15.00-25.00

             *Chef* shaker, unmarked.            Set, $8.00-10.00

             *Chef*, large. "Made in Taiwan" paper label.            $35.00-45.00

             *Chef* with blue shirt. "Made in Taiwan" on paper label.       $35.00-45.00

             *Mammy* shaker, mate to *Chef* shaker at left.            Set, $8.00-10.00

             *Chef* with blue shirt teapot. "Made in Taiwan" paper label.       $15.00-25.00

# The New Rose Collection

Rose Saxby of Warren, IL, is a long-time ceramist, applying her skills as colorist and teacher to both commercial products and her own original designs. Rose feels her collection is for today's collectors and is trying to recreate the style and quality necessary to produce an American classic. Each selection in the New Rose Collection has a production limit of one hundred pieces. Documented throughout the history of pottery, imports have squeezed out the small American entrepreneur. Rose strives to offer quality products at affordable prices.

# J C Miller

Jerry and Clarice Miller, J C Miller, of Wichita, KS, set a different tone to original design. To date, each piece modeled is in the likeness of an individual in Clarice's family, including ancestors.

Avid antiquers new to cookie jars, they became especially attracted to the Black Americana examples featured in *Book I*. The fruitless search began, but Clarice was not discouraged. If she could not find the old jars, she would have Jerry make new ones, starting with her Grandma Bell. The idea became reality. Jerry sculpts, makes molds, and pours. Clarice helps to apply the base coats, and Jerry adds the fine detail. The cards included with each limited edition tell a story unique to that family member.

**Row 1:** *Watermelon Boy*, "The New Rose Collection, #1." $125.00-130.00

*Porsha*, "J C Miller 1992 Porsha 31/250." The card reads: "Porsha is a little girl who lives in Kansas. She loves to climb trees, steal cookies, and go to McDonald's. This collectible cookie jar is hand-painted, signed "Clarice Belle Miller (in script). The model was sculptured by Jerry P. Miller." $70.00-80.00

*The Whistler*, "The Collection of Rose #66." $125.00-130.00

**Row 2:** *Baby Reece*, "J C Miller 1992 11/250" on jar. "Clarice Bell Miller was born in Enid, Oklahoma, in 1944. She was the fourth child in a family of fourteen children. She is one of over 150 grandchildren of Dottie Lampkins Bell." $75.00-85.00

*The Little Angel*, "The New Rose Collection, #12." $65.00-75.00

**Row 3:** *Grandma Bell*, "J C Miller, Grandma Bell 19/250" on jar. "Dottie Lampkins Bell was born in Dover, Oklahoma, in 1898. She was the mother of eighteen children. Her grandchildren thought she made the best biscuits in the world." $70.00-80.00

*Grandpa Washington*, "J C Miller 1992, Grandpa Washington 50/250" on jar. "George T. Washington was born March 16, 1837 in Hind County, Mississippi, at Raymond. He was a slave for Sam Herring until May 12, 1863." $80.00-90.00

*Joey*, "J C Miller 1992 - 11/250" on jar. "Joseph Michael Walker is nine years old. He loves riding his bike and going fishing. He also likes helping Grandma Reece make cookies. He is a great-great grandchild of Dottie Lampkins Bell." $65.00-75.00

**Row 1:**     *Basket Handle Mammy*, elongated body with feet, mate to *Butler with Herringbone Trousers*. Base, 5¾" H, Total height, 9". Marked "Japan" under glaze. Cauwells. (top left)     $1,500.00+

                 *Brayton Maid*, marked with black stamp, "Copyright Brayton Laguna Pottery." 12½" H. Cauwells. (top right)     $2,000.00+

**Row 2:**     *Brayton Mammy*, mark incised "Brayton Laguna Pottery©." 13" H to the top of the bow. Considered to be the rarest color discovered to date. Cauwells. (bottom left)     $1,500.00+

                 *Italian Mammy*, very similar to the Seymour Mann *Mammy*. Marked with green stamp, "Made In Italy 188." Cauwells. (bottom right)     $1,000.00+

**Below:**     *Canuck Jug,* marked "Canuck Pottery Saint John N B Canada." The mark is impressed into the pottery. 9¾" H. Cauwells.     $250.00+

                 *Bauer Mammy* on cylinder. Mark incised "Bauer USA Los Angeles." On one side, "Help Yo Self" (Some of the letters have been worn or washed off.) Cauwells.     $350.00+

                 *Googly-Eyed Man*, complete with lid, marked "Japan." 6½" H by 8" W at ears. Cauwells.     $2,500.00+

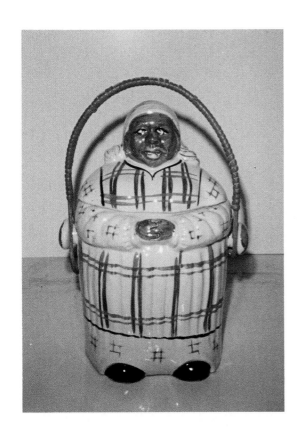

**Row 1:**   *Butler with Herringbone Trousers*, "JAPAN" stamped under glaze. Posner. (top left)                                         $1,500.00+

*Brayton Mammy*, "©Brayton Laguna California." Posner. (top rigth)                                         $900.00+

**Row 2:**   *Brayton Mammy*, "copyright 1943 by Brayton Laguna Pottery." Posner. (bottom right)                                         $900.00+

*Soldier*, unmarked. Posner. (bottom right)                                         $450.00-500.00

**Below:**   *Cream of Wheat Chef* shaker, "Japan." Posner.                                         Set, $225.00-250.00

*Cream of Wheat Chef* cookie jar, 8" H, stamped "Japan" under the glaze. Posner.                                         $1,100.00-1,200.00

*Cream of Wheat Chef* shaker, mate above.

*Cream of Wheat Chef* cookie jar, 10" H, stamped "Japan" under the glaze. Posner.                                         $1,500.00+

**Row 1:**   The *Black Clown* set featured below is sometimes referred to as minstrels rather than clowns. We see them as clowns.

*Clown* creamer, "DES PAT PEND," stamp. "Thames Hand Painted" on paper
label. Snyder.                                                  Sugar and creamer set, $25.00-30.00.

*Clown* sugar, "DES PAT PEND." stamp. "Thames Hand Painted" on paper
label. Snyder.                                                                          $12.00-15.00.

*Clown* cinnamon, unmarked. Snyder.                                             $12.00-15.00.

*Clown* cookie jar, "Thames Hand Painted, Made in Japan" on paper label.
Snyder.                                                                               $100.00-125.00.

*Clown* pepper, unmarked. Snyder.                                        Set, $10.00-12.00.

*Clown* salt, unmarked. Snyder.

*Clown* creamer, stacking "DES PAT PEND" stamp. "Thames Hand Painted,
Made in Japan" paper label. Snyder.                           Stacking set, $80.00-90.00

*Clown* sugar, stacking "DES PAT PEND" stamp. "Thames Hand Painted,
Made in Japan" paper label. Snyder.                           Stacking set, $80.00-90.00

*Clown* teapot, base of stacking set. "DES PAT PEND" stamp. "Thames
Hand Painted, Made in Japan" paper label. Snyder.             Stacking set, $80.00-90.00

**Row 2:**   *Clown* wall pocket, "TILSO Hand Painted Japan" on paper label. Wirebailed
spice containers are meant to hang from the red knobs at the base of the
wall pocket. Snyder.                                                                  $45.00-50.00

*Clown* ash tray, "DES PAT PEND" – "Thames, Hand Painted, Made in Japan."
Snyder.                                                                                 $10.00-12.00

*Clown* teapot, "DES PAT PEND" stamp. Snyder.                                  $30.00-45.00

*Clown* measuring cup = ½ cup, "DES PAT PEND" stamp. Snyder.           Set, $25.00-35.00

*Clown* measuring cup = ⅛ cup, unmarked. Snyder.                       Set, $25.00-35.00

*Clown* measuring cup = 1 cup "DES PAT PEND" stamp. Snyder.            Set, $25.00-35.00

*Clown* measuring cup = ¼ cup, "DES PAT PEND" stamp. Snyder.          Set, $25.00-35.00

# Alfano Art Pottery

Sam and Denise Alfano reside in Pearl River, LA. Sam is a metal engraver and does hand-engraving for collectors around the globe. His work has been featured in many publications and on magazine covers (his engraved knife appears on the cover of *Knives '93*) in the U.S., France, Japan, and Italy. He played music professionally for many years in New Orleans, which gave him the inspiration for the *Jazz Player*, the first in a series of musical-theme limited editions.

Denise has been a watercolor artist for many years. Her paintings are in some very prestigious southern collections. According to Sam, Denise *is* Alfano Art Pottery; she does all the work from start to finish. Sam designs and sculpts the original models and makes the molds.

Collectors of pottery and cookie jars, the Alfanos had a desire to produce something of their own. This desire grew with their collection. They first considered doing a reproduction, but after careful consideration decided to go with their own originals, each limited to one hundred pieces.

| | | |
|---|---|---|
| **Top:** | *The Jazz Player*, "© Alfano Art Pottery USA, Experimental #1 – 92." Snyder. | $150.00+ |
| | *The Jazz Player*, "© Alfano Art Pottery USA, 28/100." | $150.00+ |
| | *B-Flat Williams*, "© Alfano Art Pottery USA, 28/100." | $175.00+ |

# A Company of 2

David Brdecko was born in Deming, NM. Spending his youth on the family farm, he dreamed of greener pastures. At the age of twenty he moved to Texas where he lived for nineteen years, pursuing his life-long artistic interests.

Unable to find anyone to model his culinary sculptures, and bring them to life, he began to do his own sculpting. *Sister ChubbyCheeks* came first, followed by *Higby*.

David Brdecko now resides in Albuquerque, NM where he continues to produce original, unique cookie jars with distinct personality and character.

| | | |
|---|---|---|
| **Bottom:** | *Sister ChubbyCheeks*, "A Company of 2" in a circular mark. "David Brdecko (in script) Original Limited Editions, #1." | $125.00-130.00 |
| | *Higby*, "A Company of 2" in a circular mark. "David Brdecko (in script) Original Limited Editions, #1." | $125.00-130.00 |

# Brayton Laguna

To date there is little known about Brayton Laguna Pottery. Collectors continue to discover new items and different decorations on well-known pieces. The woodtone Provincial series designed by "Kay the Potter," the professional name of Kay Kinney, may prove to be the most extensive line ever produced at Brayton Laguna Pottery. Kay Kinney was a member of the Carmel Art Association. She designed extensively scroll bowls and accessories, ducks, birds, and boots.

It will be the Brayton collectors and lovers of California Pottery, such as Jack Chipman, author of the *Collector's Encyclopedia of California Pottery*, that will finally excavate the missing links, piece by piece. Dr. Bruce Lichtenstein, a lover of Brayton, feels there could be as many as one hundred different items in the woodtone Provincial line, and has gathered no less than thirty-five pieces including canister sets, trivets, bowls, planters, salt and pepper shakers, even a Dutch shoe and fireplace bellows.

One interesting note: there are reproductions of the Provincial cookie jar and salt and pepper shakers. Only the original cookie jar is marked "Brayton Laguna, Calif. K – 2F." Reproductions may be marked the same as the original, if someone chooses to do so.

**Row 1:** *Gingerbread Boy and Girl* salt and pepper shakers, marked "Brayton Calif. USA." There is a cookie jar to match these shakers. — Set, $35.00-45.00

*Provincial Wheelbarrow* planter, "Brayton Laguna Calif. J19." Braly. — $15.00-20.00

*Provincial Girl* bud vase, "22–178–P." — $15.00-20.00

*Provincial Covered Box* or small *Canister*. — $8.00-12.00

*Frances* bud vase, "Frances, Brayton Pottery." — $15.00-20.00

**Row 2:** *Granny*, a color variation of the *Granny* featured on page 174 of Book I. "Brayton Laguna, Calif. 40-85." — $300.00-350.00

*Provincial Lady* shaker, from what province? For years we have referred to this set as "dried apple" people, after Melva Davern sent them to us, because they were too ugly to keep in her salt and pepper collection. Thanks, Melva. "BRAYTON LAGUNA - CALIF. K26," with a green "X" applied with glaze. There has also been an "E" or "F" scratched into the pottery. — Set, $30.00-40.00

*Provincial Lady* cookie jar. We do not feel this jar is a part of Black Americana, any more than is the Twin Winton *Butler*. The woodtone coloration is a unique finish. Brayton is famous for its *Mammy* cookie jars as well as its Black Americana salt and pepper shakers. Each is hand decorated under the glaze, leaving no doubt about its origin. An old newspaper clipping calls her a *Cookie Crock*, 13" High, and lists her original price as $6.25. "Brayton Laguna Calif. K-27." Braly. — $350.00+

*Provincial Man* shaker, mate to *Lady* above. An old newspaper clipping lists the original price of these shakers at $1.75 per pair. "BRAYTON," and a green "X." — Set, $30.00-40.00

*Grandma with Wedding Band*, "Brayton Laguna Pottery ©." — $350.00-400.00

# Brush Pottery

With so many resources readily available, collectors of Brush Pottery find it relatively easy to identify. *Book I* has excellent coverage of Brush Pottery cookie jars, and omits only the rare *Elephant with Monkey on Back*.

**Row 1:**    *Clown,* "W 22 Brush USA" incised into the bottom of the base. Snyder.    $175.00-200.00

*Treasure Chest*, "W-28 Brush USA." Braly.    $160.00-180.00

*Formal Pig* with gold trim. "Brush W 7 USA." Snyder.    $450.00+

**Row 2:**    *Humpty Dumpty* with peaked hat, "W-29 Brush USA." Braly.    $160.00-180.00

*Hen on Basket*, unmarked.    $225.00-250.00

**Row 3:**    *Cylinder with Duck Finial,* "K/26 USA." Snyder.    $50.00-60.00

*Cylinder with Tulips,* "Brush – 137 USA," incised into bottom of base. Snyder.    $50.00-60.00

*Cylinder with Cat Finial,* "Brush K/26 USA."    $50.00-60.00

**Below:**    *Re-Issue Hillbilly Frog* from the original Brush Pottery mold. "Re-issue by JD." Not every re-issued *Frog* is marked; neither is the original. Reproductions have been made from the re-issue, but we cannot ascertain that they have been properly identified as reproductions.    $250.00+

Additional Brush molds known to have been purchased at auction are listed in the "Introduction."

# California Originals, Inc.

California Originals is best represented with photographic examples of its work. William Bailey, past president and general manager of California Originals has graciously shared additional company catalog sheets verifying the identity of previously unknown jars.

**Row 1:**     *Liberty Bell,* "883" in lid, and "884" on the base. Snyder.     $35.00-45.00

                *Pot Belly Stove,* with "743" on the lid, and "743 USA" on the base. Snyder.     $30.00-40.00

                *Airplane with Pilot,* "2629 USA."     $100.00-125.00

**Row 2:**     *Lion with Lollipop,* "866" on lid, and "866 USA" on the base. Snyder.     $35.00-45.00

                *Circus Wagon,* "2631" on lid and "USA 2631" on the base.     $35.00-45.00

                *Lion* with brush-on gold mane, unmarked.     $35.00-45.00

**Row 3:**     *Baseball Boy,* "875 USA" on lid and base. Snyder.     $35.00-45.00

                *Old-fashioned Phonograph,* "891 USA."     $50.00-60.00

                *Little Red Riding Hood,* "320 USA."     $225.00-250.00

**Below:**     *California Originals Display Sign,* "California Originals Stoneware by Suzi." Supnick.     $50.00-60.00

**Row 1:**    *Upside Down Turtle,* "2627 USA" on lid and base. Snyder.                    $40.00-50.00

*Rabbit Stump,* "2620-1-2-3" on lid and "2620 USA" on the base. Snyder.    $35.00-45.00

*Turtle with Top Hat,* "2640 USA."                    $35.00-45.00

**Row 2:**    *Freddie Frog,* 8½" tall, unmarked.                    $30.00-40.00

*Sitting Frog,* "877 USA."                    $50.00-60.00

*Frog bank,* unmarked.                    $15.00-20.00

**Row 3:**    *Duckbill Platypus,* "790 USA."                    $100.00-125.00

*Reclining Frog,* "704" on lid and 704 USA" on base. Snyder.    $40.00-45.00

*Duck,* "857" on base.                    $25.00-35.00

**Below:**    *Superman,* "CAL. ORIG. USA #846 © D.C. Comics, Inc., 1978." Clyde &
Takasugi.                    $225.00-250.00

*Woody Woodpecker,* "© WALTER LANTZ PROD. INC. 980 USA." Clyde &
Takasugi.                    $275.00-300.00

 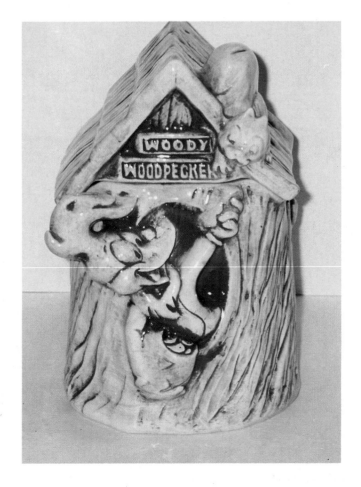

**Row 1:**   *Old-fashioned Radio*, "888" on lid, and "888 USA" on base. Snyder.   $40.00-45.00

*LiL Ole Schoolhouse*, "869" on lid and base. Snyder.   $50.00-60.00

*Coffee Grinder*, "861" on lid, and "861 USA" on base. Snyder.   $30.00-35.00

**Row 2:**   *Smiley Face House*, "741" on lid and base. Snyder.   $35.00-45.00

*Christmas House*, "857" on base. Snyder.   $40.00-45.00

*Shoe House*, "874 USA" on base. Snyder.   $30.00-35.00

**Row 3:**   *Cookie Bakery*, "863" on lid, "863 USA" on base. Snyder.   $35.00-45.00

*Napkin Lady*, "California Originals, © Manhattan Beach, Calif." on paper
label. Bass.   $60.00-75.00

*Cookie Bakery*, "863" on lid, "863 USA" on base. Snyder.   $35.00-45.00

**Below:**   *Juggling Clown*, "876" on lid and base. Snyder.   $45.00-55.00

*Lemon*, unmarked. Snyder.   $25.00-30.00

| | | |
|---|---|---:|
| **Row 1:** | *Cookie Time Clock*, "860" on lid and base. Snyder. | $30.00-35.00 |
| | *Fire Truck*, "841" on base. Snyder. | $65.00-75.00 |
| | *Rabbit*, unmarked. | $30.00-35.00 |
| **Row 2:** | *Treasure Chest*, "878" on lid, and "878 USA" on base. Snyder. | $40.00-45.00 |
| | *Pack Mule*, "2633" on lid, and "2633 USA" on base. | $125.00-150.00 |
| | *Monkey*, "884" on lid, and "884 USA" on base. Snyder. | $50.00-60.00 |
| **Row 3:** | *Yorkshire Terrier*, "937" on base. Snyder. | $45.00-55.00 |
| | *Train Engine*, "2628" on lid, and "873 USA" on base. Snyder. | $30.00-35.00 |
| | *Man in Barrel*, "873" on lid, and "873 USA" on base. Snyder. | $35.00-40.00 |

*California Originals catalog sheet. 1978-1980.*

| | | |
|---|---|---|
| **Row 1:** | *Bobby*, "GKI USA." Not a proven California Originals jar. | $35.00-45.00 |
| | *Panda*, marked C through W for Cumberland Ware but featured in the California Originals Catalog with the *Koala*. Remember, Harold Roman owned both California Originals and Roman Ceramics for a short period of time. | $100.00-125.00 |
| | *Rooster*, "CAL ORIG USA 1127" on base. Snyder. | $25.00-35.00 |
| **Row 2:** | *Puppy* salt or pepper shaker, "2628." Snyder. | Set, $10.00-15.00 |
| | *Schnauzer*, "905 USA." | $100.00-125.00 |
| | *Puppy* shaker, mate above. Snyder. | Set, $10.00-15.00 |
| | *Bunnies in Love Seat*, unmarked. | $45.00-50.00 |
| | *Squirrel Stump*, "863" on lid, and "863 USA" on base. Snyder. | $25.00-35.00 |
| **Row 3:** | *Snowman*, "872 USA." | $100.00-125.00 |
| | *Gum Ball Machine*, "890 USA." | $35.00-45.00 |
| | *Ferdinand*, "870" on base. Snyder. | $35.00-45.00 |

*A California Originals catalog sheet. 1978-1980.*

# "Celebrity" Cookie Jars

**A. BERT AND ERNIE®.** Bert and Ernie try to sell their cookies faster than Cookie Monster can grab them. Multi-color. 11" high. 8" x 6" cookie box.
**Model No. 977MC**

**B. MICKEY MOUSE®.** The world's favorite mouse leans on a big red 7-1/4" drum. Mickey is 11-1/2" high.
**Model No. 864MC**

**C. DONALD DUCK®.** Mischievous Donald stands by a big orange pumpkin. Multi-color. 11-1/2" high.
**Model No. 865MC**

**D. GOOFY®.** Goofy guards his own special cookies. Multi-color. 11-3/4" high. 6-1/4" diam. barrel.
**Model No. 862MC**

**E. SUPERMAN®.** Superman is emerging from his famous phone booth. Ideal for Superman fans of all ages. Multi-color cookie jar is 13" high x 5-1/4" square.
**Model No. 846MC**

**F. SNOW WHITE®.** Snow White shares a treasured book with a forest friend. Multi-color Snow White is 12-1/2" high and 11" wide.
**Model No. 867MC**

Cookie Monster, Bert and Ernie are trademarks of Muppets, Inc. All Rights Reserved.

© 1975 Children's Television Workshop. Sesame Street are Trademarks and Service Marks of Children's Television Workshop.

B. 864MC Mickey Mouse®
C. 865MC Donald Duck®

E. 846MC Superman®

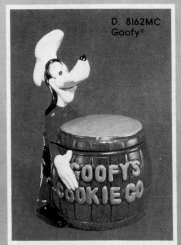

D. 8162MC Goofy®

F. 867MC Snow White®

A. 977MC
Sesame Street Bert and Ernie®

CALIFORNIA ORIGINALS
Suite 665 • 4849 Golf Road • Skokie, Illinois 60077

*California Originals Catalog Sheet.*

# Cookie Jars For One and All

A. 2620MC Squirrel     B. 2635MC Turtle

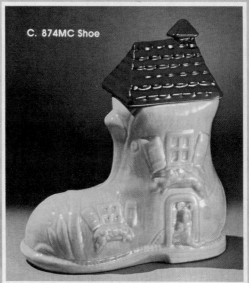

C. 874MC Shoe

D. 884MC Frog     E. 883MC Tiger     F. 886MC Cupcake

H. 873MC Christmas Tree

G. 872MC Snowman

J. 871MC Santa Claus

These whimsical charmers can sell themselves. The bright, gleaming glaze finishes are chip-resistant, and all are dishwasher safe.

**A. SQUIRREL ON A STUMP.** The busy squirrel looks for one more place to hide a nut. Brown with multi-color accents. 12-1/2" H.
**Model No. 2620MC**

**B. TURTLE.** The smiling turtle wears a decorated shell. Brown turtle, multi-color decorations. 12-1/2" high.
**Model No. 2635MC**

**C. SHOE WITH MICE.** The detailed harvest gold shoe is topped by a dark brown roof/lid. 12-1/2" high x 11-1/2" long x 6" wide.
**Model No. 874MC**

**D. FREDDIE FROG.** A tummy full of cookies will even make a frog smile. Multi-color. 8-1/2" high.
**Model No. 884MC**

**E. SMILING TIGER.** Bright yellow tiger will brighten any countertop. Multi color accent. 8-3/4" tall.
**Model No. 883MC**

**F. CUPCAKE** Sweets for the sweet — the perfect place for cookies. Multi-color. 9" high.
**Model No. 886MC**

**G. SNOWMAN.** Celebrate the snow time with our happy snowman. With red scarf and top hat. 12" high.
**Model No. 872MC**

**H. CHRISTMAS TREE.** The happiest symbol of the holiday season. 12-1/4" deep green tree is topped with a golden star and has multi color decorations.
**Model No. 873MC**

**J. SANTA CLAUS.** Jolly St. Nick leans against his bag of toys. Use for cookies and in table center pieces too. Multi-color. 11-1/2" high.
**Model No. 871MC**

*California Originals Catalog Sheet.*

# Cookie Jars with a Different Twist

A. 501MC
Taxi Cab

B. 400MC
Milk and Cookies Time

These cookie jars with a different twist are sure to cause delighted comments. All are chip-resistant and dishwasher safe.

**A. TAXI CAB.** This big yellow taxi holds dozens of favorite confections. It's 7-1/4" high x 10-3/4" long x 5-3/4" wide.
**Model No. 501MC**

**B. "MILK AND COOKIES TIME."** That says it all—so reach for the milk. Multicolor. 11-1/2"H x 5"W x 4-1/4"D.
**Model No. 400MC**

**C. "JEANS."** Now the denim look comes to the kitchen. For the teenage set. 10-1/4" high. 5-1/2" diameter.
**Model No. 502MC**

**D. DOGGY TREATS.** Cookies shaped like bones? They'd be perfect for this clever jar. Multi-color. 9-3/4" high, 7-1/4" diameter.
**Model No. 402MC**

**E. KITTY TREATS.** A real cat's meow. The kitty on the lid lounges around a bouncy ball of yarn. The multi-color jar is 9-3/4" high and 7-1/2" in diameter.
**Model No. 403MC**

C. 502MC
Jeans

D. 402MC
Doggy Treats

E. 403MC
Kitty Treats

**All Cookie Jars have
Chip-Resistant Glazes and
Are Dishwasher Safe.**

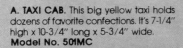

*California Originals Catalog Sheet.*
94

# CATEGORY 14

## COOKIE JARS TO TICKLE YOUR FANCY

#2637
12-1/4" H

#857
11-1/2" H

#8425-C
9" H

#8219
12-1/2" H

#869
11-1/4" H

#2756
12" H

#876
13" H

#8413-C
8-3/4" H

#875
12" H

#8218
11" H

#8214
10-3/4" H

#8215
11" H

#737
12" H

*California Originals Catalog Sheet Fall 1975.*

CATEGORY 14                                                    PAGE 37

#2623
14" H

#884
13" H

#873
12-1/2" H

#896
14-1/4" H

#891
11-1/2" H

#890
12" H

#879
11-1/2" H

#869
11-1/4" H

#726
12" H

#888
12" H

#889
10" H

#883
14" L

#2648
10-1/2" H

*California Originals Catalog Sheet Fall 1975.*

PAGE 64

Stain

DISC.

DISC.

DISC.

DISC.

# 2620
14" H
$5.50

# 2623
14" H
$5.50

# 2630
15" H
$5.50

# 1127
9" H
$4.25

# 2624
14" H
$5.50

# 2622
15" H
$5.50

DISC.

# 2621
14" H
$5.50

DISC.

*California Originals Catalog Sheet Spring 1974.*

PAGE 62

# 2645
10½'' H
$4.25

DISC.

# 2756
12'' H
$6.25

# 2751
10'' H
$4.25

# 2648
11½'' H
$4.25

# 2643
10'' H
$4.50

# 2751
10'' H
$4.25

# 1127
9'' H
$4.25

# 2648
11½'' H
$4.25

# 2645
10½'' H
$4.25

# 2628
4½'' H
$2.50

DISC.

DISC.

# 2629
5'' H
$2.50

# 2627
4¼'' H
$2.50

DISC.

# 2636
5'' H
$2.50

DISC.

*California Originals Catalog Sheet Spring 1974.*

# 856
12¼″ H
$5.50

# 738
12½″ H
$5.50

# 724
12″ H
$5.50

DISC.

# 859
13¾″ H
$5.75

# 405
12″ H
$5.50

# 869
11¼″ H
$7.00

# 728
12½″ L
$5.50

# 857
11½″ H
$7.00

# 727
4½″ H
$2.50 Set

# 726
12″ H
$5.50

DISC.

# 458
11¾″ H
$5.50

*California Originals Catalog Sheet Spring 1974.*

# 2637
12¼″ H
$6.50

# 737
12″ H
$5.50

DISC.

# 870
12″ H
$5.50

# 859
13½″ H
$5.75

# 860
13¾″ H
$5.75

# 870
12″ H
$5.50

# 871
12¼″ H
$5.75

DISC.

# 883
14″ L
$5.50

# 737
12″ H
$5.50

# 884
12″ L
$5.50

# 884
12″ L
$5.50

# 883
14″ L
$5.50

*California Originals Catalog Sheet Spring 1974.*

STONEWARE BY SUZI

#390
8'' H
$4.50

#369
8¾'' H
$4.50

#367
8¾'' H
$4.00

#9281
15½'' H
$4.00

#9291
7½'' H
$1.75

#9321
8¾'' H
$1.75

#6071
10'' H
$2.50

#6031
9¾'' H
$2.00

#3511
8'' H
$2.00

#3531
7½'' H
$2.50

#453
12'' H
$6.50

#6051
5½'' H
$1.25

#9191
7½'' H
$2.00

#366
5½'' H
$2.50

#9171
8'' H
$2.00

#3501
5½'' H
$1.25

#3521
10½'' H
$2.50

#4911
13¼'' H
$2.50

#360
5½'' H
$3.00

#368
8¾'' H
$6.50

#9181
6½'' H
$2.00

#9301
8'' H
$2.00

#6001
7'' H
$2.00

#447
9'' H
$3.00

#449
13'' L
$6.00

#448
10'' L
$4.00

#338
8¼'' L
$3.00

#337
8¼'' L
$3.75

#373
4¾'' H
$1.50

#374
6¼'' H
$2.00

#6041
3-7/8'' H
$1.25

#372
4¾'' H
$1.50

#371
3¾'' H
$1.00

#376
3½'' H
$1.00

#339
5½'' H
$2.50

*California Originals Catalog Sheet Spring 1973.*

101

*California Originals Catalog Sheet Spring 1974.*

862
12½" H

860
13½" H

861
11½" H

863    11¾" H

878
11" H

863
11¾" H

868
14½" L

DIS

*California Originals Catalog Sheet Fall 1975.*

*California Origi-nals Catalog Sheets 1976.*

Page 48
Category 14

#8425-C
9" H
RD

#583
10¼" H
FA

#M-841
11½" L
RD

#2956-F
10" H
OL

#2645
10½" H
ST

#2627
10" H
ST

#1127
8½" H
ST

#2751
10" H
ST

#2625
11¼" H
ST

#2645
10½" H
GR

Category #14

CALIFORNIA ORIGINALS
22433 S. VERMONT
TORRANCE, CALIF. 90502

#840
9-1/2" H

#975
12" H

#739
12" H

#854
13" H

#839
12" H

#858
8" H

#841
11-1/2" L

*California Originals Catalog Sheets 1976.*

105

**Row 1:**   *Rabbit in Basket of Carrots*, "703" on lid, and "703 USA" on base. Snyder.     $30.00-40.00

            *Scarecrow Turnabout*, sad side. "858" on lid and base. Snyder.     $40.00-50.00

            *Mouse on Stump*, "891-892 FS USA" on lid and base. Snyder.     $30.00-40.00

**Row 2:**   *Bert and Ernie®*, "505."     *$35.00-45.00*

            *Holly Hobbie™*, "505."     $35.00-45.00

            *Cookie Monster®*, "505."     $35.00-45.00

The number assigned the cylinder shape is 505. The catalog sheet lists *Bert and Ernie* as #515MC, *Holly Hobbie* as #509, and *Cookie Monster* as #513.

**Row 3:**   *Elf*, with paper label, "California Originals, Manhattan Beach, Calif." Snyder.     $75.00-85.00

            *Tiger* salt and pepper shaker, unmarked. Snyder.     Set, $15.00-20.00

            *Tiger* cookie jar, unmarked. Snyder.     $50.00-60.00

            *Tiger* salt and pepper shaker, mate above.     Set, $15.00-20.00

            *Elephant*, "826" on base. This is not a California Originals jar but is a Marsh Industries production. The #826 matches the number assigned in the 1967 Marsh catalog. Snyder.     $35.00-45.00

**Below:**   *Scarecrow* turnabout, happy side. Snyder.     $40.00-50.00

| | | |
|---|---|---|
| **Row 1:** | *Penguin*, "839-7" on lid, "839" on base. Snyder. | $35.00-45.00 |
| | *Caterpillar*, "853" on base. Snyder. | $35.00-45.00 |
| | *Clown*, "862" on lid and base. Snyder. | $35.00-45.00 |
| **Row 2:** | *Humpty Dumpty*, "882" on lid and base. Snyder. | $50.00-60.00 |
| | *Raggedy Andy*, "860" on lid and base. | $50.00-60.00 |
| | *Raggedy Ann*, "859" on lid and base. Snyder. | $50.00-60.00 |
| **Row 3:** | *Safe*, "482 California USA" on base. The *Safe* was not made by California Originals. It is a Marsh Industries production, listed in the 1967 catalog under #482. Snyder. | $25.00-35.00 |
| | *Clown Bust*, "859" on lid and base. Snyder. | $45.00-55.00 |
| | *Bulldog Safe*, "2630-1-2" on lid and base. Snyder. | $30.00-35.00 |
| **Below:** | *Little Girl*, unmarked. | $70.00-80.00 |
| | *Cookie Shoppe*, "2756 USA." | $35.00-45.00 |

| | | |
|---|---|---|
| **Row 1:** | *Cuckoo Clock*, "840." | $50.00-60.00 |
| | *Scarecrow*, "871 USA." | $150.00-175.00 |
| | *Teapot with Flowers*, "737" on lid and base. Snyder. | $25.00-35.00 |
| **Row 2:** | *Owl Stump*, "2620-1-2-3" on lid, "2620 USA" on base. Snyder. | $25.00-35.00 |
| | *Noah's Ark*, "881 USA." | $60.00-70.00 |
| | *Juggling Clown*, "876" on base. Snyder. | $35.00-45.00 |
| **Row 3:** | *Owl,* "856 USA" on lid and base. Snyder. | $35.00-45.00 |
| | *Hippo*, "883 USA." | $35.00-45.00 |
| | *Owl,* "856 USA." | $35.00-45.00 |

# Cardinal

| | | |
|---|---|---|
| **Below:** | *Cookie Safe*, "Cardinal 309 © USA." Snyder. | $50.00-60.00 |

# Cavanagh

Henry Cavanagh was born in 1946 in Brooklyn, NY. He grew up in Long Island, moving to rural upstate New York in 1964. He studied art education, painting, sculpture, and gold-and silversmithing at New York State University at New Paltz before going to Germany. Henry worked for two years in a bronze foundry in Dusseldorf, Germany, enabling him to travel extensively in Europe.

In 1973 he returned to the United States. Gold was $800.00 an ounce, and there was a nation-wide propane shortage. Both were key ingredients to goldsmithing and bronze casting. It was then that Henry transferred his skills to ceramics. His one-of-a-kind porcelain hippos were on display at the Smithsonian Institute and thirty other galleries from coast to coast over a seventeen year period.

Inspired by the "Diner" paintings of John Baeder, he began casting functional porcelain tableware, canisters, and mugs in 1978 under the tradename, *Diner-Ware*. Architectural subjects and building shapes became the models for *Diner* butter dishes, tea sets, and other roadside attractions. *Diner-Ware* proved to be so popular that he left the difficult-to-manage porcelain, for low-fire ceramics, which is the composition of most antique and traditional cookie jars. The low-fire clay allowed for bigger pieces, brighter colors, and more reliable results. *Diner* cookie jars were soon to follow.

In 1992 he began a line of automobile cookie jars under the tradename *Ceramicar*. The cars in this line are fantasy cars of no actual make, year, or model. Lavishly applied detail enhances every piece. Each limited edition has two hundred pieces produced in each style and color. Production of both cars and diners is a very slow, individualized process, which assures high quality and makes each piece practically one-of-a-kind.

| | | |
|---|---|---|
| **Row 1:** | *Mom's Diner* salt or pepper shaker, "H Cavanagh © 179/200." | Set, $60.00-65.00 |
| | *Mom's Diner* cookie jar, "H Cavanagh © 0/200 Sample." | $180.00+ |
| | *Mom's Diner* shaker, mate above. | Set, $60.00-65.00 |
| | *Empire Diner* salt and pepper shaker, "H Cavanagh © 196/200." | Set, $65.00-70.00 |
| | *Empire Diner* "H Cavanagh © 0/200, Sample." | $200.00+ |
| | *Empire Diner* shaker, mate above. | Set, $65.00-70.00 |
| **Row 2:** | *Taxi*, fifties style. "H Cavanagh © 6/200." | $300.00+ |
| | *Blimpmobile*, "H Cavanagh © 0/200 Sample." | $300.00+ |
| **Row 3:** | *Panel Delivery Truck*, thirties style. "H Cavanagh © 5/200." | $300.00+ |
| | *Checkered Taxi Sedan*, forties style. "H Cavanagh © 5/200." | $300.00+ |

Cavanagh on car construction from beginning to end...

Henry considers his research into real cars and period toy cars more fun than work. Taking various elements from a variety of sources, he synthesizes them into an original design or drawing. The drawing is rendered into a three-dimensional clay sculpture, purposely larger than the finished project to allow for shrinkage. A plaster mold that might have eight to ten parts and weighs up to one hundred pounds is made from this sculpture.

A clay casting is made from the plaster mold, using only proven commercial materials and guaranteed lead-free clays, colors, and glazes. The clay casting, lid, and base, are hand-fit and cleaned of seam lines and other casting marks, then dried thoroughly, and fired to 1,900℉ which results in a pure white, hard bisque piece.

The bisque piece is then colored. Most coloring requires three hand applied applications with drying time is between. Two applications of glaze are applied to the outside and one application is applied to the inside, which totals six hand-applied coats. The piece is fired around 1,800℉, but the glossy, brightly colored piece is not finished yet!

Silver highlights and details are hand-painted. An expensive platinum luster is used because silver would tarnish. The platinum is "fixed" with a low firing of 900°F. Further detail, such as decals or hand-painted areas, are done in china paints (over the glaze) and the whole thing is fired one last time at 1,200°F.

At the completion of each step, the lid and matching base are coded with a letter or number, so they can be kept together throughout the various processes. Some of these marks may remain visible on the finished piece. Finally, the platinum ©, the H Cavanagh signature, and the date are fired. When the protective felt pads are put on the bottom, the piece is numbered with a permanent marker (i.e., 15/200) and is entered into records. Pieces are numbered at the last moment, because of the loss potential in each step of the process.

# Characters

## Teenage Mutant Ninja Turtles

The Teenage Mutant Nunja Turtles send an ecological message to all of us. A large corporation carelessly discard a canister of green colloidial gel that has been exposed to a series of radiated waves. Four small pet turtles land in the ooze and are rescued by Splinter, the pet rat of a Ninja master, who contaminates himself in the process. Splinter adopts the turtles, giving them names he chooses from a Renaissance art book, which he had found in a storm drain. The turtles learn the way of the Ninja, and become a kick-stomping fighting team for the side of good.

**Row 1:**  *Raphael™,* "Teenage Mutant Ninja Turtles ®, International Silver Company, Made in Korea, © 1990 Mirage Studios, Exclusively licensed by Surge Licensing Inc."   $40.00-50.00

*Donatello* cereal bowl, "® & © 1990 Mirage Studios USA. Exclusively Licensed by Surge Licensing Inc., Made in China D13."   $5.00-7.00

*Michelangelo™,* "Teenage Mutant Ninja Turtles®, International Silver Company, Made in Korea, ©1990 Mirage Studios, Exclusively licensed by Surge Licensing Inc."   $40.00-50.00

*Raphael* cereal bowl, "® & © 1990 Mirage Studios USA. Exclusively Licensed by Surge Licensing Inc., Made in China D24."   $5.00-7.00

*Leonardo™,* "Teenage Mutant Ninja Turtles®, International Silver Company, Made in Korea. ©1990 Mirage Studios, Exclusively licensed by Surge Licensing Inc."   $40.00-50.00

**Row 2:**  *Raphael™,* "Teenage Mutant Ninja Turtles ©1991 Mirage Studios U.S.A. Exclusively Licensed by Surge Licensing Inc., International Silver Company, Made in Taiwan." Paper label, "Taiwan."   $40.00-50.00

*Michelangelo™,* "Teenage Mutant Ninja Turtles ©1991 Mirage Studios U.S.A. Exclusively Licensed by Surge Licensing Inc., International Silver Company, Made in Taiwan." Paper label, "Taiwan."   $40.00-50.00

*Leonardo™,* "Teenage Mutant Ninja Turtles © 1991 Mirage Studios U.S.A. Exclusively Licensed by Surge Licensing Inc., International Silver Company, Made in Taiwan." Paper label, "Taiwan."   $40.00-50.00

**Row 3:**  *Leonardo* cereal bowl, "® & © 1990 Mirage Studios USA. Exclusively Licensed by Surge Licensing Inc., Made in China A14."   $5.00-7.00

*Donatello™,* "Teenage Mutant Ninja Turtles ©1991 Mirage Studios U.S.A. Exclusively Licensed by Surge Licensing Inc., International Silver Company, Made in Taiwan." Paper label, "Taiwan."   $40.00-50.00

*Turtle* mug, mask changes color when liquid is added. "® & © Mirage Studios USA Exclusively by Surge Licensing Inc., Made in China C13."   $5.00-7.00

*Leonardo,* plastic coin bank, originally filled with chocolate chip cookies. "Distributed by Delicious Cookie Co. Inc., Des Plaines, Ill. 60018, ® & ©1990 Mirage Studios, Teenage Mutant Ninja Turtles."   $8.00-10.00

*Donatello™,* "Teenage Mutant Ninja Turtles®, International Silver Company, Made in Korea." ©1990 Mirage Studios USA. Exclusively Licensed by Surge Licensing Inc."   $40.00-50.00

*Michelangelo* cereal bowl, "® & © 1990 Mirage Studios USA. Exclusively Licensed by Surge Licensing Inc., Made in China D1."   $5.00-7.00

**Row 1:**    *Chef Nerd*, "Nerds®, ©1984 Willie Wonka Brands, exclusively distributed
by United Silver and Cutlery Co., Made in Taiwan." Snyder.                          $35.00-45.00

*Pound Puppy* with cane and derby, "Pound Puppies Lovable, Huggable exclusively distributed by United Silver and Cutlery Co., ©1987, Tonka Corp.
Made in Taiwan."                                                                    $55.00-65.00

*Pound Puppy* (Girl with Teddy Bear), unmarked. The paper label has probably
been removed.                                                                       $55.00-65.00

**Row 2:**    *Santa Nerd*, "Nerds®, ©1984 Willie Wonka Brands, exclusively distributed by
United Silver and Cutlery Co., Made in Taiwan."                                     $35.00-45.00

*Skateboard Nerd*, "Nerds®, ©1984 Willie Wonka Brands, exclusively distributed by United Silver and Cutlery Co., Made in Taiwan." Snyder.                     $35.00-45.00

*Baseball Nerd*, "Nerds®, ©1984 Willie Wonka Brands, exclusively distribut-
ed by United Silver and Cutlery Co., Made in Taiwan."                               $35.00-45.00

**Row 3:**    *Santa Pound Puppy*, "Pound Puppies Lovable, Huggable exclusively  distributed by United Silver and Cutlery Co., ©1987, Tonka Corp. Made in Taiwan."            $55.00-65.00

*Nose Marie*, "Pound Puppies Lovable, Huggable exclusively distributed by
United Silver and Cutlery Co., ©1987, Tonka Corp. Made in Taiwan."                  $55.00-65.00

*Howler*, "Pound Puppies Lovable, Huggable exclusively distributed by
United Silver and Cutlery Co., Made in Taiwan."                                     $55.00-65.00

**Below:**    *Chef Nerd*, "Nerds®, ©1984 Willie Wonka Brands, exclusively distributed by
United Silver and Cutlery Co., Made in Taiwan."                                     $35.00-45.00

*Baseball Nerd*, "Nerds®, ©1984 Willie Wonka Brands, exclusively distributed
by United Silver and Cutlery Co., Made in Taiwan." Snyder.                          $35.00-45.00

**Row 1:** *Ziggy*, paper label, "Designer Collection, Ziggy™, by Tom Wilson Press Syn., Text © MCMLXXXII WWA, Inc., WWA, Inc. Cleveland, USA 44144, Made in Korea."  $75.00-85.00

*Ernie the Keebler Elf* bank, "®." Unmarked. McCoy.  $35.00-45.00

*Garfield*, "©1978, 1981 United Features Syndicate, Inc. All Rights Reserved Worldwide. Licensee Enesco Corporation. Made in Indonesia" on paper label.  $40.00-50.00

**Row 2:** *Olive Oyl* shaker, re-issue of 1980 set for Popeye's birthday celebration. "Vandor © 1980 KFS."  Set, $40.00-50.00

*Tuffy*, a.k.a. Bluto, unmarked. An original by JD.  $125.00-150.00

*Popeye* shaker, mate to *Olive Oyl* above.  Set, $40.00-50.00

*Paddington Bear*, "Eden's Toys Inc. 1978." Braly.  $150.00-175.00

*Davy Crockett, Jr.* shaker, "Davy Crockett Jr." on paper label. Another paper label covers the hole in one foot, "After filling use Scotch or adhesive tape over hole."  Set, $100.00-125.00

*Davy Crockett* canister, "Handpainted Japan."  $80.00-90.00

*Davy Crockett, Jr.* shaker, mate above.  Set, $100.00-125.00

**Row 3:** *Alf,* "Handpainted, Made in USA."  $55.00-65.00

*Fred Flintstone*, "JD 1992."  $90.00-100.00

*Alf*, unmarked. Braly.  $55.00-65.00

**Below:** *Barney and Bam-Bam,* "JD 1992."  $90.00-100.00

*Garfield on Cookies*, "Garfield ©1978, 1981 United Features Syndicate Inc., Licensee Enesco" on transparent decal. "Enesco designed giftware, Korea" on foil label. Posner.  $150.00-175.00

*Miss Piggy* bank, "HA!" incised above the hole in the bottom of the bank. "Sigma" incised on opposite side of hole. "Tastesetter © Sigma…Made in Japan." Posner.  $50.00-75.00

# Jetsons

Vandor sent the Jetson catalog sheet to a few select customers in the fall of 1990. Samples were produced for spring shows, but licensing was never procured from Hanna Barbera. It is believed there were six cookie jars; twelve sets of Jetson shakers; possibly six sets of Spacely Sprockets shakers; and a limited run of figural mugs. The possibility that the bookends were never produced, even as samples, exists. Pricing is next to impossible on the Jetson line. It is a seller's market, with the exception of the baseball mugs, which are readily available. Characters rank among the hottest collectibles today. It would be a well envied collector that could claim ownership of the cookie jar or either set of salt and pepper shakers.

**Row 1:**    *George Jetson* mug, catalog number 2233. "©Hanna Barbera Productions
Inc. Licensed by Hamilton Projects Inc. Vandor®, ©1990, Made in Korea."          $20.00-30.00

*Jane* mug, catalog number 2235. "©Hanna Barbera Productions Inc.
Licensed by Hamilton Projects Inc. Vandor®, ©1990, Made in Korea."          $20.00-30.00

*Baseball* mug, catalog number 2226. "The Jetson ©1989 Hanna Barbera
Productions Inc., Licensed by Hamilton Projects Inc., Vandor, Made in Korea
©1990," on paper label.          $7.00-10.00

*Elroy* mug. Catalog number 2236. "©Hanna Barbera Productions Inc. Licensed by
Hamilton Projects Inc. Vandor®, © 1990, Made in Korea."          $20.00-30.00

*Judy* mug. Catalog number 2234. "©Hanna Barbera Productions Inc. Licensed by
Hamilton Projects Inc. Vandor, Made in Korea ©1990," on paper label.          $20.00-30.00

**Row 2:**    *Jetson* shakers, unmarked. Very rare, only twelve sets were ever produced.    Set, $350.00+

*Jetson* cookie jar featuring Elroy and Astro. Extremely rare, only six sample
jars ever produced.          Too rare to price

*Jetsons Catalog Sheet, Fall 1990.*

| | | | |
|---|---|---|---|
| #2225 | *Jetsons* decal mug. | $7.00-10.00 | |
| #2226 | *Baseball* mug. | $7.00-10.00 | |
| #2227 | *Office* mug. | $7.00-10.00 | |
| #2228 | *Soda Shop* mug. | $7.00-10.00 | |
| #2230 | *Spacely Sprocket* shakers. Extremely rare. | | |
| #2231 | *George and Astro* bookends. Extremely rare | | |

#2232    *Jetsons* shakers, very rare, only 12 pairs produced.

#2233    *George Jetson* figural mug.

#2234    *Judy* their daughter, figural mug.

#2235    *Jane* his wife, figural mug.

#2236    *Elroy* their son, figural mug.

#2237    *Jetsons* cookie jar. Extremely rare, only six samples produced.

**Row 1:**   *Fred Flintstone* mug, "Vandor, Made in Japan" on paper label.          $15.00-20.00

*Fred Flintstone*, standing. "Vandor ©1989."          $90.00-110.00

*Wilma Flintstone* mug, "Vandor, Made in Japan" on paper label.          $15.00-20.00

*Fred and Pebbles* cookie jar, "Vandor ©1989." Made in Japan" on paper label.          $275.00-325.00

**Row 2:**   *Fred and Wilma* bookends, "©1989 Vandor." Paper label, "Made in Japan."          $35.00-45.00

*Bam-Bam* salt or pepper shaker. "Vandor© Made in Korea" on paper label.          Set, $30.00-40.00

*Fred Flintstone* bank, "Vandor®, © Made in Korea" on paper label.          $15.00-20.00

*Pebbles* salt or pepper shaker, mate to *Bam-Bam* above.          Set, $30.00-40.00

*Dino and Pebbles* bank. "©1989 Vandor." Paper label, "Vandor © Made in Japan."          $35.00-45.00

*Barney* mug, "Vandor Made in Japan" on paper label.          $15.00-20.00

**Row 3:**   *Popeye* salt or pepper shaker. "Vandor ©1980 KFS."          Set, $40.00-50.00

*Swee' Pea* egg cup, "Vandor, Made in Japan" on paper label.          $10.00-15.00

*Olive Oyl* salt or pepper shaker, mate to *Popeye* above.          Set, $40.00-50.00

*Swee' Pea* bank, unmarked.          $80.00-100.00

*Howdy Doody* spoon rest, "Vandor, Made in Japan" on paper label.          $15.00-20.00

*Howdy Doody* bookends, "Vandor, Made in Japan" on paper label.          Set, $35.00-45.00

*Howdy Doody* covered box, "Vandor, Made in Japan" on paper label.          $25.00-35.00

**Below:**   *Sylvester and Tweety Bird*, "Warner Bros. Inc. 1989, the Good Company, City of Industry, CA 91749." Saxton.          $250.00+

The popular children's show *Howdy Doody* aired on NBC from December 1947 through September 1960. Howdy Doody remains highly collectible today in the nineties, perhaps more so than when Howdy was alive and well and not just a memory.

*1989 Vandor Catalog Sheet*

| #0578 | Howdy Doody Cookie Jar | $275.00+ |
|---|---|---|
| #0586 | Howdy Doody TV Bank | $25.00-35.00 |
| #0587 | Howdy Doody Picture Frame | $12.00-15.00 |
| #0590 | Howdy Doody Spoon Rest | $15.00-20.00 |
| #0577 | Howdy Doody Face Mask | $30.00-40.00 |
| #0592 | Howdy Doody Wall Hook | $25.00-35.00 |
| #0585 | Howdy Doody Salt and Pepper | $25.00-35.00 |
| #0583 | Howdy Doody Bank | $15.00-20.00 |
| #0588 | Howdy Doody Pin Tray | $12.00-15.00 |
| #0584 | Howdy Doody Magnets | $4.00-6.00 |

#0581    Howdy Doody Covered Box...................................................$25.00-35.00
#0593    Howdy Doody Clock (The catalog sheet assigns the same
             number, 0593, to the clock and wood cut-out on right.)........$30.00-40.00
#0597    Howdy Doody Wristwatch Clock.............................................$30.00-40.00
#0593    Howdy Doody Wood Cut-out ................................................$25.00-35.00

*Vandor Catalog Sheet*

#0595    Howdy Doody Mike Music Box................................................$20.00-30.00
#0579    Howdy Doody Bookends .....................................................$35.00-45.00
#0574    Howdy Doody Bumper Car Cookie Jar .........................................$250.00+
#0594    Howdy Doody Jukebox Music Box............................................$40.00-50.00
#0580    Howdy Doody Music Box......................................................$25.00-35.00
#0576    Howdy Doody Decal Mugs ....................................................$7.00-12.00
#0572    Howdy Doody Water Ball .....................................................$20.00-30.00
#0575    Howdy Doody Sculptured Mug ..............................................$15.00-20.00
#0599    Howdy Doody Deep Dish Decal ...............................................$8.00-10.00

All Howdy Doody items were discontinued by Vandor in 1990.

# Harry James

All Harry James items are licensed and distributed in England. Most of the manufacturing is accomplished in the Far East for HJ.

**Row 1:**  *Garfield,* "©1978, 1981 United Features Syndicate, Inc. All rights reserved worldwide. LICENSEE ENESCO CORPORATION, MADE IN INDONESIA," decal on bottom.  $55.00-65.00

*Beny,* distributed in England, 7" tall. "©1990 Hanna Barbera Productions Inc. On the box, "Harry James Design ® ™."  $50.00-60.00

*Top Cat,* distributed in England, 10" tall. "©1990 Hanna Barbera productions Inc." On the box. "Harry James Design ® ™."  $65.00-75.00

*Garfield, Loose in the Kitchen,* England. "Garfield ©1978, 1981 United Syndicate Features Inc., Made in Taiwan for Molly Housewares Limited."  $70.00-90.00

**Row 2:**  *Tom and Jerry,* England, 7" tall. "Tom and Jerry ™© 90 Turner Entertainment Co., Exclusive Harry James Design ®™."  $50.00-60.00

*Tom and Jerry,* England, 10" tall. "Tom and Jerry ™©90 Turner Entertainment Co., Exclusive Harry James Design ®™."  $65.00-75.00

*Smokey Bear* salt or pepper shaker, unmarked. Made in Japan. Okamoto.  Set, $60.00-75.00

*Smokey Bear* cookie jar, unmarked, Norcrest.  $450.00+

*Smokey Bear* shaker, mate above. Unmarked. Okamoto.  Set, $60.00-75.00

*Barney Rubble,* England. "Made in Taiwan. An Exclusive Harry James Design ®™."  $50.00-60.00

*Fred Flintstone,* England. "©1990 Hanna Barbera Productions Inc., An Exclusive Harry James Design ®™."  $85.00-95.00

**Row 3:**  *Yogi Bear,* England, 10" tall. "©1990 Hanna Barbera Productions, Inc., An Exclusive Harry James Design ®™."  $65.00-75.00

*Boo-Boo,* England, 7" tall, "©1990 Hanna Barbera Productions, Inc., An Exclusive Harry James Design.®™."  $50.00-60.00

*Smokey Bear* bank, unmarked. Okamoto.  $110.00-135.00

*Bart Simpson* tin bank. "©1992 Nestlé Chocolate and Confection Company."  $5.00-8.00

*Homer Simpson* cookie jar, England. "©1990 Twentieth Century-Fox Film Corp." On the box, "Harry James Design®™, Taiwan."  $250.00+

**Characters** ─────────────────────────────────────────────────────

**Row 1:**   *Human Beans™* figurine, "Moms are Special." "HUMAN BEANS ©1981 Morgan Inc. Lic. Enesco Imports" decal. "ENESCO DESIGNED GIFTWARE SRI LANKA" on paper label. Snyder.   $7.00-10.00

*Human Beans™* bank, "My needs are simple, but my wants are very expensive." "HUMAN BEANS © 1981 Morgan Inc. Lic. Enesco Imports" decal. "ENESCO DESIGNED GIFTWARE SRI LANKA" on paper label. Snyder.   $10.00-15.00

*Human Beans™* figurine, "This HUMAN BEAN™ is on the ball." "HUMAN BEANS ©1981 Morgan Inc. Lic. Enesco Imports" decal. "ENESCO DESIGNED GIFTWARE SRI LANKA" on paper label. Snyder.   $7.00-10.00

*The World of Beatrix Potter – Peter Rabbit Cookies* tin.   $7.00-9.00

*Human Beans™* figurine, "Bosses are HUMAN BEANS™ too." "HUMAN BEANS ©1981 Morgan Inc. Lic. Enesco Imports" decal. "ENESCO DESIGNED GIFTWARE SRI LANKA" on paper label. Snyder.   $7.00-10.00

*Human Beans™* pen holder, "Happy Birthday Grandpa." "HUMAN BEANS ©1981 Morgan Inc. Lic. Enesco Imports" decal. "ENESCO DESIGNED GIFTWARE SRI LANKA" on paper label. Snyder.   $7.00-10.00

*Human Beans™* snow bank. "Human Bean ©1981 Morgan Inc. LTD ENESCO Imports."   $10.00-15.00

**Row 2:**   *Human Beans™* figurine, "You're my type of ... HUMAN BEAN™." "HUMAN BEANS ©1981 Morgan Inc. Lic. Enesco Imports" decal. "ENESCO DESIGNED GIFTWARE SRI LANKA" on paper label. Snyder.   $7.00-10.00

*Human Beans™* figurine, "Be nice to me...I'm a HUMAN BEAN™." Unmarked, labels have been removed. Snyder.   $7.00-10.00

*Human Bean™* bank, "This is a RETIRED HUMAN BEAN." "HUMAN BEAN ©1981 Morgan Inc. Lic. Enesco Imports" decal. "KOREA" on paper label. Snyder.   $10.00-15.00

*Human Beans™* cookie jar. "Human Bean ©1981 Morgan Inc. LTD, Enesco Imports."   $35.00-45.00

*Human Beans™* bank, "This is a RETIRED HUMAN BEING." "HUMAN BEANS © 1981 Morgan Inc. Lic. Enesco Imports" decal. "Korea" on paper label. Snyder.   $10.00-15.00

*Human Beans™* figurine, "EXECUTIVES ARE SUCCESSFUL HUMAN BEANS™." Unmarked, labels are missing. Snyder.   $5.00-7.00

*Human Beans™* bank, "This HUMAN BEAN™ ... LOVES ALL." "HUMAN BEANS ©1981 Morgan Inc. Lic. Enesco Imports" decal. "ENESCO DESIGNED GIFTWARE SRI LANKA" on paper label. Snyder.   $10.00-15.00

**Row 3:**   *Strawberry Shortcake* tin, "Checo Housewares, J. CHEIN & Co."   $8.00-10.00

*Frosty the Snowman* salt or pepper shaker, range size. "™/© Warner/Chappell Music 1990, Made in Taiwan" on paper label. Snyder.   Set, $15.00-20.00

*Frosty the Snowman* magnet, unmarked.   $2.00-4.00

*Frosty the Snowman* cookie jar, "™/© Warner/Chappell Music 1990. Made in Taiwan" on paper labe.   $35.00-45.00
*Frosty the Snowman* salt or pepper shaker, mate above.   Set, $15.00-20.00

*Frosty the Snowman* candy dish. "™/© Warner/Chappell Music 1990. Made in Taiwan on paper label. Snyder.   $15.00-20.00

*Frosty the Snowman* magnet, unmarked. Same as above.   Set, $2.00-4.00

*Frosty the Snowman* utensil holder. "™/© Warner/Chappell Music 1990. Made in Taiwan" on paper label. Snyder.   $15.00-20.00

**Row 1:**    *E.T.*, unmarked. Snyder.                                                    $25.00-35.00

*Davy Crockett* mug by Brush, unmarked.                                $40.00-50.00

*Woodsey Owl* by McCoy. "®" on base.                                   $40.00-50.00

*Cinderella and Fairy Godmother*, "© Applause" on paper label. "©Applause
Inc. Made in China 33254."                                             $50.00-60.00

**Row 2:**    *Sherman on the Mount*, "Sherman on the Mount™ MCMLXXXIII, American
Greeting Corp. Cleveland Ohio 44144 Made in Korea." Snyder.            $65.00-75.00

*Weiss Red Riding Hood*, Portugal.                                    $125.00-150.00

*Jack and the Beanstalk* cookie jar, "© Made in Japan" stamped under glaze.
Snyder.                                                                $35.00-45.00

*Jack and the Beanstalk* salt or pepper shaker, unmarked. Japan. Snyder.    Set, $10.00-12.00

**Row 3:**    *Cookie Monster* by California Originals. "505 USA." Snyder.            $35.00-45.00

*Davy Crockett* cylinder. "RANSBURG GENUINE HAND PAINTED INDIAN-
APOLIS U.S.A." incised into bottom. Snyder.                            $30.00-40.00

*Cool Cookie Penguin*, "Made in Taiwan ©1981 Hallmark Cards Inc." stamped
on bottom. Snyder.                                                     $65.00-75.00

**Below:**   *Oliver Hardy* decanter, "Heritage China, 25-35 1976 R.H.-66, Ezra Brooks ©
Larry Harman Pictures Corp." Heritage China was a trade name used by
Roman Ceramics for Ezra Brooks.                                        $25.00-35.00

*Stan Laurel* decanter, "Heritage China, 25-35 1976 R.H.-66, Ezra Brooks ©
Larry Harman Pictures Corp."                                           $25.00-35.00

*Oliver Hardy* cookie jar, "C through W, U.S.A." C through W is Cumberland
Ware, a trade name used by Roman Ceramics of Mayfield, KY.              $350.00+

Polynesian Arts, founded in 1943, was Harold Roman's
original company. Sikeston Ceramics was an extension of
Polynesian Arts, with Roman Ceramics an extension of Sikeston Ceramics. All divisions were closed in 1982.

## Characters

**Row 1:**   *Popeye Spinach Can*, produced by Shirley Corl.                          $150.00+

                 *Swee' Pea* reproduction, "G 67/200." Gerds.                          $150.00-160.00

**Row 2:**   *Popeye* reproduction, "G 71/200." Gerds.                          $150.00-160.00

                 *Olive Oyl* reproduction, "G 35/200." Gerds.                          $150.00-160.00

**Row 3:**   *Tar Baby*, an original by Shirley Corl.                          $130.00-150.00

                 *Baby Huey* reproduction, "G 39/200." Gerds.                          $150.00-160.00

                 *Porky Pig*, "1975 Warner Bros."                          $80.00-90.00

**Below:**   *Garfield* salt and pepper shakers. "Enesco designed giftware, Japan."
Foil label and transparent decal "Garfield ©1978 1981 United Features
Syndicate Inc. Licensee Enesco." Posner.                          Set, $55.00-65.00

                 *Garfield and Arlene* salt and pepper shakers. Hanging tag, "One
hundred percent pure Garfield." "Brought to you by Enesco, Garfield
©1978, United Features Syndicate Inc., Licensee Enesco Corporation."
Posner.                          Set, $65.00-85.00

                 *Garfield* bookends. Transparent decal "Immovable object, Garfield by
Jim Davis, G 1978, 1981 United Features Syndicate Inc. Licensee
Enesco E5913." "Enesco designed giftware, Japan." Posner.                          Pair, $125.00-150.00

"Garfield ©1978, 1981 United
Features Inc. Licensee Enesco,"
"Enesco designed giftware, Korea."

**Row 1:** *Muppets' Old Men in Balcony,* "Sigma the Tastesetter © Henson and Assoc." Posner. (top left photo, left)     $195.00-225.00

*Kermit and Miss Piggy* salt and pepper shakers. "Sigma The Tastesetter © Henson and Assoc. Made in Japan." Posner. (top left photo, right)     $75.00-85.00

*Snoopy* candy jar, "Snoopy © 1958-1966 United Feature Syndicate Inc." Posner. (top right photo, left)     $100.00-125.00

*Woodstock,* covered container. Posner. (top right photo, center)     $35.00-45.00

*Snoopy* jam jar, "SNOOPY © 1958, 1966 United Feature Syndicate Inc." Posner. (top right photo, right)     $55.00-75.00

**Row 2:** *Smokey Bear* salt or pepper shaker, unmarked. Made in Japan. Posner. (center left photo, left)     Set, $60.00-75.00

*Smokey Bear* candy jar, unmarked, Norcrest. Posner. (center left photo, center)     $350.00+

*Smokey Bear* shaker, mate above. Unmarked. Posner. (center left photo, right)     Set, $60.00-75.00

*Smokey Bear* ash tray, foil label "Reg. Pat. Off. Norcrest Japan." Posner. (center right photo)     $95.00-125.00

**Row 3:** *Swee' Pea* bank by the American Bisque Comapny, unmarked. Posner. (bottom left photo)     $600.00-800.00

*Raggedy Ann,* "© 1972 The Bobbs Merrill Co. Ltd." Posner. (bottom right photo)     $300.00-400.00

A 0603 Waitress Cutout
B 0605 Pot Pourri
C 0606 Magnets (asst. 4)
D 0609 Boat Salt & Pepper
E 0610 Diner Salt & Pepper
F 0611 Salt & Pepper & Napkin Holder
G 0613 Car Pouch (asst. 3)
H 0615 Eyeglass Case
I 0616 Juke Box Music Box
J 0617 Palm Music Box
K 0626 Wall Hooks (asst. 4)
L 0627 Surfer Frame
M 0628 Music Notes Frame
N 0653 Hula Covered Box
O 0662 T-Bird Covered Box
P 0664 Mugs (asst. 4)
Q 0666 Tin-Box w/Candle
R 0667 Tin Boxes (asst. 4)
S 0668 Juke Box Bank
T 0673 Picture Frame
U 0434 Clock

*1989 Vandor Catalog Sheet*
Betty Boop

| | | | | | | |
|---|---|---|---|---|---|---|
| A - | #0603 | Waitress Cut-out | $30.00-35.00 | L - #0627 | Surfer Frame | $20.00-25.00 |
| B - | #0605 | Pot Pourri | $20.00-25.00 | M - #0628 | Music Notes Frame | $20.00-25.00 |
| C - | #0606 | Magnets (asst. 4) | $12.00-16.00 | N - #0653 | Hula Covered Box | $20.00-25.00 |
| D - | #0609 | Boat salt and pepper | $15.00-20.00 | O - #0662 | T-Bird Covered Box | $20.00-25.00 |
| E - | #0610 | Diner salt and pepper | $20.00-25.00 | P - #0664 | Mugs (asst. 4) | $20.00-25.00 |
| F - | #0611 | Salt & Pepper & Napkin | $20.00-25.00 | Q - #0666 | Tin-Box w/Candle | $20.00-25.00 |
| G - | #0613 | Car Pouch | $5.00-10.00 | R - #0667 | Tin Boxes (asst. 4) | $20.00-25.00 |
| H - | #0615 | Eyeglass Case | $5.00-10.00 | S - #0668 | Juke Box Bank | $20.00-25.00 |
| I - | #0605 | Juke Box Music Box | $45.00-55.00 | T - #0673 | Picture | $20.00-25.00 |
| I - | #0617 | Palm Music Box | $45.00-55.00 | U - #0434 | Clock | $20.00-25.00 |
| J - | #0626 | Wall Hooks (asst. 4) | $6.00-10.00 | | | |

*1989 Vandor Catalog Sheet*
Betty Boop

| A - #0106 | Mask | $30.00-40.00 | N - #2025 | 60th Anniversary Mug | $20.00-30.00 |
|---|---|---|---|---|---|
| B - #0107 | Mini Mask | $15.00-20.00 | O - #2026 | 60th Anniversary Plate | $35.00-45.00 |
| C - #0600 | Face Mask | $18.00-26.00 | P - #2027 | 60th Anniversary Box | $25.00-35.00 |
| D - #0601 | Piano Music Box | $40.00-50.00 | Q - #2035 | Bath Box | $40.00-50.00 |
| E - #0618 | Piano Music Box | $40.00-50.00 | R - #2036 | Bookends | $65.00-70.00 |
| F - #0629 | Piano Ashtray | $22.00-30.00 | S - #2037 | 3-Piece Bath Set | $50.00-60.00 |
| G - #0630 | Piano Vase | $20.00-25.00 | T - #2038 | Hand Mirror | $40.00-50.00 |
| H - #0635 | Heart Box | $14.00-20.00 | U - #2039 | Federal Reserve Bank | $30.00-40.00 |
| I - #0661 | Heart Frame | $20.00-25.00 | V - #2040 | Book Music Box | $45.00-55.00 |
| J - #0672 | Tophat Jar | $75.00-85.00 | W - #2041 | Face Box | $25.00-35.00 |
| K - #0674 | Pencil Holder | $25.00-35.00 | X - #2042 | Moon Planter | $35.00-45.00 |
| L - #0675 | Testarosa Box | $35.00-45.00 | Y - #2048 | Flower Vase | $35.00-45.00 |
| M - #0676 | Moon Dish | $20.00-30.00 | Z - #2049 | Electric Night-light | $75.00-85.00 |

# Christmas

**Row 1:**    *Santa,* "The Cook's Bizarre, Made in Taiwan" on paper label. Snyder.    $30.00-40.00

               *Bear with Muff,* "Made in Taiwan ROC" on paper label. Snyder.    $25.00-35.00

               *Santa,* "Made in Taiwan" on paper label. Snyder.    $20.00-30.00

The Dayton-Hudson Santa tradition began in 1981 with a new and different Santa scheduled for release each year. The Santa jars produced prior to 1984 are dated and marked "Hudson." Even after Dayton bought Hudson in 1984, the tradition continued. Marshall Field was added to the Dayton-Hudson holdings in 1990 further expanding the market availability of these wonderful Santas to collectors.

**Row 2:**    *1987 Dayton-Hudson Santa,* "Made in Japan" paper label. "Dayton's 1987" stamped under glaze. Snyder.    $65.00-75.00

               *Christmas Mouse,* unmarked. Snyder.    $25.00-35.00

               *Santa Snowman,* "Made in Taiwan" paper label. Snyder.    $25.00-35.00

**Row 3:**    *Santa with Teddy Bear,* "Made in China" paper label. Snyder.    $25.00-35.00

               *Boots with Toys,* "The Cook's Bizarre, Made in Taiwan" paper label. Snyder.    $20.00-30.00

               *Santa Gnome,* unmarked. Snyder.    $20.00-30.00

**Below:**    *Santa,* "Made in Taiwan" paper label.    $20.00-30.00

               *Roly-Poly Santa,* salt or pepper shaker, "Made in Taiwan" paper label.    Set. $8.00-10.00

               *Black Santa,* "Handpainted, Made in USA."    $90.00-100.00

               *Roly-Poly Santa,* salt or pepper shaker, mate above.    Set, $8.00-10.00

               *Roly-Poly Santa* cookie jar, "Made in Taiwan" paper label.    $20.00-30.00

**Row 1:**     *Mrs. Santa* salt and pepper shaker. "Napco Ceramic Japan" on paper label.
Stamped "AX920P – AX9205." Snyder.              Set, $10.00-15.00

*Santa*, "Reg. US Pat Off Norcrest Japan" paper label. Stamped "X – 14."
Snyder.        $30.00-40.00

*Santa* salt or pepper shaker, mate to *Mrs. Santa* above. Snyder.     Set, $10.00-15.00

*1992 Dayton-Hudson Snowman*, "Japan" decal.     $45.00-50.00

*Sleigh*, "Made in Taiwan" paper label.     $15.00-20.00

**Row 2:**     *Santa* candy dish or planter, unmarked. Snyder.     $15.00-20.00

*Santa* candy container or planter, stamped "S 413 A." Snyder.     $20.00-25.00

*Santa* cookie jar, stamped "©1965 Snarco Cleve, Ohio E – 2079." Snyder.     $40.00-45.00

*Santa* bank, unmarked. Snyder.     $12.00-15.00

*Santa with Teddy Bear*, small. "Made in Taiwan" paper label. Snyder.     $10.00-12.00

**Row 3:**     *1992 Dayton-Hudson Santa*, a Jim Smith design. "©Dayton's 1992,
© Marshall Field's 1992 ©Hudson's 1992. Made in Japan."     $50.00-60.00

*Dayton-Hudson Snowman*, distributed by Dayton-Hudson Corporation,
Minneapolis, MN 55402. "Made in Taiwan" paper label.     $45.00-50.00

*1991 Dayton-Hudson Santa*, a Jim Smith design. "© Dayton's 1991, ©
Marshall Field's 1991, © Hudson's 1991, Made in Japan."     $65.00-75.00

**Below:**     *Skating Rabbit*, "Japan."     $30.00-40.00

*Christmas Tree with Mice*, "OCI."     $65.00-75.00

*Mrs. Kringle*, "Christmas Kringles, Department 56" on paper label. Paper
label, "Made in Japan © for Department 56."     $70.00-80.00

# Cleminsons

The California Cleminsons began in 1941 in El Monte, CA. Cleminsons' business venture outgrew the confines of the family's garage, making it necessary to build a factory to house the pottery. Larger quarters enabled the hiring of additional employees, many of whom were decorators. The lively Pennsylvania Dutch Cleminsons style is highly acclaimed and sought by collectors today.

**Below:**    *Pot Belly Stove*, "The California Cleminsons © Hand painted."      $60.00-80.00

              *House,* "The California Cleminsons © Hand painted." Snyder.      $60.00-80.00

              *Cook Book*, "The California Cleminsons, Hand painted ©."      $60.00-80.00

# DeForest of California

DeForest is another small family based venture that prospered and grew. Several new jars have surfaced since Book I with the collectibility of DeForest being recognized. Don Winton states he did design work for DeForest but cannot remember if this included cookie jars.

**Row 1:**    *Calorie Sally*, "© 1959 DeForest of California USA." Snyder.      $35.00-45.00

              *Rabbit*, "DeForest of Calif © 58." Snyder.      $30.00-35.00

              *Sailor Girl Elephant*, "DeForest of Calif. USA © 1964-506."      $45.00-50.00

**Row 2:**    *Weather House*, "19 © 60 DeForest of Calif USA." Snyder.      $35.00-45.00

              *Owl*, "DeForest of California 5537-5545." Snyder.      $30.00-35.00

              *Tuggle*, "California."      $35.00-45.00

**Row 3:**    *Dachshund,* "DeForest of Calif 518."      $50.00-75.00

              *Pig Head* salt or pepper shaker, unmarked. Snyder.      Set, $15.00-20.00

              *Pig Head* cookie jar, "DeForest of California Handpainted." Snyder.      $30.00-40.00

              *Pig Head* salt or pepper shaker, mate above.      Set, $15.00-20.00

              *Pig Goody Bank*, with cookie jar base. "DeForest of California © 1965."      $125.00-150.00

**Row 1:**  *Onions* condiment, "DeForest of California, Hand Painted." Snyder.  $15.00-20.00

*Garlic* condiment, "DeForest of California Hand Painted." Snyder.  $15.00-20.00

*Snappy Gingerbread Boy*, "DeForest of California © #6, Made in USA." Snyder.  $100.00-125.00

*Mustard* condiment, unmarked. Snyder.  $15.00-20.00

*Jam* jar, "DeForest of California Hand Painted." Snyder.  $15.00-20.00

**Row 2:**  *Monk,* "1964 © DeForest of California USA."  $65.00-75.00

*Onions* condiment, "DeForest of California Hand Painted." Snyder.  $15.00-20.00

*Buddha*, "USA DeForest of California #527." Snyder.  $65.00-75.00

*Mr. and Mrs. Garlic*, "DeForest of California Hand Painted." Snyder.  $20.00-30.00

*Nun*, "DeForest of California."  $150.00-200.00

**Row 3:**  *Chipmunk*, "DeForest 514."  $40.00-45.00

*Cheese* condiment, unmarked. Snyder.  $15.00-20.00

*Cheese* shaker, single, unmarked. Snyder.  $8.00-10.00

*Monkey*, "DeForest of California 5516." Snyder.  $30.00-40.00

*Owl* salt or pepper shaker, unmarked.  Set, $8.00-10.00

*Owl* cookie jar, "DeForest of California."  $30.00-35.00

*Owl* shaker, mate above.  Set, $8.00-10.00

# Department 56 Inc.

Department 56 Inc. is an importer/distributor based in Eden Prairie, MN.

**Row 1:**  *Mirage Cactus* cookie jar, "Mirage © Dept. 56." Snyder. ............... $35.00-40.00

*Mirage Cactus* shaker, unmarked. Snyder. ............... Set, $10.00-15.00

*Mirage Cactus* teapot, "Mirage © Dept. 56." Snyder. ............... $28.00-32.00

*Short-Order Toaster* cookie jar, "Short-Order Made in Japan Exclusively
for © Department 56 Inc." Snyder. ............... $45.00-55.00

**Row 2:**  *Ugly Stepsisters*, "Tea Time Ugly Stepsisters  Dept. 56, 1989." Snyder. ............... $50.00-60.00

*Witch,* unmarked, paper label missing. ............... $40.00-50.00

*Le Chef Cuisine* salt or pepper shaker. "Le Chef Cuisine, Dept. 56" on paper
label. ............... Set, $20.00-25.00

*Le Chef Cuisine* cookie jar. "Le Chef Cuisine, Dept. 56" on paper label.
"© Linda Massopust Design, Made in Japan © Dept. 56." ............... $150.00-175.00

*Le Chef Cuisine* shaker, mate above. ............... Set, $20.00-25.00

**Row 3:**  *McNutts Egg* covered sugar, "McNutts © 1988 Schlaifer Nance & Co Inc.
Dept 56 Japan." Snyder. ............... Set, $25.00-30.00

*McNutts Chicken* creamer, "McNutts © 1988 Schlaifer Nance & Co Inc. Dept.
56 Japan." Snyder. ............... Set, $25.00-30.00

*McNutts Chicken* teapot, "McNutts © 1988 Schlaifer Nance & Co Inc. Dept.
56 Japan." Snyder. ............... $40.00-50.00

*McNutts Egg* cookie jar, "McNutts © 1988 Schlaifer Nance & Co Inc. Dept.
56 Japan." ............... $50.00-60.00

*McNutts Egg* salt and pepper shakers. "Made in Japan for © Dept. 56" on
paper label. Snyder. ............... Set. $15.00-20.00

*McNutts Corn* butter dish, "McNutts © 1988 SN & Co. Inc. Dept. 56 Japan."
Snyder. ............... $30.00-35.00

*McNutts Chicken Coop* cookie jar, "McNutts Dept. 56 Japan, © 1988
Schialfer Nance & Co. Inc." ............... $125.00-150.00

# Desert Notions

Desert Notions was established in 1980 at Apache Junction, AZ, by Tom Williams. Tom froze his retirement with Ford Motor Company and moved to Arizona after his wife developed health problems. He had always loved to make things; now fate handed him the perfect opportunity to try his hand at creativity as a livelihood. Tom does all of the designing and manufactures the Desert Notions line with the aid of his wife and their ten employees.

**Below:**   *Navajo and Child*, "Hand painted and manufactured by Desert Notions, Apache Junction, AZ., 22K Gold trim."          $40.00-50.00

*Pueblo* cookie jar, "Hand painted and manufactured by Desert Notions, Apache Junction, AZ., 22K Gold trim."          $40.00-50.00

# Doranne of California

The Doranne of California corporation was dissolved April 1, 1991. This is becoming the all too familiar demise of American potteries.

| | | |
|---|---|---|
| **Row 1:** | *Basket of Lemons*, "J - 20 © USA." Wells. | $35.00-45.00 |
| | *Frog*, unmarked. | $35.00-45.00 |
| | *Hippo*, "CJ 6 © USA." | $30.00-40.00 |
| **Row 2:** | *Wide Mouth Jar* salt or pepper shaker, unmarked. | Set, $15.00-20.00 |
| | *Wide Mouth Jar* cookie jar, unmarked. | $35.00-45.00 |
| | *Wide Mouth Jar* salt or pepper shaker, mate above. | Set, $15.00-20.00 |
| | *Fire Hydrant,* "CJ 50 USA." | $35.00-45.00 |
| | *Dog*, unmarked. | $40.00-50.00 |
| **Row 3:** | *Deer*, unmarked. | $35.00-45.00 |
| | *Crook-Neck Squash*, "CJ © USA." | $35.00-45.00 |
| | *Mother Goose*, "USA." Snyder. | $100.00-125.00 |

**Row 1:**   *Donkey*, "USA" on back. This *Donkey* can also be found in a decorated version. Braly.                                                                                  $75.00-85.00

*Van*, "118 CJ USA©."                                                                                  $60.00-75.00

*Pumpkin*, unmarked. Braly.                                                                       $30.00-35.00

**Row 2:**   *Ice Cream Soda*, "J 66 © USA."                                                         $45.00-50.00

*Volkswagen*, "117 CJ USA©."                                                                     $150.00-175.00

*Lackadaisical Dog*, unmarked.                                                                   $55.00-65.00

**Row 3:**   *Cat and Mouse*, "CJ 4 USA."                                                             $45.00-55.00

*4 X 4 Pick-up*, "Doranne, CA CJ 119 © USA."                                           $100.00-125.00

*Bear Essentials* cookie jar, unmarked.                                                      $45.00-55.00

**Below:**   *Leprechaun Pot*, "J 42 USA." Clyde/Takasugi.                                     $75.00-85.00

*Jeep*, "Doranne Calif CJ 115." Darrow.                                                      $60.00-75.00

**Row 1:**    *Cup Cake,* "J 54." Snyder.                                    $30.00-35.00

               *Cookie,* "USA J55." Snyder.                                  $30.00-40.00

               *Pure Cane Sugar,* unmarked. Snyder.                          $30.00-35.00

**Row 2:**    *Lemon,* unmarked. Snyder.                                    $25.00-35.00

               *Apple,* "USA J 111." Snyder.                                 $25.00-35.00

               *Mug of Beer,* "USA J 72©." Snyder.                          $30.00-40.00

**Row 3:**    *Orange,* "USA J 112." Snyder.                                 $25.00-35.00

               *Pineapple,* "J 115." Snyder.                                 $25.00-35.00

               *Strawberry,* unmarked. Snyder.                              $25.00-35.00

**Below:**    *Antique Milk Can,* "USA J 16. Snyder.                        $25.00-35.00

               *Strawberry Pie,* "USA J 55." Snyder.                         $40.00-45.00

               *Deer,* unmarked. Snyder.                                     $35.00-45.00

**Row 1:**    *Cat*, flat unglazed bottom, unmarked. We feel this jar was erroneously placed in the Doranne section. Holiday Design?      $35.00-45.00

              *Rabbit in Hat*, "CJ 74."      $35.00-45.00

              *Shaggy Dog*, unmarked.      $40.00-45.00

**Row 2:**    *Humpty Dumpty*, "© USA CJ 47." Snyder.      $60.00-80.00

              *Hound Dog*, "USA." Snyder.      $35.00-40.00

              *Sniffing Dog*, "USA GK4." Snyder.      $35.00-40.00

**Row 3:**    *Shoe House*, "USA." Snyder.      $30.00-35.00

              *Cat*, "J 5 USA." Snyder.      $30.00-35.00

              *Owl*, "© USA J 62." Snyder.      $30.00-35.00

**Below:**    *Dragon*, "USA."      $75.00-85.00

              *Snowman* "J 52 USA." Snyder.      $100.00-125.00

| | | |
|---|---|---|
| **Row 1:** | *Hippo,* "California USA 18." Snyder. | $35.00-40.00 |
| | *Cable Car,* "Doranne Calif. CJ 116 USA." Snyder. | $45.00-55.00 |
| **Row 2:** | *Ice Cream Cone,* unmarked. Snyder. | $30.00-35.00 |
| | *Clown,* "USA." Snyder. | $45.00-55.00 |
| | *Ice Cream Sundae,* "USA J 66G©." Snyder. | $35.00-45.00 |
| **Row 3:** | *Walrus,* "Calif." Snyder. | $30.00-35.00 |
| | *Pinocchio/Court Jester,* "C J 46 © USA." Snyder. | $175.00-195.00 |
| | *Die,* "J 70 © USA." Snyder. | $25.00-35.00 |
| **Below:** | *Slot Machine,* "J 64© USA." | $30.00-35.00 |
| | *Turtle,* "USA 14 ©." Snyder. | $30.00-35.00 |

**Row 1:** *Koala Kate*, unmarked but purchased in the original box, leaving no
doubt as to the manufacturer. $30.00-35.00

*Fish*, unmarked. $30.00-35.00

*Bear Essentials* bank, unmarked. Snyder. $15.00-18.00

**Row 2:** *Duck with Yarmulke*, unmarked. $35.00-45.00

*Brown Bagger*, "USA." $25.00-35.00

*Cookies and Milk Carton*, unmarked. $25.00-35.00

**Row 3:** *Mouse,* "M-450-USA." $30.00-35.00

*Lion*, unmarked. $30.00-40.00

# Ely

To date, no information is available on I.G. Ely and Company.

**Below:** *Ye Olde Outhouse,*"© I.G. Ely & Co., 1959," on the lid and base. This piece
has a china body and characteristics very similar to Regal China. Could
this be the mystery manufacturer of *Harpo Marx?* $125.00-150.00

# Enesco

Enesco is an Elk Grove, IL based importer/distributor.

The Mother-in-the-Kitchen line is sometimes called Prayer Lady. The shakers were found in the original box, complete with label, giving us the actual product name. An ad found in the 1967-68 *Helen Gallager Foster House* catalog gives us dating. When we say any of these pieces are unmarked, it simply means the small red and gold oval label is missing.

**Row 1:**   *Mother-in-the-Kitchen* napkin holder. Paper label, "Imports, Enesco, Japan." Wooldridge.  $30.00-35.00

*Mother-in-the-Kitchen* mug, unmarked. Wooldridge.  $12.00-15.00

*Mother-in-the-Kitchen* salt and pepper shakers. Wooldridge.  Set, $12.00-15.00

*Mother-in-the-Kitchen* spoon holder. "Imports, Enesco, Japan" on paper label.  $30.00-35.00

*Mother-in-the-Kitchen* look-a-like salt and pepper shakers, plastic, "Hong Kong." Wooldridge.  Set, $5.00-7.00

*Mother-in-the-Kitchen* instant coffee, unmarked. Wooldridge.  $35.00-45.00

**Row 2:**   *Mother-in-the-Kitchen* covered sugar, part of tea set, unmarked. Wooldridge. Three-piece set: teapot, sugar, and creamer.  3-piece Set, $100.00+

*Mother-in-the-Kitchen*, creamer, the second part of the tea set, Wooldridge.

*Mother-in-the-Kitchen* timer. "Imports, Enesco, Japan" on label. Wooldridge.  $40.00-45.00

*Mother-in-the-Kitchen* salt or pepper shaker, "Imports, Enesco, Japan." Wooldridge.  Set, $10.00-12.00

*Mother-in-the-Kitchen* teapot completes the three-piece tea set. "Imports, Enesco, Japan" on paper label. Wooldridge.

*Mother-in-the-Kitchen* instant coffee, "Imports, Enesco, Japan" on paper label. The pottery loop on the right holds a spoon.  $30.00-35.00

*Mother-in-the-Kitchen* picture frame. "Imports, Enesco, Japan" on paper label. Wooldridge.  $45.00-45.00

*Mother-in-the-Kitchen*  crumb brush, unmarked.  $45.00-55.00

**Row 3:**   *Mother-in-the-Kitchen* spoon rest. Stamped "E - 3347."  $15.00-20.00

*Mother-in-the-Kitchen* vase/planter. "Imports, Enesco, Japan" on paper label.  $40.00-45.00

*Mother-in-the-Kitchen*  string holder. "Imports, Enesco, Japan" on label. Wooldridge.  $50.00-60.00

*Mother-in-the-Kitchen* ring holder. "Imports, Enesco, Japan" on label. Wooldridge.  $28.00-32.00

*Mother-in-the-Kitchen* cookie jar, unmarked.  $175.00-225.00

*Mother-in-the-Kitchen* salt or pepper shaker, mate above on Row 2.  Set, $10.00-12.00

*Mother-in-the-Kitchen* scouring pad holder. "Imports, Enesco, Japan" on label.  $12.00-15.00

*Mother-in-the-Kitchen* bud vase. "Imports, Enesco, Japan."  $28.00-32.00

*Mother-in-the-Kitchen* toothpick holder. "Imports, Enesco, Japan."  $15.00-18.00

*Mother-in-the-Kitchen* napkin holder. "Imports, Enesco, Japan."  $15.00-18.00

# Fitz & Floyd

Founded in 1960, Fitz & Floyd is headquartered in Dallas, TX, and is widely regarded as an industry leader in fashion-forward fine china dinnerware and giftware. The company enjoys an outstanding reputation for its exclusive and innovative designs and product quality. Its products are well established in the marketplace and are retailed through leading specialty and department stores throughout the United States, Canada, and in certain international markets. Fitz & Floyd products are prominently featured in numerous mail-order catalogues. The company is known for the originality of its highly acclaimed in-house design staff.

Omnibus Collections International (OCI), a division of Fitz & Floyd, brings additional diversification to the rapidly growing company. OCI began as a medium-priced gift and gourmet item line. In recent years, however, it has grown substantially and now includes dinnerware and large-scale decorative accessories in addition to the beautiful giftware for which it is so well known.

The company's approach to the dinnerware is unique. Fitz & Floyd is renowned as the creator of the "mix and match" concept in table design. The Fitz & Floyd product is considered high fashion in its field. Kenneth R. Marvel, chairman and chief executive officer of the company, states "Tabletop is a forum for fun. When people entertain, as they do with more and more frequency today, they want to create a table dressed with self-expression and creativity. We provide them with a vast assortment of components to recreate that expression in numerous combinations of pattern and color every time they set their table."

| | | |
|---|---|---|
| **Row 1:** | *Clown,* "Fitz & Floyd, Inc. © MCMLXXIX FF" stamped under glaze. Snyder. | $100.00-110.00 |
| | *Adam and Eve,* "© FF 1987." Paper label, "FF Japan." Banuelos. | $250.00+ |
| | *Kangaroo,* stamped "Fitz & Floyd Inc. 1977 Inc. 1977 FF." Kaulbach. | $60.00-70.00 |
| **Row 2:** | *The Runaway,* stamped "The Fitz & Floyd Inc. CMCMLXXVII FF." | $175.00-195.00 |
| | *The Cookie Factory,* stamped "Fitz & Floyd © FF 1987." On paper label, "FF Japan." Snyder. | $115.00-125.00 |
| | *Grandma,* "© FF" incised into bottom of base. | $90.00-110.00 |
| **Row 3:** | *Cookie Thief,* stamped "Fitz & Floyd 1976 FF." Kaulbach. | $65.00-75.00 |
| | *Fat Lady,* "© OCI" impressed, "Made in Japan" paper label. Braly. | $100.00-125.00 |
| | *Old Woman In a Shoe,* "Fitz & Floyd © 1986" incised, "FF Japan" paper label. Snyder. | $85.00-95.00 |
| **Below:** | *Spotted Dog,* stamped "Fitz & Floyd © MCMLXXIX FF." Paper label "FF Japan." Snyder. | $45.00-55.00 |
| | *Owl,* stamped "Fitz & Floyd Inc. © MCMLXXVIII FF." Paper label "FF Japan." Snyder. | $40.00-50.00 |

**Row 1:**  *Halloween Hoedown Witch*, "Fitz & Floyd © FF 1992" impressed. "F & F Korea" on paper label. Snyder.                                          $130.00-140.00

*Halloween Witch* candy jar. "© FF 1988" incised. "F & F Korea" on paper label.                                          $45.00-50.00

**Row 2:**  *Halloween Hoedown Witch/Cauldron* salt and pepper shaker. "Fitz & Floyd © FF 1992" incised. "FF Korea" paper label. Snyder.                         Set, $20.00-25.00

*Haunted House* cookie jar, "Fitz & Floyd © FF 1987" incised. "F & F Taiwan" on paper label. Snyder.                                          $100.00-125.00

*Ghost/Pumpkin* cookie jar, "© FF 1987" impressed. "FF Korea" on paper label.                                          $60.00-70.00

**Row 3:**  *Polka Dot Witch*, "Fitz & Floyd © MCMLXXVII" impressed.                    $250.00-300.00

*Halloween Witch* "© F & F 1987" impressed. "F & F Korea" on paper label. Inside the bottom of the base is a large spider web with "BOO" on it.      $120.00-130.00

**Below:**  *Fat Cat*, "Fitz & Floyd Inc. © MCMLXXVII" incised. "FF Japan" on paper label. Snyder.                                          $65.00-75.00

*Hershel Hippo* salt or pepper shaker, "Fitz & Floyd © FF" incised. "FF Taiwan" paper label. Snyder.                                          Set, $10.00-12.00

*Hershel Hippo* cookie jar. "Fitz & Floyd © FF" incised into the bottom of the base. "FF Taiwan" on paper label.                                  $60.00-70.00

*Hershel Hippo* salt or pepper shaker, mate above. Snyder.              Set, $10.00-12.00

*Rabbit*, stamped "Fitz & Floyd Inc. 1977 FF." Kaulbach.                         $75.00-95.00

Fitz & Floyd is known to be pricey. The opening of temporary outlets in some key cities has enabled collectors to enhance their collections at bargain prices.

**Row 1:**   *Christmas Car* candy jar from the Robert C. Floyd Signature Collection. 6" H, "© FF 1987" incised, "FF Japan" paper label. Snyder.  $150.00-175.00

*Christmas Car* cookie jar from the Robert C. Floyd Signature Collection. 8" H X 15⅜" L X 8½" W, "FF Japan" on paper label. The first in the line to be discontinued.  $350.00+

*Santa Car* teapot, "© FF 32 oz." incised. "FF Japan" on paper label. Snyder.  $100.00-125.00

**Row 2:**   *Spirit of St. Nicholas* candy jar, 7½" H X 11" L X 9⅝" W. "© F & F" incised. "FF Japan" on  paper label. Snyder.  $150.00-175.00

*Spirit of St. Nicholas* cookie jar from the Robert C. Floyd Signature Collection. 9¾" H X 15½" L X 15¾" W. "© FF" Incised. "Robert C. Floyd" in script. "FF Japan" on paper label. Snyder. The second in the line to be discontinued.  $350.00+

**Row 3:**   *Snowman* teapot, "© FF 34 oz." incised. "FF Japan" on paper label. Snyder.  $50.00-75.00

*Santa Cycle* cookie jar, the third and final jar in the Robert C. Floyd signature collection. 9¾" H X 13 ¾" L X 10¾" W. "© F&F" Incised. "Robert C. Floyd" in script. "FF Japan" on paper label. This was the third jar to be discontinued, ending the Robert C. Floyd Signature Collecton.  $300.00+

*Snowman* pitcher, "© F & F 1¾ Qt." impressed. "FF Japan" on paper label. Snyder.  $60.00-80.00

**Below:**   *Christmas Teddy Bear with Holly Wreath* cookie jar. "© MCMLXXXIII FF" stamped under glaze. Snyder.  $60.00-80.00

*Southwest Santa*, 15" H X 13" W. "© FF" impressed. "FF Japan" on paper label.  $325.00-350.00

*Gift Box*, "© FF" incised. "FF Korea" on paper label. Snyder.  $40.00-50.00

# Foxfield Ltd.

The Foxfield Atelier is where Tim Kelly began creating designs in the red fox motif, labeled Functional Foxware in 1980. The *Fox* jar was one of the early designs. Others included bowls, platters, napkin rings, salt and pepper shakers, and Christmas ornaments.

An idea was sparked, the model made, then a plaster mold was made, followed by test casting and painting. For small pieces master models were made from the first mold out of rubber to enable making working molds for production. Painting technique and coloring evolved over the decade from the original yellow-orange to the overlaying of multiple colors used on current productions. The paint is made in the studio using a ceramic stain base.

All designs were limited production with marketing geared toward the horse show populace as well as equine jewelry gift boutiques that catered to them.

The studio name changed to Foxfield Ltd. in 1989. At that time, nearly all designs were discontinued due to other pursuits. The *Fox* jar, napkin rings, ornaments, and refrigerator magnets are currently all that are available. Recently, more serious sculptures have been cast in limited edition bronze.

**Row 1:**   *Rascally Reynard,* "© Foxfield," in terra cotta.          $60.00-70.00

   *Rascally Reynard,* "© Foxfield."          $100.00-125.00

# Frankoma Pottery

Frankoma Pottery is located in Sapulpa, OK. Though still an active pottery, it is no longer a family owned business. The president of Frankoma is Kyle Costa, who is assisted by Joniece Frank, daughter of the founding Frank family, as vice-president and designer.

**Left:**   *Barrel* cylinder, "Frankoma." Wooldridge.          $25.00-35.00

# Gilner & Gonder

Gilner Potteries burned in 1957. The day after the fire, Gilner management approached California Originals about producing Gilner's line. They had received many orders at summer gift shows and needed to fill the orders. California Originals agreed, providing the items would not interfere with their own lines. After several months, Gilner decided not to rebuild. California Originals absorbed Gilner's best numbers into its line, and Gilner went out of business. California Originals hired all of the key Gilner people.

The stars of Gonder, whether cookie jars or banks, are the *Sheriff* and *Pirate.*

opposite page:
**Row 2:**   *Rooster,* "Gilner G-622." Snyder.          $35.00-45.00

   *Hen,* "Gilner G-610."          $35.00-45.00

**Row 3:**   *Gonder Sheriff,* "Gonder Original 950."          $500.00+

   *Rabbit,* "Gilner."          $40.00-50.00

this page:
**Left:**   *Gonder Pirate* bank, unmarked. Supnick.          $250.00+

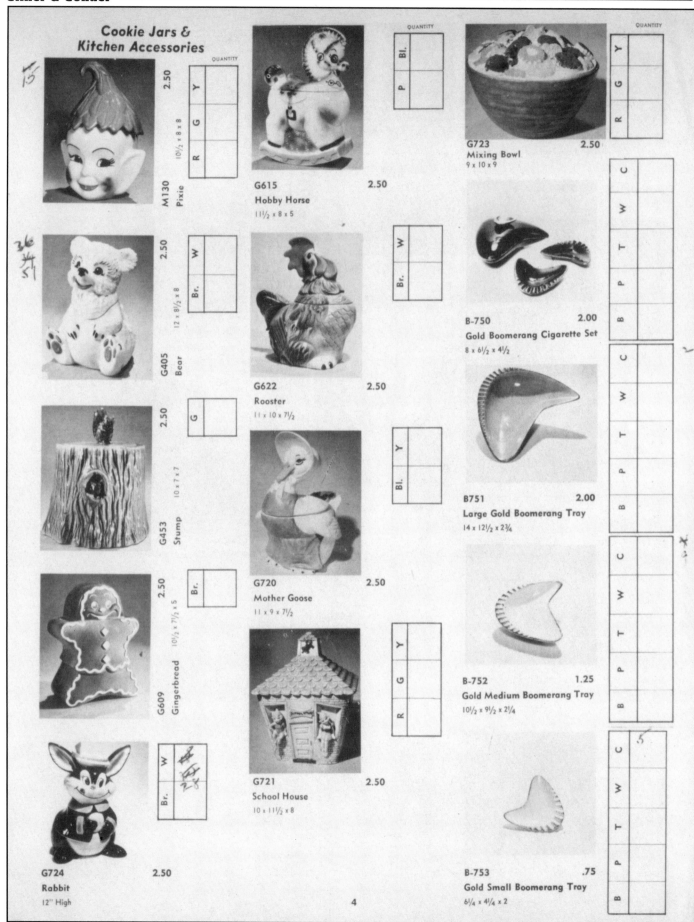

## Cookie Jars & Kitchen Accessories

**M130**    2.50
Pixie
$10\frac{1}{2}$ x 8 x 8

| Y | | |
|---|---|---|
| G | | |
| R | | |

**G405**    2.50
Bear
12 x $8\frac{1}{2}$ x 8

| W | |
|---|---|
| Br. | |

**G453**    2.50
Stump
10 x 7 x 7

| G | |
|---|---|

**G609**    2.50
Gingerbread
$10\frac{1}{2}$ x $7\frac{1}{2}$ x 5

| Br. | |
|---|---|

**G724**    2.50
Rabbit
12" High

| W | |
|---|---|
| Br. | |

**G615**    2.50
Hobby Horse
$11\frac{1}{2}$ x 8 x 5

QUANTITY

| P | Bl. | |
|---|---|---|

**G622**    2.50
Rooster
11 x 10 x $7\frac{1}{2}$

| W | |
|---|---|
| Br. | |

**G720**    2.50
Mother Goose
11 x 9 x $7\frac{1}{2}$

| Y | |
|---|---|
| Bl. | |

**G721**    2.50
School House
10 x $11\frac{1}{2}$ x 8

| Y | |
|---|---|
| G | |
| R | |

**G723**    2.50
Mixing Bowl
9 x 10 x 9

QUANTITY

| Y | | |
|---|---|---|
| G | | |
| R | | |

**B-750**    2.00
Gold Boomerang Cigarette Set
8 x $6\frac{1}{2}$ x $4\frac{1}{2}$

| C | W | |
|---|---|---|
| T | P | |
| B | | |

**B751**    2.00
Large Gold Boomerang Tray
14 x $12\frac{1}{2}$ x $2\frac{3}{4}$

| C | W | |
|---|---|---|
| T | P | |
| B | | |

**B-752**    1.25
Gold Medium Boomerang Tray
$10\frac{1}{2}$ x $9\frac{1}{2}$ x $2\frac{1}{4}$

| C | W | |
|---|---|---|
| T | P | |
| B | | |

**B-753**    .75
Gold Small Boomerang Tray
$6\frac{1}{4}$ x $4\frac{1}{4}$ x 2

| C | W | |
|---|---|---|
| T | P | |
| B | | |

4

*Gilner Catalog Sheet, 1955.*

## Compotes

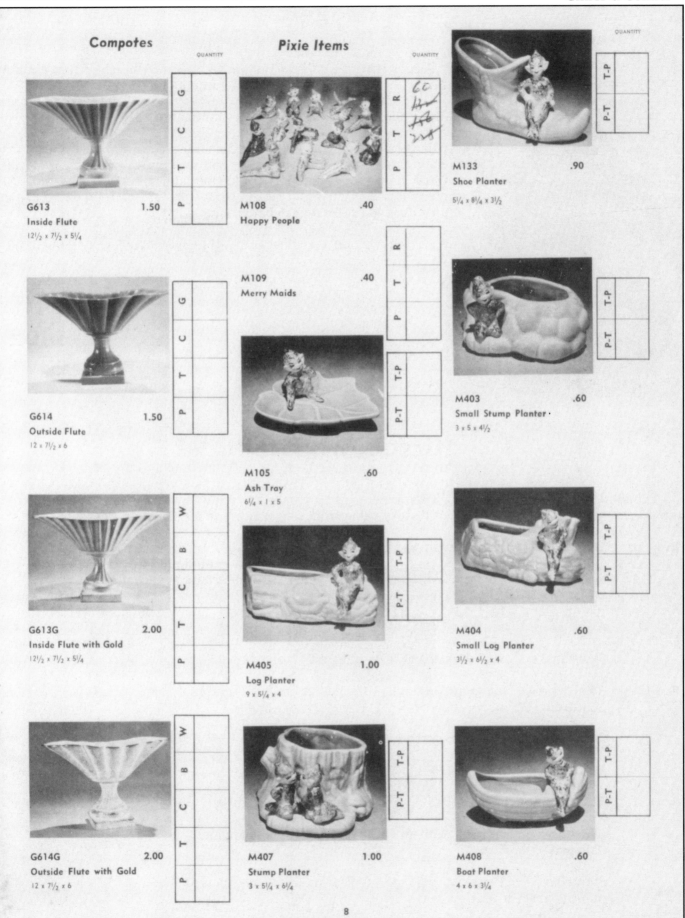

**G613**                    1.50
Inside Flute
12½ x 7½ x 5¼

| G | C | T | P |
|---|---|---|---|
| | | | |

**G614**                    1.50
Outside Flute
12 x 7½ x 6

| G | C | T | P |
|---|---|---|---|
| | | | |

**G613G**                   2.00
Inside Flute with Gold
12½ x 7½ x 5¼

| W | B | C | T | P |
|---|---|---|---|---|
| | | | | |

**G614G**                   2.00
Outside Flute with Gold
12 x 7½ x 6

| W | B | C | T | P |
|---|---|---|---|---|
| | | | | |

## Pixie Items

QUANTITY

**M108**                    .40
Happy People

| R | T | P |
|---|---|---|
| 6C | | |
| | | |

**M109**                    .40
Merry Maids

| R | T | P |
|---|---|---|
| | | |

**M105**                    .60
Ash Tray
6¼ x 1 x 5

| T-P | P-T |
|---|---|
| | |

**M405**                    1.00
Log Planter
9 x 5¼ x 4

| T-P | P-T |
|---|---|
| | |

**M407**                    1.00
Stump Planter
3 x 5¼ x 6¼

| T-P | P-T |
|---|---|
| | |

QUANTITY

**M133**                    .90
Shoe Planter
5¼ x 8¼ x 3½

| T-P | P-T |
|---|---|
| | |

**M403**                    .60
Small Stump Planter
3 x 5 x 4½

| T-P | P-T |
|---|---|
| | |

**M404**                    .60
Small Log Planter
3½ x 6½ x 4

| T-P | P-T |
|---|---|
| | |

**M408**                    .60
Boat Planter
4 x 6 x 3¼

| T-P | P-T |
|---|---|
| | |

*Gilner Catalog Sheet, 1955.*

# Haeger

Haeger Potteries of East Dundee, IL, drawing much of the rebuilding business following the Chicago fire, began as a brick factory in 1871. In 1914 the company expanded into art pottery. Today, the company makes decorative pottery in East Dundee and the floral line at their Macomb, IL, plant.

Haeger management is extremely careful about taking on debt based on fads. This means emphasizing contract work, making promotional pottery such as the *Keebler* cookie jar and a *Harley-Davidson "Hog"* (motorcycle) piggy bank. It seems companies are more likely to use premiums during a recession to boost sales.

**Left:**   *Nummy Cookies*, "Haeger © ...," incised. Snyder.   $40.00-50.00

# Hirsch, William H.

Though listed as William H. Hirsch Manufacturing Company, Hirsch was a jobber that carried the Winton line in the 1950's. This brief bit of history came from Don Winton of Twin Winton Ceramics.

**Row 1:**   *Smiling Bear with Badge* salt and pepper shakers. "W.H. Hirsch Mfg. Co., California USA ©," incised on the pepper shaker only. How could anyone ever doubt that this is a Winton design? All one has to do is look at the Brush *Smiling Bear* on page 81, Book I. Snyder.   Set, $35.00-40.00

*Monk*, "W.H. Hirsch Mfg. Co., Calif. USA." incised.   $35.00-45.00

*Monk* shakers, "W.H. Hirsch Mfg. Co., Calif. USA," on one shaker.   $20.00-25.00

**Row 2:**   *Raggedy Ann*, stamped "William H. Hirsch Mfg. Co., Los Angeles © California."   $60.00-65.00

*Smiling Bear with Badge*, unmarked. Snyder.   $40.00-50.00

*Hen on Nest*, "Hirsch Mfg. WH © '61 Made in USA."   $25.00-35.00

**Row 3:**   *Rooster*, incised mark "19©60 Wm. Hirsch California USA."   $50.00-60.00

*Cuckoo Clock*, stamped "William H. Hirsch Mfg. Co. Los Angeles, California." Snyder.   $50.00-60.00

*Pinocchio* "W.H. Hirsch Mfg. Co., L A California USA © 60" incised into the base. Snyder.   $150.00-160.00

# House of Webster

It all started with a paper route. In the early 1930's, Roy Webster took a 125-mile newspaper route for the *Southwest American* out of Fort Smith, AR. Soon he decided he might as well be carrying more than just the paper and worked out a deal to deliver bread for the Harris Baking Company along the same route. While these two enterprises did not exactly make him rich, he made enough money to marry his sweetheart Evelyn who became his partner. She decided she could bake pies for Roy to sell on his route. In the winter of 1934-35, Evelyn baked and Roy delivered 17,000 two-crust pies to grocery stores along his route. Next, they were selling butter and then chocolate milk!

At the end of the thirties, a bakery in Rogers became available, so Roy and Evelyn went into the bakery business. Roy discovered Evelyn had a talent for cake decorating and sent her to Chicago to study with a "master." The bakery business was good when the war emerged; sugar was being rationed, and people found fruitcakes were just the thing for mailing to soldiers. Would their business continue to be strong after the war? Roy decided he needed an idea. What resulted was a gift package: a small wooden chest (with a padlock and a key) containing a 1½-pound fruitcake and ceramic jugs of sorghum and honey. "Rare Gift of Arkansas" found a market with commercial buyers. The next year it was another product and another booklet for the same customers and more.

And so it began.... In 1934 the Websters began to design replica containers for some of their food gifts. The replicas were of things that were a part of the way of life of their parents and grandparents. The old-time ceramic containers are made in the House of Webster Ceramic plant in Eastland, TX. Everything is packaged and shipped from the headquarters in Rogers, AR.

In 1957, The House of Webster began developing "Country Charm," early American electric appliances designed to capture the charm of country living with the automatic conveniences of the most modern kitchen. The House of Webster is another Arkansas success story, perhaps not as big as the late Sam Walton's, but every bit as ingenious.

| | | |
|---|---|---|
| **Row 1:** | *Bushel Basket*, "House of Webster Ceramics, Eastland, Texas" stamped on bottom. Snyder. | $12.00-15.00 |
| | *Log Cabin*, "House of Webster Ceramics, Eastland, Texas" stamped on bottom. Snyder. | $12.00-15.00 |
| | *Cream Can*, unmarked. Snyder. | $12.00-15.00 |
| | *Covered Wagon*, "House of Webster Ceramics, Eastland, Texas" stamped on bottom. Snyder. | $12.00-15.00 |
| | *Wishing Well*, unmarked. Snyder. | $12.00-15.00 |
| **Row 2:** | *Burlap Bag*, "House of Webster Ceramics, Eastland, Texas" stamped on bottom. Snyder. | $12.00-15.00 |
| | *Stoneware Churn*, "House of Webster Ceramics, Eastland, Texas" stamped underglaze. Snyder. | $12.00-15.00 |
| | *Strawberry*, "House of Webster Ceramics, Eastland, Texas" stamped underglaze. Snyder. | $12.00-15.00 |
| | *Box of Strawberries*, "House of Webster Ceramics, Eastland, Texas" stamped on bottom. | $12.00-15.00 |
| | *Apple*, "House of Webster Ceramics, Eastland, Texas" stamp. Snyder. | $12.00-15.00 |
| | *Thimble* stamped "House of Webster Ceramics, Texas." Snyder. | $12.00-15.00 |
| **Row 3:** | *Shock of Wheat*, stamped "House of Webster Ceramics, Eastland, Texas." Snyder. | $12.00-15.00 |
| | *Cook Stove*, unmarked, or the mark is illegible on the black. Snyder. This is NOT a McCoy salesman sample. | $12.00-15.00 |
| | *Schoolhouse*, unmarked. Snyder. | $12.00-15.00 |
| | *Wall Telephone*, stamped "House of Webster Ceramics, Eastland, Texas," Snyder. | $12.00-15.00 |
| | *Liberty Bell*, stamped "House of Webster Ceramics, Eastland, Texas." Snyder. | $12.00-15.00 |

"OLD RIP" 1897-1929

In 1897 when the cornerstone of Eastland County Courthouse was dedicated, Earnest Wood, a justice of the peace, placed a West Texas horned toad, "Old Rip," along with a Bible and several other subjects of interest in the cornerstone. Here "Old Rip" lived for thirty-one years.

On Febuary 8, 1928, when a wrecking crew began to demolish the thirty-one year old courthouse to make way for a new one, 3,000 persons were on hand to witness the opening of the corner stone. After Judge Ed S. Pritchard removed the Bible and the other objects, Eugene Day, a local oil man, thrust his hand into the cavity of the cornerstone and lifted out the dust covered toad, "Old Rip"... holding him up by the hind leg to show him to the crowd. The toad's other hind leg twitched..."Old Rip" was alive. The crowd cheered and "Old Rip" awoke from a thirty-one year slumber.

"Old Rip" was exhibited in various parts of the country including a visit to President Coolidge in Washington.

"Old Rip" died of pneumonia January 19, 1929. His body was embalmed and can be seen today in his plush-lined casket in the lobby of the Eastland County Courthouse. You are invited to see him.

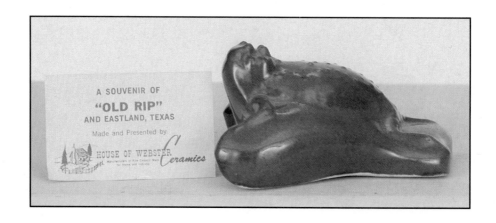

# PEACHES AND CREAM

Once upon a time there was a cream can on the back porch of most farm homes in America. They were made of metal and much larger but they looked sorta like this 7½ x 4½ inch ceramic can...this one is bright, cheerful and gifty, filled with bright yellow peach preserves. Peaches get ripe around here in August. They are peeled, sliced, sprinkled with sugar and frozen, then preserved to fill your order.

## PEACHES & CREAM-PLUS
*Ceramic Cream Can-Plus*
3 lbs. Peach preserves
(2) 1 lb. bags Flaky Buttermilk Biscuit mix
2 lb. slab War Eagle country-cured and hickory smoked bacon.
**Gift No. P-CP**

*Peaches & Cream-Biscuits*
Ceramic can filled with
3 lbs. Peach preserves
(2) 1 lb. bags biscuit mix
**Gift No. P-C2B**

*Peaches & Cream*
Ceramic cream can filled with
3lbs. Peach preserves
**Gift No. P-C**

## CERAMIC LOG CABIN

Filled with good tasting Elberta Peach Preserves and a small 20 page booklet. Saturated with a warmheated first person account of four 11 and 12 year old boys totally immersed in one summer building, a log cabin, and the anticipation of our first supper and first night. We had built it all with our own hands. We were the happiest boys on the earth and ate the best vegetable soup in the world that night.

After supper we discussed the future of our vast empire. In our imagination we envisioned thousands of acres of land, great herds of cattle, large apple and peach orchards, large strawberry fields and hundreds of employees, operating the whole thing straight from our log cabin...Headquarters March 21, 1925.

*Ceramic Log Cabin – Plus*
2 lbs. 12 oz. Peach preserves
(2) 1 lb. bags Flaky Buttermilk Biscuit Mix
2 lbs. slab War Eagle country-cured and hickory smoked bacon.
**Gift No. LCP**

*Log Cabin-Biscuits*
2 lbs. 12 oz. Peach preserves
(2) 1 lb. bags biscuit mix
**Gift No. LC2B**

*Log Cabin*
2 lbs. 12 oz. Peach preserves
**Gift No. LC**

18

## EARLY AMERICAN REPLICA SET

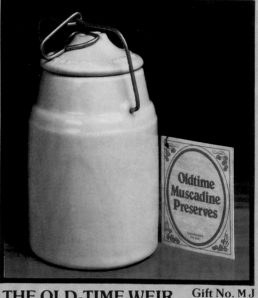

Cast iron for enjoyable outdoor living...dandy for cream and sugar, sauce and relish, or decorative for indoor use. A natural cast iron finish but treated to resist rust.

The Ole Set'ler tea kettle (4½" x 4") is filled with 2 lbs. bright red strawberry preserves made as fresh as a morning dew and the most pleasant and tastiest preserves we make.

The Ole Colony pot (4½" x 4") is filled with 2 lbs. wild huckleberry preserves...truly a favorite 'mongst hill folks.

Copies of "Ole Set'ler" and "Ole Colony," included, couch each gift in an old-time atmosphere that will not be soon forgotten. They're "surenuf" conversation pieces...mailable.
**Gift No. OSOC**

**OLE SET'LER**
Miniature teakettle with strawberry preserves
**Gift No. OS**

**OLE COLONY POT**
Miniature 3-legged pot with huckleberry preserves
**Gift No. OC**

### THE OLD-TIME WEIR CERAMIC JAR...     Gift No. M J

...Filled with old-time seedless muscadine whole fruit preserves... **Contains 2 lbs. 8 ozs.**

The Weir jar was developed for home food preserving in the late 17th century. This antique jar was patented in 1803...reproduced in our ceramic plant in Eastland, Texas.

The wild and wonderful muscadines grow on grape-like vines that travel from tree to tree, resembling but larger than a grape. Their domain begins mostly in the Dismal Swamp of North Carolina through the southeastern and southern states to east Texas. In recent years research in most southern state universities has improved the yield and flavor of the muscadine.

### WEBSTER'S WISHING WELL
#### filled with 2 lbs. 8 oz. strawberry preserves

This brown ceramic well platform, with its bucket, rope, windlass, and its "Wishing Well" booklet, reflects one of my strongest childhood memories of hand-dug wells in our neighborhood. Where we lived, a vein of water was usually found from 40 to 60 feet deep. At that depth, the water was always pure, clear, cold and refreshing.

In the summer, jugs of milk and pails of butter would be hung in wells on ropes to keep them cool.

The "Wishing Well" is about 5 inches wide and 7 inches high...earthen brown with dark trim.
**Gift No. WW**

### THE ONE ROOM SCHOOL HOUSE
#### loaded with 2 lbs. 8 oz. strawberry preserves

Here is how to capture the imagination of your friends and associates. A most attractive, red-roofed ceramic school house (4 x 6½ x 8 inches tall) with bell that rings and it's filled with preserved bright red mountain grown strawberries. The one room school of yesteryear now basks in the sublimity of a wonderful past...a shrine of learning that helped form the mighty precepts which are still the very foundation of our freedom loving America.

A copy of the "Epoch of the One Room School House" is included. Written in the first person, it will trigger the warm image of school days...put you behind the geography with an apple in your hand.

It's true, many successful people can be traced to a one room, rural school. Mailable in an attractive carton. **Gift No. SH**

26

## STRAWBERRY PRESERVES

Here is a gift idea that is older than you are... strawberry preserves in square one-half pint Mason fruit jars, gold lacquered lids, paraffin wax and labeled in longhand. Downright old-fashioned flavor too.

12-11 oz. jars Strawberry
   Preserves
**Gift No. S12**

8-11 oz. jars Strawberry
   Preserves
**Gift No. S8**

6-11 oz. jars Strawberry
   Preserves
**Gift No. S6**

4-11 oz. jars Strawberry
   Preserves
**Gift No. S4**

in old-time ½ pint Mason fruit jars

**each filled with rare and special treats!**

### Old-fashioned REPLICA CONTAINERS

MOM'S THIMBLE...always in Mom's sewing basket, is a tribute to Moms everywhere for their tireless needlework and mending...then and now. Bright cherry preserves fill this 5¼" high ceramic thimble. "MOM'S THIMBLE," a booklet, recalls the experiences of a boy and his Mom. 1 lb. 14 oz.
**Gift No. TH**

THIS IS IT!...jug five inches in diameter by seven inches high — three pounds of Wild Honey from

a summers parade of 25 or more flowers blended into a delicately flavored, bright amber colored honey. A symbol of love and appreciation ever since Jacob sent his gift of honey to Joseph in Egypt in 1708 B.C., Genesis 43:11. Mailable.
**Gift No. TI**

THE PEACH BASKET...and two pounds, four ounces of bright yellow peach preserves. We do our best to have whole slices in every basket ...surely look and taste good on a

hot biscuit or toast. This eye catching ceramic basket is about 4¾ inches high and 5½ inches in diameter... a mailable gift.
**Gift No. PCBK**

FIRE PLUG...this bright red ceramic fire plug stands 8 inches high and is filled with 3 lbs. Wild Catsclaw Honey. Catsclaw, a wild flowering, honey producing shrub, grows 25 feet tall and thrives in arid regions of the Southwest.
**Gift No. FP**

29

# Hull

The Hull Pottery Company of Crooksville, OH is best known for originating *Little Red Riding Hood.* Numerous lines of Hull artware, mostly designed by Louise Bauer, are highly acclaimed by collectors. Though Hull did produce cookie jars, they are not necessarily its strong point, with the exception of *Little Red Riding Hood.*

**Left:**   *Hen*, "Hull Ware USA 968." This 1940 jar is approximately 11½" high. Skillman.    $200.00-225.00

# Hutula

Mystery still surrounds the origin of Helen's Ware, or Helen Hutula Originals. One theory suggests Hawaii, another Nebraska. We feel confident that some day, a relative or former employee will enlighten us as to who Helen Hutula is. She deserves recognition.

*Pitcher*, "Helen's Ware." Bass.    $125.00-150.0

*Tat-L-Tale* cookie jar, "© Helen's Tat-L-Tale, Helen Hutula Original." Supnick.    $350.00+

*Jewelry* container, felt over bottom of base. Supnick.    $175.00+

*Tat-L-Tale* cookie jar, "©Helen's Tat-L-Tale, Helen Hutula Original." Paper label "I'm the Original TAT-L-TALE – Tip my head upside down."    $300.00+

# Imports

**Row 1:**   *Country Kin*, stamped "HAND PAINTED TAKAHASHI SAN FRANCISCO." Paper label, "Takahashi® SAN FRANCISCO 94103 MADE IN JAPAN." Snyder.    $18.00-22.00

*Lilkins House*, stamped "HAND PAINTED TAKAHASHI SAN FRANCISCO. Snyder.    $25.00-30.00

*Granny*, stamped "HAND PAINTED TAKAHASHI." Snyder.    $30.00-40.00

**Row 2:**   *Hen with Egg*, stamped "GALLERY ORIGINALS."    $18.00-22.00

*Owl*, "Hand painted, Made in Brazil."    $12.00-15.00

*Pinocchio*, "V BASSANO."    $50.00-60.00

**Row 3:**   *World Globe* minus finial on lid. "Made in Italy."    $35.00-45.00

*Frog*, "4961 Made in Italy."    $35.00-45.00

*Italian Lady*, stamped "2249 O.G. GJ ITALY."    $35.00-45.00

**Row 1:** *Basketball Player*, unmarked. "Colony Crafted™, Made in Taiwan" on the box.  $18.00-28.00

*Football Player*, unmarked. "Colony Crafted™, Made in Taiwan" on the box.  $18.00-28.00

*Baseball Player*, unmarked. "Colony Crafted™, Made in Taiwan" on the box.  $18.00-28.00

**Row 2:** *Clown*, "Schmid Hand painted © 1979" stamped inside lid. "The Candyman Schmid No. 243 Japan" on paper label inside lid. Snyder.  $35.00-45.00

*Squirrel*, "Made in Taiwan ROC" on paper label, base. Snyder.  $20.00-30.00

*Cow*, "Taiwan."  $8.00-12.00

**Row 3:** *Cat with Bonnet*, from Wal Mart. "Made in Thailand" on paper label.  $10.00-15.00

*Franciscan Monk*, "Mexico" stamped under glaze.  $40.00-50.00

*Cat with Kittens in Basket*, from Wal-Mart. "Made in Thailand" on paper label.  $10.00-15.00

**Left:** *St. Nicholas*, "Handmade Exclusively for SILVESTRI®, Chicago, IL. 60614, Made in Taiwan." Braly.  $100.00-125.00

# Imperial Porcelain

Imperial Porcelain Corporation was located in Zanesville, OH from 1946 through 1960. Paul Webb, the creator of *Li'l Abner* and *Daisy Mae,* was instrumental in the design of the popular Mountain Boys produced by Imperial.

*Daisy Mae,* "Imperial Porcelain Corp. USA, Zanesville, O." Skillman.  $300.00-400.00

*The Bum,* "Imperial Porcelain Corp. USA, Zanesville, O." Skillman.  $150.00-200.00

# Japan

Even Japan, once the biggest competition to American industry, is being left behind in the race to produce cheap jars for the American based importer/distributors.

**Row 1:**    *Spotted Jersey*, (Well, almost! So, she has a white body. She has a black nose.) "Made in Japan" paper label.    $25.00-35.00

*Holstein Cow*, "Japan."    $50.00-60.00

**Row 2:**    *Holstein Cow in Pasture*, "Made in Taiwan" paper label. Snyder.    $25.00-35.00

*Haldon Dairy* mug, "Haldon Dairy Co. LTD."    $3.00-5.00

*Haldon Dairy Milk Carton*, "2000 Mi Haldon Dairy Co LTD, Pasteurized, Homogenized. Made in Japan." Paper label. "The Haldon Group."    $15.00-18.00

*Haldon Dairy* mug, "Haldon Dairy Co. LTD."    $3.00-5.00

*Cook Books*, "Shafford Japan" paper label. Okamoto.    $35.00-45.00

**Row 3:**    *Shoe House,* "Made in Japan" paper label. Okamoto.    $10.00-15.00

*Cow in Dress*, "Japan."    $15.00-20.00

*Cowboy Frog*, "© Sears Roebuck & Co. 1981, Made in Japan."    $25.00-35.00

**Below:**    *City Cab*, "Japan" incised into the bottom of the base. This cab is another *Home Shopper's* special.    $100.00-125.00

| | | |
|---|---|---:|
| **Row:1** | *Robot*, "Japan." Snyder. | $35.00-45.00 |
| | *Robot*, "Japan." | $35.00-45.00 |
| | *Robot*, "Japan." | $35.00-45.00 |
| **Row 2:** | *Robot*, "Japan." | $35.00-45.00 |
| | *Robot*, "Japan." Snyder. | $35.00-45.00 |
| | *Robot*, "Japan." | $35.00-45.00 |
| **Row 3:** | *Man*, stamped "60/153 JAPAN." Snyder. | $35.00-45.00 |
| | *Rainbow Cylinder*, "Japan" incised into bottom. Snyder. | $20.00-30.00 |
| | *World Globe*, unmarked. Kaulbach. | $25.00-35.00 |

Though some of the *Robots* above may appear to be Transformers we hesitate to label them as such. Transformer is a registered trademark, and none of the above demonstrate licensing.

# Lane

Lane was a Los Angeles based manufacturer and jobber. We have not documented many jars for Lane, but a few keep surfacing. The most recent is a *Teapot* (not pictured) marked with a paper label similiar to the one on the clock. How would we ever identify some of these jars without these paper labels? The most valuable Lane to date is the *Indian,* featured in Book I, followed by the *Sheriff*. The Lane *Sheriff* has been reproduced.

| | | |
|---|---|---:|
| **Below:** | *Clown*, "Lane and Co. Los Angeles © 1950." | $150.00-175.00 |
| | *Clock*, paper label on lid "Distinctive American Craftsmanship for over twenty-five years, Lane Ceramics." | $65.00-75.00 |
| | *Rocking Horse*, "Lane Ceramics" embossed on the bottom of the base. Grace. | $150.00-175.00 |

# Lefton

George Z. Lefton China is an importer/distributor based in Chicago, IL.

**Row 1:**   *Cat* salt or pepper shaker, stamped "1521."  Set, $12.00-15.00

*Cat* creamer, stamped "1508."  3-piece Tea Set, $55.00-65.00

*Cat* cookie jar, stamped "1502."  $35.00-45.00

*Girl Cook*, stamped "2360." Paper label, "Lefton Reg. US Pat. OFF Exclusive, Japan."  $35.00-45.00

*Cat* teapot, part of 3-piece tea set.  $25.00-35.00

*Cat* sugar, the third part of the 3-piece tea set.  $15.00-20.00

*Cat* salt or pepper shaker, mate above.  Set, $12.00-15.00

**Row 2:**   *Blue Bird* creamer, unmarked.  $8.00-10.00

*Blue Bird* egg cup, stamped "286."  $3.00-5.00

*Blue Bird* planter, unmarked.  $5.00-8.00

*Blue Bird* teapot, "© Geo. Z. Lefton 438."  $20.00-30.00

*Blue Bird* shaker, stamped "282."  Set, $12.00-15.00

*Blue Bird* cup, "284 GEO. Z. Lefton ©."  $3.00-5.00

*Blue Bird* cup, "284 GEO. Z. Lefton ©."  $3.00-5.00

*Blue Bird* cup, "284 GEO. Z. Lefton ©."  $3.00-5.00

**Row 3:**   *Young Lady* salt or pepper shaker.  Set, $12.00-15.00

*Young Lady* teapot, stamped "321."  3-piece Tea Set, $55.00-65.00

*Young Lady* salt or pepper shaker, mate above.  Set, $12.00-15.00

*Young Lady* cookie jar, "© Geo. Z. Lefton 040A."  $35.00-45.00

*Young Lady* sugar, "322 Lefton Reg US Pat. OFF, Exclusive Japan." Part of the 3-piece tea set.  $15.00-20.00

*Young Lady* creamer, "322 Lefton Reg US Pat. OFF, Exclusive Japan." Third part of the 3-piece tea set.  $15.00-20.00

*Young Lady* jam jar, "323."  $8.00-10.00

# Lotus International, Inc.

Lotus International, Inc. is a Dallas, TX based importer/distributor.

**Row 1:**   *Airplane Santa,* "Exclusively for Lotus, Made in China 1991" on paper label. Snyder.   $20.00-25.00

*Car Santa,* "Exclusively for Lotus Made in China 1991" on paper label. Snyder.   $20.00-25.00

**Row 2:**   *Sleigh Santa,* "Exclusively for Lotus, Made in China 1991" on paper label.   $20.00-25.00

*Ship Santa,* "Exclusively for Lotus, Made in China 1991" on paper label.   $20.00-25.00

*Train Santa,* "Exclusively for Lotus, Made in China 1991" on paper label.   $20.00-25.00

**Row 3:**   *Santa* cookie jar, 10" H, "Exclusively for Lotus, Made in China 1991" on paper label. The original Santa is 13" H and has been discontinued. Snyder.   $25.00-35.00

*New York* cookie jar, "Exclusively for Lotus, Made in China 1991" on paper label.   $20.00-25.00

*Cowboy* cookie jar, "Exclusively for Lotus, Made in China 1991" on paper label.   $20.00-25.00

**Below:**   *Halloween Pumpkin,* 10½" H – Discontinued. "Exclusively for Lotus, Made in Taiwan © 1989" on paper label.   $60.00-65.00

*Halloween Witch,* "Exclusively for Lotus, Made in Taiwan © 1989" on paper label.   $35.00-40.00

*1989 Lotus International catalog sheets on pages 194 and 195.*

# Santa I — Hand Painted Ceramic

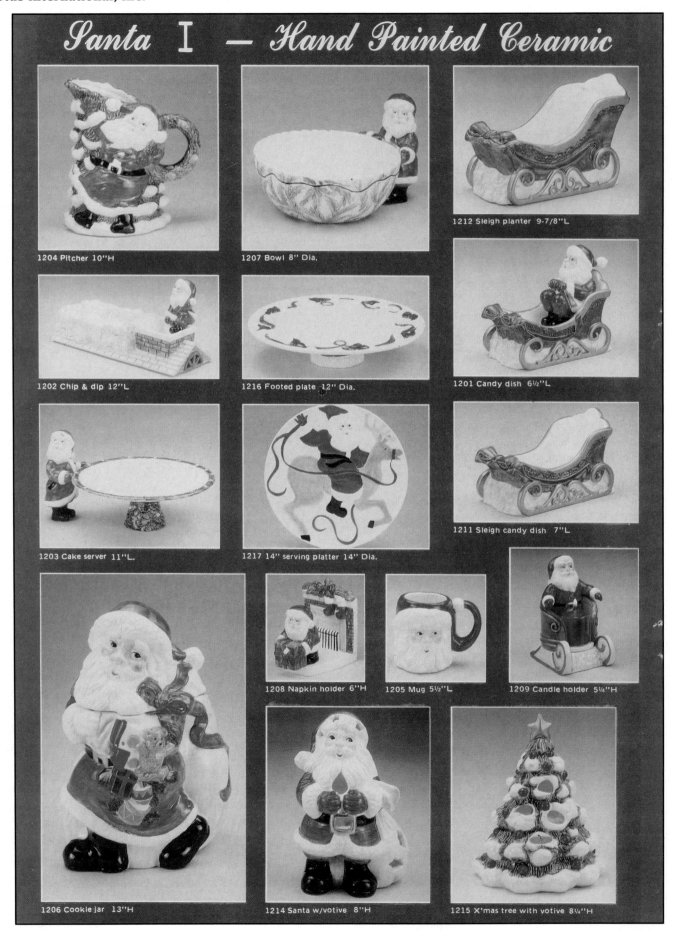

1204 Pitcher 10"H

1207 Bowl 8" Dia.

1212 Sleigh planter 9-7/8"L

1202 Chip & dip 12"L

1216 Footed plate 12" Dia.

1201 Candy dish 6½"L

1203 Cake server 11"L.

1217 14" serving platter 14" Dia.

1211 Sleigh candy dish 7"L

1208 Napkin holder 6"H

1205 Mug 5½"L

1209 Candle holder 5¼"H

1206 Cookie jar 13"H

1214 Santa w/votive 8"H

1215 X'mas tree with votive 8¼"H

*Lotus International Catalog Sheet.*

# Santa II — Hand Painted Ceramic

1304 Fisherman cookie jar 10"H

1303 Florida cookie jar 10¾"H

1305 Cowboy cookie jar 9¾"H

1302 Santa Fe cookie jar 10"H

1301 New York cookie jar 10"H

1309 Bowl 9¾" Dia.

1307 Vase/Candy dish 7"H   1308 Box 6"H

1306 Candy dish 10½"W

2204 Mug 6"H

1310 Tid bid server 13"L

## Snowman

2201 Napkin/card holder 6"H

2206 Cookie jar 10½"H   2202 Pitcher 10½"H

2203 2-section server 14"L

2205 Votive 5½"H

*Lotus International Catalog Sheet.*

195

# Marsh Industries

Marsh Industries was located at 224 East 16th Street in Los Angeles, CA. Lois Lehner supplied catalog sheets for 1956, 1965, and 1967. At the bottom of the catalog sheets are the names Art Marpet and Mike Shein, who according to Lehner started Marsh Industries in Glendale, CA in 1950. One interesting note: The catalog sheets offer an attractive selection of cookie jars – all hand decorated on backgrounds of maple color. One more company to sort through that used the wood grain finish. We know they did wonderful underglaze colors as well. The company was in business in 1986, but it has since closed.

**Row 1:**  *Toy Soldier*, unmarked, but listed as #112 in the catalog sheets. Snyder.  $50.00-60.00

*Cookie Chef*, unmarked, listed in catalog as #110. Although not shown in photo, "Cookie" is written on the hat's band. Snyder.  $100.00-125.00

*Toy Soldier*, unmarked. Snyder.  $50.00-60.00

# Maurice of California

Maurice of California is still located in Los Angeles, CA. Careful research with numerous company heads (California Originals, Hondo Ceramics, Treasure Craft, and Twin Winton) tells us Maurice is a jobber and has never been a manufacturer.

**Row 2:**  *Mrs. Hen*, "Maurice Ceramics of Calif. USA 19©76 PG 60 USA."  $75.00-90.00

*Owl with Guitar*, "Maurice © Calif. USA 19©76 PG 62."  $100.00-125.00

*Frog*, "Maurice Ceramics."  $40.00-50.00

**Row 3:**  *Rabbit*, "Maurice of Calif. USA ... ©." Snyder.  $30.00-40.00

*Clown*, "Maurice © Calif. USA" incised into base. Snyder.  $225.00+

*Owl*, "Maurice of © Calif USA 1?1" incised into base. Snyder.  $30.00-40.00

# Marcia of California

Marcia of California was owned by George Siegel. He named the company for his daughter. Siegel was a jobber buying from numerous companies, including Hondo Ceramics. Siegel owned a small pottery company, but never manufactured cookie jars.

# Maddux of California

The Maddux pottery was established in 1937 at 3020 Fletcher Drive, Los Angeles, CA. The plant was located in Los Angeles on the Southern Pacific Railroad. It had one tunnel kiln, one periodic kiln, one bisque kiln, and a glost kiln. They used natural gas as the fuel. The plant made artware birds, horses, and dogs and produced 120,000 pieces of ware annually in 1947. According to correspondence from Maddux to Rena London, Maddux closed at the first of 1980.

**Row 1:**    *Covered Wagon*, "Marcia of California." Snyder.     $20.00-30.00

               *Queen*, "Maddux of Calif USA © 210" incised in back of base. The catalog number for the Queen is "2104." Snyder.     $100.00-125.00

               *Scottie*, "Marcia/NAC USA" incised into bottom. Snyder.     $50.00-60.00

**Row 2:**    *Snowman*, "Marcia of California."     $50.00-60.00

               *Grapes Cylinder*, "Maddux of Calif. 8412 USA" incised on bottom. Snyder.     $25.00-35.00

               *Calory Hippy*, "USA MARCIA" incised into back of base. Snyder.     $35.00-45.00

**Row 3:**    *Walrus*, "Maurice Ceramics MP 23" (The MP is believed to stand for Manuel Provenzaro, a manufacturer in the San Fernando Valley.)     $40.00-50.00

               *Strawberry,* "MARCIA CJ 2 CAL USA" incised into bottom. Snyder.     $18.00-22.00

               *Koala*, "Maurice Ceramics MP 20 USA."     $50.00-60.00

**Below:**    *Raggedy Ann*, "Maurice Ceramics Calif. U.S.A. WO 38." It is believed that this jar was also produced by Pottery Gulch for Maurice.     $65.00-75.00

# McCoy

The first known McCoy pottery was established in 1848 by the ancestors of the former Nelson McCoy Pottery Company of Roseville, OH. The W. Nelson McCoy Pottery was founded by W. Nelson McCoy, and his uncle W. F. McCoy in Putnam, OH. Today, Putnam is a part of Zanesville, OH.

The second generation McCoy Pottery was the J.W. McCoy Pottery founded by James W. McCoy the father of Nelson McCoy. In 1911 the J. W. McCoy Pottery became Brush-McCoy Pottery following a merger with George Brush. The Brush pottery, located in Zanesville, OH, had been destroyed by fire in 1908, approximately one year after the opening. James W. McCoy died in 1914, but his son and business partner, Nelson McCoy, continued to represent the family's interest in Brush-McCoy until 1918, when Nelson resigned from the Brush-McCoy board.

James W. McCoy, and his son, Nelson, founded the Nelson McCoy Sanitary Stoneware Company in 1910, just prior to the J. W. McCoy and Brush merger. The McCoy interest in Brush-McCoy was sold in 1925 at which time the stoneware company was expanded. The company name was changed in 1922 to the Nelson McCoy Company. Nelson McCoy died in 1945 leaving the company in the capable hands of his nephew, Nelson McCoy Melick. Melick remained president until 1954 when, upon his death, the reins were passed to twenty-nine year old Nelson McCoy, Jr. Thus, the cookie jar story unfolds ....

Nelson McCoy, Jr. continued as president of the Nelson McCoy Pottery Company until his retirement in 1981. Though the company was sold three times during this time frame, the Nelson McCoy Pottery Company name was retained. The first sale came in 1967 to David T. Chase and Chase Enterprises of Hartford, CT. The second sale came in 1974 to the Lancaster Colony Group, the owners of Indiana Glass. The third and final sale was in 1985 to Designer Accents of New Jersey.

It has been recorded that financial woes were plaguing the multi-faceted conglomerate as early as 1988. The pottery was closed "for the holidays" toward the end of 1990. The doors were never reopened after the 1990 holiday season and fire claimed the office complex in the fall of 1991, ending the tradition that had spanned four generations.

**Row 1:**  Cabbage salt or pepper shaker, "McCoy USA." Braly. — Set, $30.00-40.00

Cabbage grease jar (It is every bit as large as the Tomato cookie jar.), "McCoy USA." Braly. — $125.00-150.00

Cabbage salt or pepper shaker, mate above. — Set, $30.00-40.00

Leprechaun, unmarked. Braly. — $1,000.00+

Kittens on Ball of Yarn, "McCoy USA." — $65.00-85.00

**Row 2:**  Basket of Potatoes, minus one. "0274 McCoy USA." — $55.00-60.00

Western Box, "USA." Braly. — $150.00-175.00

Pine Cones, "McCoy USA." Braly. Only example known. — Too rare to price.

**Row 3:**  Grandma, "159 USA." — $125.00-150.00

Bamboo cylinder, "188 209L McCoy USA." — $50.00-60.00

Bear, unmarked Design Accent. — $45.00-50.00

**Row 1:**  *Pear (flat leaves)*, unmarked.  $100.00-125.00

*Grandfather Clock*, "USA" on back corner.  $125.00-150.00

*Crayola Kids* cylinder, "McCoy USA."  $45.00-50.00

**Row 2:**  *Lunch Box*, "377 USA."  $25.00-35.00

*Kittens on Ball of Yarn*, "McCoy USA."  $65.00-85.00

*Fruit* cylinder, "1123 USA."  $30.00-35.00

**Row 3:**  *Garbage Can*, "350."  $40.00-45.00

*Ice Cream Cone*, unmarked.  $25.00-30.00

*Indian* (Reproduction of original Pontiac Indian), "COMMEMORATIVE ISSUE 1990 McCoy U S A, LIMITED EDITIONS, 295/300." Produced by Cookson Pottery, Roseville, Ohio for George D. Williams III.  $125.00-150.00

**Below:**  *Goose with Scarf*, unmarked.  $35.00-45.00

*Teddy and Friend*, "154 USA."  $30.00-40.00

*Rooster*, umarked.  $45.00-50.00

**Row 1:** *Aladdin* teapot, "McCoy USA" on bottom of base. Snyder. $40.00-50.00

*Pirate's Chest*, "252 McCoy USA ©" on bottom. Snyder. $80.00-90.00

*Liberty Bell*, "McCoy, LCC, USA" on bottom. Snyder. $40.00-50.00

**Row 2:** *Baa Baa Black Sheep*, unmarked. Snyder. $55.00-65.00

*Humpty Dumpty*, unmarked. Snyder. $55.00-65.00

*Little Miss Muffet*, unmarked. Snyder. $55.00-65.00

*Mary, Mary, Quite Contrary*, unmarked. Snyder. $55.00-65.00

**Row 3:** *Apple*, "256, McCoy, USA." Snyder. $35.00-40.00

*Harley-Davidson Hog*, undecorated white blank (probably a second – See the decorated version in Advertising.). Braly. $200.00-225.00

*Pepper*, "McCoy." Snyder. $35.00-40.00

**Below:** *Little Boy Blue*, unmarked. Lindberg. $55.00-65.00

**Row 1:**  *Penguin*, unmarked Designer Accents.                                    $45.00-55.00

*Panda and Swirl*  undecorated blank, "141USA."                 $125.00-150.00

*Panda*, unmarked Designer Accents. Snyder.                      $40.00-50.00

**Row 2:**  *Clyde Dog*, "182, McCoy, LC USA."                              $150.00-175.00

*Bear and Beehive*, "143, USA."                                         $35.00-45.00

*Orange*, "257, USA."                                                          $40.00-50.00

**Row 3:**  *Rabbit*, unmarked Designer Accents. Snyder.                 $40.00-50.00

*Hamm's Bear*, "148, USA."                                               $150.00-175.00

*Pig*, unmarked Designer Accents. Snyder.                          $40.00-50.00

**Below:**  *Jewel Box*, no "Cookie Box" on front. Marked "USA."    $100.00-125.00

**Row 1:**   *Gay Time, Standing People* (1974), "McCoy, USA." Lindberg.          $50.00-60.00

*Sack of Cookies* (1961), "McCoy, USA." Lindberg.                             $35.00-45.00

*Gay Time, Kneeling People* (1974), "McCoy, USA." Lindberg.                   $45.00-55.00

**Row 2:**   *Mediterranean* (1967-68), "USA, 200." Lindberg.                 $40.00-45.00

*Modern Pineapple* (1967-71), "USA." Lindberg.                               $90.00-100.00

*Honeycomb* (1968-69), "250, 19©68, USA." Lindberg.                          $50.00-60.00

**Row 3:**   *Tulip – Flowerpot Shape* (1958-59), "McCoy, USA." Lindberg.     $200.00-225.00

*Gingerbread Boy* (1961), "USA." Lindberg.                                   $45.00-55.00

*Flower Burst* (1972-73), "USA 156." Lindberg.                               $35.00-45.00

**Below:**   *Dem Cookies Shor Am Good Mammy* (1991), "Commemorative Issue 1991, McCoy, Limited Edition." Available in white, yellow, turquoise, and blue. This is a reproduction with variations of the elusive *Dem Cookies Mammy*. Produced by Cookson Pottery in Roseville, Ohio. Wooldridge.                                                                  $100.00-105.00

The jars on Row 1 are not McCoy jars. The pottery building is an original design; the Mammy and Indian are reproductions, which were sold as commemoratives.

**Row 1:**  *Nelson McCoy Pottery Co. Building,* "Donaldson, Ltd. Edition, 500©1992." Lindberg.                                                          $125.00-130.00

*Dem Cookies Shor am Good Mammy* (1991), "Commemorative Issue 1991, McCoy, Limited Edition, #22 of 250." Reproduction by Cookson Pottery, Roseville, OH. Lindberg.                                            $100.00-105.00

*Indian* (Reproduction of original Pontiac Indian – 1990), painted face, "Commemorative Issue, 1990, McCoy, USA, Limited Editions, 1-5-91, #6 GW." Decorated by Rick Wisecarver, Roseville, OH. Lindberg.                    $160.00+

**Row 2:**  *Clown in Barrel* (1953-55), "McCoy, USA." Lindberg.              $90.00-110.00

*Clown in Barrel* (1953-55), "McCoy, USA." Lindberg.              $90.00-110.00

*Clown in Barrel* (1953-55), "McCoy, USA." Lindberg.              $90.00-110.00

**Row 3:**  *Cookstove* (1963-69), "McCoy, USA." Lindberg.                    $20.00-25.00

*Cat* (1986), unmarked, wearing original ribbon. Lindberg.          $50.00-60.00

*Pot Belly Stove* (1963-69), unmarked. Lindberg.                    $20.00-25.00

**Below:**  *Dem Cookies Shor Am Good, Mammy,* back view of *Mammy* on Row 1. Cookson Pottery, Roseville, OH. Lindberg.

**Row 1:**   *Traffic Light* (1978-87). "351, USA." Lindberg.                                    $35.00-45.00

*Basketweave* (1978-87), "1109, USA." Lindberg.                              $35.00-45.00

*Lamb on Cylinder*, "McCoy, USA." Lindberg.                              $225.00-275.00

**Row 2:**   *Frog on Stump* (1972), "216, McCoy, USA." Lindberg.                     $50.00-60.00

*Owl*, short (1976), "219, McCoy, USA." Lindberg.                              $25.00-35.00

*Cookie Bell* (1953-66), unmarked. Lindberg.                              $25.00-35.00

**Row 3:**   *Clown Bust* (1945-47), "McCoy." Lindberg.                                    $40.00-55.00

*Mouse on Clock* (1968-73), unmarked. Lindberg.                              $30.00-40.00

*Polar Bear*, without "Cookies" (1945), "McCoy." Lindberg.                     $30.00-40.00

**Below:**   *Mammy – Dem Cookies Sho Got Dat Vitamin A*, "McCoy." This jar is believed
by many to be the original *Dem Cookies... Mammy*. With all of the photos
of this elusive *Mammy* showing only a front view, it is easy to assume what
is on the back. Two examples have recently surfaced, the first one yellow
with underglaze paint on the hands and face and this undecorated aqua jar.
Lichtenstein.                                                           Too rare to value.

**Row 1:**   *Cookie Pot* (1964), "McCoy, USA." Lindberg.                                              $35.00-45.00

            *Lemon* (1972), "262, McCoy, USA." Lindberg.                                         $40.00-45.00

            *Cookie Pot* (1964), "McCoy, USA." Lindberg.                                              $35.00-45.00

**Row 2:**   *Brown Bear* (1945), "McCoy." Lindberg.                                             $275.00-300.00

            *Bear and Barrel* (1978), "142, USA." Lindberg.                                      $60.00-70.00

            *Panda and Swirl* (1978), "141, USA." Lindberg.                                      $225.00-275.00

**Row 3:**   *Goodie Goose* (1986-87), "166, USA." Lindberg.                                    $35.00-45.00

            *Brown and Gray Canister* (1978-79), "214, McCoy, USA." Lindberg.          $20.00-25.00

            *Painted Rooster*, unmarked, made in Sebring Studio. Lindberg.              $60.00-75.00

**Below:**  *Hillbilly Bear* (Early 1940's), "McCoy, USA." This photo was taken in the Ohio Ceramic Center by Chiquita Prestwood. It is part of the personal collection of Nelson and Billie McCoy.                                    Too rare to value.

            *Apollo* (1970-71), "260 McCoy © USA."                                                  $1,000.00+

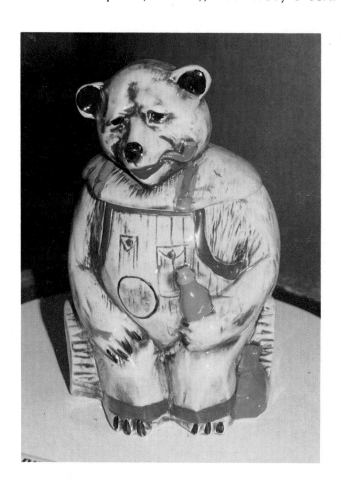

**Row 1:**   *Soccer Ball* (1978), unmarked. Lindberg.                        $550.00-650.00

              *Uncle Sam's Hat* (1973), unmarked. Lindberg.           $600.00-700.00

              *Jack-O'-Lantern* (1955) "McCoy, USA." Lindberg      $450.00-550.00

**Row 2:**   *Dog House* (1983), unmarked. Lindberg.                         $200.00-250.00

              *Quaker Oats* (1970), unmarked. Lindberg.               $350.00-450.00

              *Dog House* (1983), unmarked. Lindberg.                   $150.00-175.00

**Row 3:**   *House* (1966-68), unmarked. Lindberg.                          $250.00-350.00

              *Penguin* (1940-43), "McCoy." Lindberg.                 $200.00-250.00

              *Three-Banded Churn* (1961), unmarked. Lindberg.    $225.00-275.00

**Below:**   *Basketball*, unmarked. Skillman.                         Too rare to value.

**Row 1:**  *Grandfather Clock* (1962-64), "USA." Lindberg.                                     $60.00-80.00

*Koala Bear* (1983), "216, McCoy, USA." Lindberg.                                 $85.00-115.00

*Grandfather Clock* (1962-64), "USA." Lindberg.                                   $100.00-125.00

**Row 2:**  *Hen on Basket* (1958-59), "7110, McCoy USA." Lindberg.               $50.00-65.00

*Wren on Birdhouse* (1958-60), "McCoy, USA." Lindberg.                            $125.00-175.00

*Tilt Pitcher* (1939), unmarked. Lindberg.                                       $35.00-55.00

**Row 3:**  *Chilly Willy* (1986-88), "155 USA." Lindberg.                                       $40.00-45.00

*Winking Pig*, undecorated white (1972), "150, USA." Lindberg.                   $125.00-150.00

*Chilly Willy* (1986-88), " 155, USA." Lindberg.                                 $40.00-45.00

**Below:**  *Cookie Tug*, "McCoy USA." Skillman.                                  Too rare to value.

**Row 1:**  *Cookie Jug* (1971-78), unmarked. Lindberg.  $20.00-25.00

*Cookie Barrel* (1969-72), "146, McCoy, USA." Lindberg.  $30.00-35.00

*Cookie Jug* (1971-78), unmarked. Lindberg.  $20.00-25.00

**Row 2:**  *Bushel of Fruit* (1958-59), "McCoy, USA." Lindberg.  $50.00-60.00

*Modern*  (1958), "McCoy, USA." Lindberg.  $35.00-45.00

*Picnic Basket* (1961-63), "USA." Lindberg.  $40.00-45.00

**Row 3:**  *Burlap Sack* (1985), "207, McCoy, USA." Lindberg.  $30.00-35.00

*Burlap Bag* (1973-77), "158, McCoy, USA." Lindberg.  $30.00-35.00

*Coffee Grinder* (1961-68), "McCoy U.S.A." Lindberg.  $25.00-35.00

**Below:**  *Original Pontiac Indian*, without "Cookies" on the front. "McCoy." Firestone.  Too rare to value.

| | | |
|---|---|---|
| **Row 1:** | *Pot Belly Stove Lamp*, "McCoy, USA." Lindberg. | $30.00-35.00 |
| | *Tea Kettle Lamp*, "McCoy, USA." Lindberg. | $30.00-35.00 |
| **Row 2:** | *Cork Lid* (1975-76), "178, McCoy, USA." Lindberg. | $175.00-275.00 |
| | *Tan and Brown*, random brush strokes (1975), "3106, McCoy, USA." Lindberg. | $75.00-100.00 |
| | *Nibble Kettle*, unmarked. Lindberg. | $150.00-200.00 |
| **Row 3:** | *Turkey*, green and brown (1945), "McCoy." Lindberg. | $275.00-325.00 |
| | *Mother Goose*, brown tones (1948-52), "McCoy, USA." Lindberg. | $100.00-125.00 |
| | *Turkey*, white (1945), "McCoy." Lindberg. | $300.00-350.00 |
| **Below:** | *Engine*, orange blank with silver paint (1962-64), "McCoy, USA." Lindberg. | $150.00-175.00 |

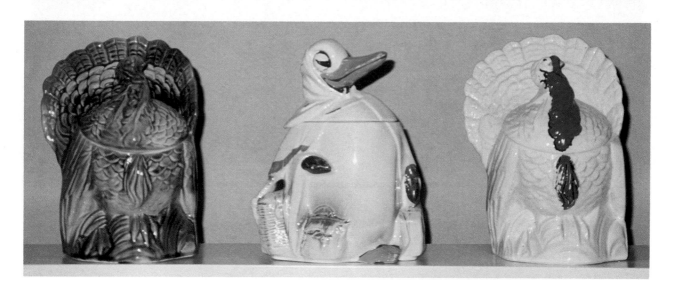

**Row 1:**   *Blue Fruit,* milk can (1978), "253, McCoy, USA." Lindberg.                   $30.00-40.00

*Rosemary* , milk can (1977), "253, McCoy, USA." Lindberg.                   $30.00-40.00

*Fruit,* milk can (1980-85), "253, USA." Lindberg.                   $30.00-40.00

**Row 2:**   *Happy Time,* milk can (1975), "333, McCoy." Lindberg.                   $35.00-45.00

*Ask Grandma,* milk can (1973), "USA." Also stamped "Made in England."
Lindberg.                   $50.00-60.00

*Happy Time,* milk can, "253, McCoy, USA." Lindberg.                   $35.00-45.00

**Row 3:**   *Seagram's,* milk can, "253, McCoy, USA." Lindberg.                   $40.00-50.00

*Blue Willow,* milk can (1973), "USA." Lindberg.                   $40.00-50.00

*Farm Scene,* milk can, "253, McCoy, USA." Lindberg.                   $40.00-50.00

**Below:**   *Spirit of '76,* milk can (1973-75), "9, USA." Eagle decal taken from the
Carved Wooden Eagle, artist unknown, National Gallery of Art,
Washington, D.C. Lindberg.                   $30.00-40.00

*Cow,* milk can, "9, USA." Lindberg.                   $40.00-50.00

*Yorkville,* milk can, (1974), "McCoy, USA, 174."                   $30.00-40.00

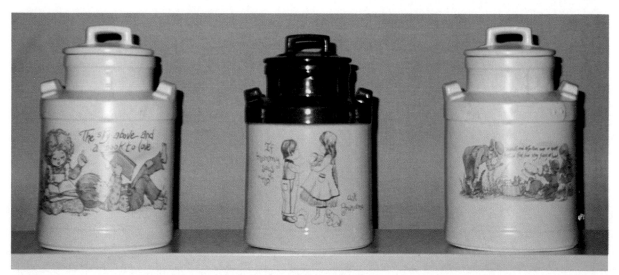

**Row 1:**    *Pink Roses*, cylinder (1946-54), "McCoy, USA." Lindberg.      $30.00-40.00

           *Apple*, cylinder (1946-54), "McCoy, USA." Lindberg.      $30.00-40.00

           *Red Roses*, cylinder (1946-54), "McCoy, USA." Lindberg.      $30.00-40.00

**Row 2:**    *Vegetables*, cylinder (1946-54), "McCoy." Lindberg.      $30.00-40.00

           *Wheat on Pearl Glaze*, cylinder (1946-54), "McCoy." Lindberg.      $40.00-50.00

           *Chef*, cylinder (1946-54), "McCoy, USA." Lindberg.      $30.00-40.00

**Row 3:**    *Yellow/Black lid*, cylinder (1946-54), "McCoy." Lindberg.      $40.00-50.00

           *Red Poppies*, cylinder (1946-64), "McCoy." Lindberg.      $30.00-40.00

           *Black/Pink lid*, cylinder (1946-54), "McCoy." Lindberg.      $50.00-60.00

**Below:**    *"Snitch the Cookies,"* cylinder (1946-54), "McCoy, USA." Lindberg.      $65.00-75.00

           *Amber*, cylinder (1946-54), "McCoy, USA." Lindberg.      $30.00-40.00

           *Cookie Express*, cylinder (1946-54), "McCoy, USA."      $65.00-75.00

| | | |
|---|---|---:|
| **Row 1:** | *Peanut* (1976-77) "260, McCoy, USA." Lindberg. | $30.00-40.00 |
| | *Pennsylvania Dutch*, cylinder (1946-54), "McCoy." Lindberg. | $40.00-50.00 |
| | *Peanut* (1976-77), "260, McCoy, USA." Lindberg. | $30.00-40.00 |
| **Row 2:** | *Yellow/Flower Panels*, modern cylinder (1970-71), "254, McCoy, USA." Lindberg. | $30.00-35.00 |
| | *Black/No Panels*, modern cylinder (1970-71), "254 McCoy, USA." Lindberg. | $30.00-35.00 |
| | *Brown/Flower Panels*, modern cylinder (1970-71), "254 McCoy, USA." Lindberg. | $30.00-35.00 |
| **Row 3:** | *Spice Delight*, canister (1975-76), "216 L, McCoy, USA." Lindberg. | $30.00-35.00 |
| | *Gingham Patchwork*, canister (1975-76), "216, McCoy, USA." Lindberg. | $30.00-35.00 |
| | *Violets*, canister (1975-76), "216, McCoy, USA." Lindberg. | $35.00-40.00 |
| **Below:** | Mustard color cylinder, "USA, 28." Lindberg. | $30.00-35.00 |
| | Cobalt Blue cylinder, "USA, 28." Lindberg. | $30.00-35.00 |
| | Mustard/Green drip glaze cylinder, "USA, 28." Lindberg. | $40.00-45.00 |

| | | |
|---|---|---|
| **Row 1:** | *Tilted Strawberry*, unmarked (SS). Lindberg. | $30.00-40.00 |
| | *Red Grid* (1986 – NMC), "4253, USA." Lindberg. | $30.00-35.00 |
| | *New Apple* (1986 – NMC), "8161." Lindberg. | $30.00-35.00 |
| **Row 2:** | *Strawberry Basket*, dark (1978), unmarked. Lindberg. | $75.00-90.00 |
| | *Lunch Bucket*, green lid (1978-87), unmarked. Lindberg. | $50.00-60.00 |
| | *Strawberry Basket*, light (1978), unmarked. Lindberg. | $60.00-80.00 |
| **Row 3:** | *Red Apple*, green leaf (1958), "McCoy, USA." Lindberg. | $50.00-60.00 |
| | *Yellow Apple* (1950-64), "McCoy, USA." Lindberg. | $30.00-40.00 |
| | *Red Apple*, gold leaf (1956-57), "McCoy, USA." Lindberg. | $75.00-95.00 |
| **Below:** | *Happy Face*, all yellow/raised letters (1972-79), "235, McCoy, USA." Lindberg. | $30.00-40.00 |
| | *Cookie Jug*, brown (1978-79), "213, McCoy, USA." Lindberg. | $30.00-35.00 |
| | *Pepper*, yellow (1956-57), "157, McCoy, USA." Lindberg. | $30.00-40.00 |

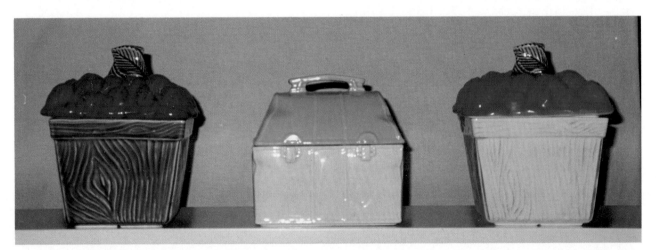

**Row 1:**   *Canyon* (1979), "1402L, McCoy, USA." Lindberg.                    $40.00-50.00

          *New Yellow Cookie*, "214, McCoy." Lindberg.                    $30.00-40.00

          *Blue Field* (1979), "200, McCoy, USA." Lindberg.                 $40.00-50.00

**Row 2:**   *Canister, Strawberries*, "McCoy, USA." Lindberg.                $30.00-35.00

          *Indian Design*, "131, USA." Lindberg.                           $40.00-50.00

          *Daisy Delight*, "McCoy, USA." Lindberg.                        $35.00-40.00

**Row 3:**   *Grandma's Cookies* (SS), unmarked. Lindberg.                 $30.00-35.00

          *Duck Family* (LDCCJ), unmarked. Lindberg.                      $30.00-35.00

          *Dancing Bears* (LDC), "1018." Lindberg.                        $30.00-35.00

**Below:**   *Wildflower* (LDC), "4253, USA." Lindberg.                      $30.00-35.00

          *Kid's Stuff Dog* (1989-90), "1501, USA." Lindberg.             $35.00-45.00

          *Wildflower* (LDC), "4253, USA." Lindberg.                      $30.00-35.00

| | | |
|---|---|---|
| **Row 1:** | *Chuck Wagon* (1974-75), "186, McCoy, USA." Lindberg. | $50.00-60.00 |
| | *Canister*, small (1985), "214, McCoy, USA." Lindberg. | $20.00-25.00 |
| | *Chuck Wagon, Spice Delight* (1974-75), "186, McCoy, USA." Lindberg. | $50.00-60.00 |
| **Row 2:** | *Gypsy Pot* (1975), unmarked. Lindberg. | $30.00-35.00 |
| | *Canister, Children at Play* (1978), "360, McCoy, USA." Lindberg. | $30.00-40.00 |
| | *Little Red Bean Pot* (1971), "McCoy, USA." Lindberg. | $30.00-35.00 |
| **Row 3:** | *Lantern/Lamp* (1962-63), "McCoy, USA." Lindberg. | $55.00-65.00 |
| | *Cookie Kettle* (1965-68), unmarked. Lindberg. | $35.00-40.00 |
| | *Yosemite Sam* (1971-72), stamped, "McCoy, USA." Lindberg. | $125.00-150.00 |
| **Below:** | *Pagoda* (1974-75), "208L, McCoy, USA." Lindberg. | $30.00-40.00 |
| | *Hammered Tea Kettle* (1974), "185, McCoy, USA." Lindberg. | $35.00-40.00 |
| | *Madrid* (1974), "USA." Lindberg. | $35.00-45.00 |

**Row 1:**    *Old Milk Can* (1939-44), unmarked. Lindberg.    $30.00-35.00

*Round Basketweave* (Late 1930's), unmarked. Lindberg.    $50.00-60.00

*Concave Lilies* (Mid 1930's), "USA." Lindberg.    $30.00-40.00

**Row 2:**    *Floral* (1956-57), stamped "McCoy USA." Lindberg.    $45.00-55.00

*Hot Air Balloon* (1985-86), "353, USA." Lindberg.    $35.00-40.00

*Floral* (1956-57), stamped "McCoy USA." Lindberg.    $45.00-55.00

**Row 3:**    *Bean Pot, Garden Girl*, "342, McCoy, USA, Ovenproof." Lindberg.    $65.00-75.00

*Bean Pot,* Re-issue, "McCoy, USA." Lindberg.    $40.00-45.00

*Bean Pot, Four Owls*, "342, McCoy, USA, Ovenproof." Lindberg.    $65.00-75.00

**Below:**    *Concave* (1942), unmarked. Lindberg.    $35.00-40.00

*Cope Market Lady* (1991), modeled by Sidney Cope, former McCoy
designer. Produced by Sidney's son, Leslie Cope, of Cope Studio in
Roseville, OH. We feel this jar defines perfectly a commemorative
jar, though it was never called a commemorative. Lindberg.    $175.00-185.00

*Thinking Puppy* (1977-79), "...USA." Lindberg.    $25.00-30.00

**Row 1:**  *Fruit,* tilt cookie/candy jar (1977-80), unmarked. Lindberg.  $30.00-35.00

*Colonial Scene,* old-fashioned milk can – AUTHENTIC McCoy Reproductions "Circa 1911 by McCoy."  $30.00-40.00

*Canister,* (1969-79), "7024, McCoy, USA." Lindberg.  $25.00-30.00

**Row 2:**  *Yorkville,* pitcher (1974), "202, McCoy, USA." Lindberg.  $30.00-40.00

*Spice Delight,* pitcher (1976), "202, McCoy, USA." Lindberg.  $30.00-40.00

*Fruit,* pitcher (1975-77), "202, McCoy, USA." Lindberg.  $30.00-40.00

**Row 3:**  *Country Kitchen* (1977-80), "0269, USA." Lindberg.  $75.00-85.00

*English Ivy,* round (1964), "McCoy, USA." Lindberg.  $70.00-80.00

*Soup Tureen* (1965), "McCoy, USA." Lindberg.  $50.00-60.00

**Below:**  *Reclining Cow* for "Cookies and Milk." Marked in mold "McCoy USA." Lindberg. Too rare to price!

**Row 1:**    *Hexagon* (1947-49), "McCoy." Lindberg.                                      $50.00-60.00

          *Square, V-Finial* (1947), "McCoy." Lindberg.                           $35.00-45.00

          *Hexagon* (1947-49), "McCoy."                                           $50.00-60.00

**Row 2:**    *Heart-Shaped Hobnail* (1940), unmarked. Lindberg.                  $350.00-400.00

          *Pineapple* (1957), "McCoy, USA." Lindberg.                          $125.00-175.00

          *Heart-Shaped Hobnail* (1940), unmarked. Lindberg.                  $350.00-400.00

**Row 3:**    *Round Hobnail* (1940), unmarked. Lindberg.                          $75.00-100.00

          *Honey Bear* (1953-55), "McCoy, USA." Lindberg.                     $150.00-175.00

          *Round Hobnail* (1940), unmarked. Lindberg.                          $75.00-100.00

**Below:**    *Corn* (1977), "275, McCoy, USA." Lindberg.                          $45.00-50.00

HAND DECORATED COOKIE JARS

Ass't. 227

No. 253

Ass't. 254

KOOKIE KETTLE

No. 171

No. 236

COOKIE JUG

No. 144

No. 7024

No. 255

Ass't. 228

No. 225 Assortment

Ass't. 229

No. 250

Wish I Had a Cookie

No. 180

No. 252

No. 178

No. 213

COOKIES

The Nelson McCoy Pottery Company

Area Code 614 697-7331    Roseville, Ohio 43777

*McCoy Catalog Sheet, 1968-1970.*

### HAND DECORATED COOKIE JARS

No. 257

No. 256

Ass't. 117

No. 846

Ass't. 231

No. 823

No. 847

No. 848

No. 258

No. 260

No. 220

Hand Decorated
AMERICAN
COOKIE
JAR
for Gracious
Living
MCP

### CANISTER SETS

No. 925

**The Nelson McCoy Pottery Company**
*Subsidiary of Mount Clemens Pottery Company*
Area Code 614 697-7331          Roseville, Ohio 43777

No. 926

Page 3

*McCoy Catalog Sheet, 1968-1970.*

# McCoy Pottery
## Antique Reproductions

The registered McCoy trademark was first used by Roger Jensen in Rockwood, TN on January 1, 1991. Because the original McCoy trademark was never registered by the founding Ohio potters, Jensen was able to legally qualify the trademark in Tennessee simply by using it for one year. He filed for federal trademark registration August 31, 1992, receiving approval on March 9, 1993.

**Row 1:**    *Clown,* "McCoy #93."                                                             $35.00-45.00

                  *Little Red Riding Hood,* "McCoy #93."       $90.00-110.00

**Row 2:**    *Pearl Mammy,* unmarked. Available in white, yellow, blue, green, or pink.    $65.00-70.00

                  *Luzianne Mammy,* "USA."                    $65.00-70.00

**Row 3:**    *Aunt Jemima,* "McCoy."                           $35.00-45.00

                  *Aunt Jemima,* "McCoy."                           $35.00-45.00

                  *Aunt Jemima,* "McCoy."                           $35.00-45.00

*Aunt Jemima* is available in traditional white, antique green, precious pink, antique yellow, walnut brown, or country blue with regular or antique crackle glaze; face and hands are decorated with brown or black paint over the glaze.

Not all of the items produced by McCoy Pottery of Rockwood, TN, have a two-digit number mark (i.e. #93) indicating the year of production, incised into the pottery. McCoy Pottery first started making jars without realizing the impact it might have on the collectible market. After concerned individuals explained the importance of properly identifying the new McCoy Pottery line, Jensen stressed his main concern is that his products be represented for what they are, antique reproductions. His original purpose was to provide the people who could not afford an antique cookie jar a reproduction that would look similar, but be much less expensive.

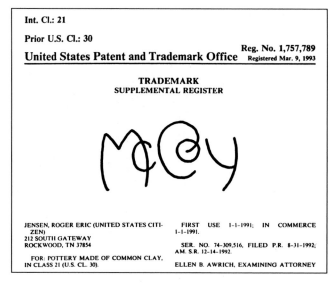

Int. Cl.: 21

Prior U.S. Cl.: 30

Reg. No. 1,757,789

**United States Patent and Trademark Office**  Registered Mar. 9, 1993

**TRADEMARK**
**SUPPLEMENTAL REGISTER**

JENSEN, ROGER ERIC (UNITED STATES CITIZEN)
212 SOUTH GATEWAY
ROCKWOOD, TN 37854

FOR: POTTERY MADE OF COMMON CLAY, IN CLASS 21 (U.S. CL. 30).

FIRST USE 1-1-1991; IN COMMERCE 1-1-1991.

SER. NO. 74-309,516, FILED P.R. 8-31-1992; AM. S.R. 12-14-1992.

ELLEN B. AWRICH, EXAMINING ATTORNEY

# Metlox

Would you associate tile and neon signs with dinnerware and cookie jars? The only familiarity of early Metlox to today's collector would be "Poppytrail," the name assigned to one of three clay dinnerware lines created to help survive the Depression when the sale of neon signs began to go "soft."

Metlox was originally a division of Proutyline Products Company founded by T.C. Prouty in 1921. The Metlox division opened in 1927 to manufacture insulated bases for neon signs. One of the procedures Prouty had invented was to adhere metal to tile. During the Depression, Americans escaped their troubles by going to the movies, which created good demand for neon signs. T. C. Prouty died in 1931. Soon after, the demand for signs slowed down, plus many of those who had ordered signs on credit found they could no longer pay the bill. Metlox switched to dinnerware.

Evan K. Shaw purchased Metlox in 1946 after his Los Angeles, California-based American Pottery burned to the ground. The year 1946 was truly the birth of Metlox. Shaw was able to pull Metlox out of the red with a $600,000 gross in the first year and go on to become a world leader in ceramic ware.

**Left:**   "Poppytrail, Made in California." Firestone.       $100.00-125.00

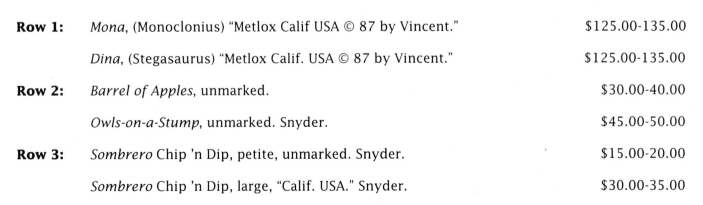

The Johnny Carson show commissioned many companies to make things that had the colors and markings of cows for a special show with a cow theme. It was to be for a skit on *The Tonight Show.* Unfortunately, the skit was scrapped, but Metlox did design several of the *Cow-Dinosaur* jars.

**Right:**   *Cow-Painted Rex* (Tyrannosaurus Rex)
"Metlox Calif USA © 87 by Vincent."
Clyde and Takasugi.       $250.00-270.00

| | | |
|---|---|---|
| **Row 1:** | *Mona*, (Monoclonius) "Metlox Calif USA © 87 by Vincent." | $125.00-135.00 |
| | *Dina*, (Stegasaurus) "Metlox Calif. USA © 87 by Vincent." | $125.00-135.00 |
| **Row 2:** | *Barrel of Apples*, unmarked. | $30.00-40.00 |
| | *Owls-on-a-Stump*, unmarked. Snyder. | $45.00-50.00 |
| **Row 3:** | *Sombrero* Chip 'n Dip, petite, unmarked. Snyder. | $15.00-20.00 |
| | *Sombrero* Chip 'n Dip, large, "Calif. USA." Snyder. | $30.00-35.00 |

**Row 1:**  *Cookie Boy*, unmarked. The original red paint is missing from his cap, mouth, and stripes between the collar edges.    $300.00-350.00

*Strawberry Box*, "Made in USA Poppytrail Calif."    $50.00-60.00

*Candy Girl*, "Made in California, Poppytrail Pottery by Metlox" on paper label.    $300.00-350.00

**Row 2:**  *Watermelon*, "Made in Poppytrail Calif."    $200.00-225.00

*Space Rocket*, "Made in USA."    $400.00+

*Calf,* or *Calf – says "Moo,"* paper label, "Made in California Poppytrail Pottery by Metlox."    $200.00-225.00

**Row 3:**  *Teddy Bear*, unmarked, designed by Helen McIntosh, a former Disney designer. The *Teddy Bear* is Metlox's oldest character design and, therefore, the most plentiful.    $40.00-45.00

*Happy the Clown*, unmarked.    $325.00-375.00

*Ballerina Bear*, "Metlox Calif. USA."    $100.00-125.00

**Below:**  *Little Pig*, "Metlox Calif USA." Clyde and Takasugi.    $150.00-175.00

*Beau Bear* canister set, "METLOX CALIF. USA" on all three pieces.    3-Piece Set, $100.00-125.00

**Row 1:**   *Grapes*, "Made in USA."   $125.00-150.00

*Poncho Bear with Sombrero* salt or pepper shaker, "Metlox, Calif. USA."   Set, $25.00-30.00

*Poncho Bear with Sombrero* cookie jar, "Metlox, Calif. USA."   $70.00-80.00

*Poncho Bear with Sombrero* salt or pepper shaker, mate above.   Set, $25.00-30.00

*Raccoon Cookie Bandit*, "Made in Poppytrail, Calif. USA."   $100.00-125.00

**Row 2:**   *Gingerbread*, "Made in Poppytrail Calif. USA."   $60.00-75.00

*Rose* salt or pepper shaker, unmarked, but made in Japan. Metlox never made figural shakers to match their *Rose*. This Japanese set blends in well.   Set, $10.00-12.00

*Rose*, "Made in USA." Paper label, "Made in California, Poppytrail Pottery by Metlox."   $275.00-300.00

*Rose* salt or pepper shaker, mate above.   Set, $10.00-12.00

*Lamb* or *Lamb - says "Baa,"* "Made in Poppytrail Metlox Calif. U.S.A."   $100.00-125.00

**Row 3:**   *Daisy Topiary*, "Made in Poppytrail Calif."   $50.00-60.00

*Wheat Shock*, "Made in Poppytrail Calif."   $40.00-50.00

*Cookie Girl*, "Made in Poppytrail Calif. USA."   $55.00-65.00

**Below:**   *Red Rooster* cookie cylinder, "Poppytrail by Metlox, Made in Calif." Supnick.   $35.00-45.00

*Cow* bank, "Metlox Calif. USA."   $40.00-45.00

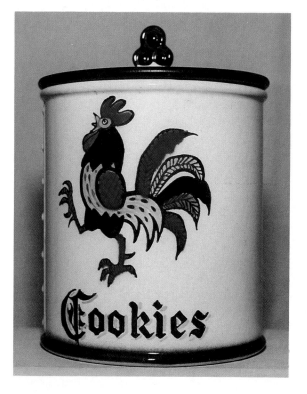
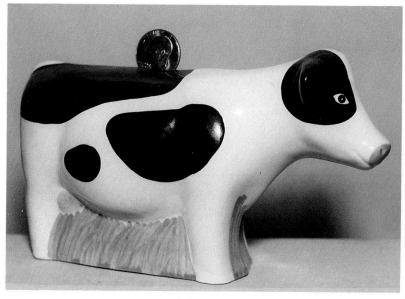

**Row 1:**    *Chef Pierre*, "Metlox Calif. USA."                                       $100.00-125.00

*Pescado Fish*, stamped "Pescado by Metlox, California Pottery, Manhattan Beach, Est. 1927."         $60.00-80.00

*Humpty Dumpty*, "Metlox Calif. USA."         $125.00-150.00

**Row 2:**    *Puddles*, "Metlox Calif USA."         $50.00-60.00

*Kangaroo*, "Made in California, Poppytrail Pottery by Metlox."         $500.00+

*Puddles*, "Metlox Calif USA."         $50.00-60.00

**Row 3:**    *Koala Bear*, "Made in Poppytrail Calif USA."         $100.00-125.00

*Roller Bear*, "Metlox USA."         $100.00-125.00

*Koala Bear*, "Made in Poppytrail Calif USA."         $100.00-125.00

**Below:**    *Humpty Dumpty*, unmarked. Hawks.         $300.00-350.00

**Row 1:**   *Lamb with Flowers,* "Made in Poppytrail Calif."                                $175.00-200.00

*Rabbit* (clover bloom finial), "Metlox, Made in USA."                $100.00-125.00

*Chicken, Mother Hen,* "Made in USA."                                      $40.00-50.00

**Row 2:**   *Whale,* "Made in Poppytrail Calif USA."                                  $275.00-300.00

*Owl* salt or pepper shaker, "Metlox" on rubber stopper.          Set, $12.00-15.00

*Owl* cookie jar, "Made in Poppytrail Calif."                            $40.00-45.00

*Owl* salt or pepper shaker, mate above.                                  Set, $12.00-15.00

*Blue Bird* on Stump, "Made in USA."                                       $40.00-50.00

**Row 3:**   *Apple,* "Made in USA."                                                        $35.00-45.00

*Bubbles,* unmarked.                                                            $175.00-225.00

*Raccoon Cookie Bandit,* "Made in Poppytrail Calif. USA."         $70.00-90.00

**Below:**   *Bubbles the Hippo,* "USA." Clyde and Takasugi.                   $225.00-250.00

*Bubbles* was plagued with production problems and had to be redesigned many times. The flower on the lid was top-heavy. Not many of these jars were ever made due to lack of consumer interest at the time. *Bubbles* was issued a second time in the late 1980's as *Dottie Hippo.* This time she wore dots rather than the soft gray or yellow solid color. Dots are far easier to apply, thus, more cost effective.

**Row 1:**    *Tulip*, "Made in USA."                                                                        $300.00+

               *Little Piggy*, "Poppytrail Calif. USA." Braly.       $100.00-125.00

               *Walrus*, "Made in Poppytrail Calif. USA."      $200.00-225.00

Did you know there are two sizes of the *Walrus?* The brown is a full size larger than the cream-colored with blue tie and hat. Helen McIntyre was a wonderful designer, but sometimes her finished product would not fit into the standard-size box. The *Walrus* is a perfect example. The brown Walrus became the model for the cream, one size down – Voilá, perfect fit!

**Row 2:**    *Scottie*, "Metlox Calif USA."                             $100.00-125.00

               *Flamingo*, "Metlox Calif. USA." The *Flamingo* was one of the most unpopular jars with the consumer. It was designed and produced, and nobody bought it! Consequently, there was a very limited production.    $250.00+

               *Ballerina Bear*, "Metlox Calif. USA."       $100.00-125.00

**Row 3:**    *Nut and Chipmunk Barrel*, unmarked. Snyder.      $70.00-85.00

               *Mother Goose*, "Made in Poppytrail Calif." Paper label, "Made in Calif, Poppytrail Pottery by Metlox."      $150.00-175.00

               *Cow*, "Made in Calif Poppytrail."            $300.00-350.00

**Below:**    *Circus Bear,* "Metlox Made in U.S.A." Potter.      $150.00-175.00

| | | |
|---|---|---|
| **Row 1:** | *Noah's Ark*, "Made in Poppytrail Calif." Paper label, "Made in Calif, Poppy-trail Pottery by Metlox." | $100.00-125.00 |
| | *Kitten – Says "Meow,"* paper label "Made in California, Poppytrail by Metlox." | $100.00-125.00 |
| | *Mouse Mobile*, unmarked. | $125.00-150.00 |
| **Row 2:** | *Orange,* "Made in USA." | $40.00-45.00 |
| | *Drummer Boy*, "Made in Calif. USA." | $225.00-250.00 |
| | *Nun*, "Metlox Calif USA." | $300.00+ |
| **Row 3:** | *Lucy Goose*, "Metlox Calif USA." | $50.00-60.00 |
| | *Teddy Bear*, "Made in Poppytrail USA." | $30.00-40.00 |
| | *Uncle Sam Bear*, "Metlox Calif. USA." | $400.00+ |
| **Below:** | *Flower Basket*, unmarked. | $30.00-40.00 |
| | *Mammy Scrub Woman*, unmarked. | $1,200.00+ |

The *Mammy Scrub Woman* was made in multiple colors including burgundy, blue, and yellow. She was first made after 1946 and discontinued in the late 1940's according to Doris Caffazza who was head of the decorating department at Metlox for almost fifty years.

The jar and lid were poured with slip and then removed from the mold and finished after drying for nearly 24 hours. The finishing involved using a wet cloth to smooth away any imperfections. This created a piece of greenware. At this point, the decorators took the finished piece of greenware and painted it with colored slip called on-go. This eliminated the need for a second firing. After the on-go had been applied, the jar was glazed and fired.

The *Mammy Scrub Woman* has a lid with a small hole in the bottom. This was done to keep the shape, according to Caffazza. There had been a problem with the greenware losing its shape because of the extensive handling before the firing. She further explained that most of the tops did not fit the bottoms of the jars before the process, which left the hole in the bottom of the lid.

Few cookie jars were made by Metlox in the 1940's. They worked primarily on dinnerware.

258

**Row 1:**   *Bassett Dog*, "Metlox Calif. USA."                                      $250.00+

        *Ali Cat* salt or pepper shaker. "Metlox U.S.A."                  Set, $30.00-35.00

        *Ali Cat* cookie jar. "Metlox Calif. U.S.A."                       $125.00-150.00

        *Ali Cat* salt or pepper shaker, mate above.                    Set, $30.00-35.00

        *Lion*, "Made in Poppytrail Calif."                               $150.00-175.00

**Row 2:**   *Beau Bear*, "Metlox, Calif USA."                                 $40.00-50.00

        *Bucky Beaver*, "Metlox, Made in USA."                           $100.00-125.00

        *Fido Dog*, "Made in Poppytrail U.S.A."                          $60.00-70.00

**Row 3:**   *Parrot*, "Made in Poppytrail Calif. USA."                        $150.00-175.00

        *Sir Francis Drake* salt or pepper shaker.                       Set, $20.00-25.00

        *Francine Duck,* "METLOX CALIF USA."                             $100.00-125.00

        *Sir Francis Drake* salt or pepper shaker, mate above.           Set, $20.00-25.00

        *Frosty Penguin*, "Metlox Calif. U.S.A."                         $70.00-80.00

**Below:**   *Dutch Girl*, antique finish, "Metlox Calif. USA © By Vincent." Clyde and
Takasugi.                                                                      $100.00-125.00

        *Hen*, (matching *Rooster* has open beak, as if crowing) "Made in Poppy-
trail Calif." Clyde and Takasugi.                                              $100.00-125.00

**Row 1:**      *Strawberry*, "Made in U.S.A."         $35.00-45.00

               *Boy on Pumpkin*, unmarked.         $400.00+

               *Apple*, "Metlox Calif. U.S.A." Snyder.         $35.00-45.00

**Row 2:**      *Broccoli*, second in a canister set. "Metlox Calif. U.S.A."         $70.00-90.00

               *Corn*, first in a canister set. "Made in Poppytrail Calif."         $50.00-60.00

               *Tulip Time*, "Made in Poppytrail Calif. U.S.A."         $35.00-45.00

There are at least five variations of this cookie jar. Additional designs include *Feathered Friends, Chickadee, Sunflowers,* and *Children of the World.*

**Row 3:**      *Pineapple*, "Made in U.S.A."         $35.00-45.00

               *Fruit Basket*, unmarked. Snyder.         $40.00-50.00

               *Pretzel Barrel*, unmarked.         $60.00-70.00

**Below:**      *Squash*, "Made in Poppytrail Calif. U.S.A."         $125.00-150.00

               *Pumpkin*, "Metlox Calif. U.S.A."         $30.00-35.00

**Row 1:**  *Squirrel with Acorn*, "Made in U.S.A." Snyder.                                  $225.00-250.00

*Walrus*, "Metlox Calif. U.S.A."                                                     $90.00-100.00

*Panda with Lollipop*, "Made in Poppytrail Calif. U.S.A." Snyder.      $175.00-200.00

**Row 2:**  *Cookie Girl*, unmarked. Snyder.                                              $70.00-90.00

*Cookie Girl*, "Made in Poppytrail Calif. U.S.A."                             $70.00-90.00

*Pretty Ann*, "Made in Poppytrail Calif. U.S.A."                          $100.00-125.00

**Row 3:**  *Calico Cat*, "Made in Poppytrail Calif. U.S.A." Snyder.             $125.00-135.00

*Blue Bird on Pine Cone*, "Made in U.S.A."                                 $50.00-60.00

*Gingham Dog*, "Made in Poppytrail Calif. U.S.A." Snyder.          $125.00-135.00

**Below:**  *Ferdinand Calf*, "Metlox Calif. U.S.A."                                        $400.00+

**Row 1:** *Happy Time* canister base (missing wooden lid). "POPPYTRAIL BY METLOX MADE IN CALIFORNIA" stamped on bottom. There is also a number "13" stamped on the bottom. $8.00-10.00

*Red Rooster* and *Hen* salt and pepper shakers. Set, $10.00-15.00

*Santa* candy or planter, "Metlox Calif. U.S.A." Stamped "Original Calif. Pottery by Metlox." $50.00-60.00

**Row 2:** *Dutch Boy*, "Metlox Calif. U.S.A. © 87 by Vincent." $150.00-175.00

*Dutch Girl*, "Metlox Calif. U.S.A. © 87 by Vincent." $150.00-175.00

**Row 3:** *Jolly Chef*, paper label, "Made in California, Poppytrail Pottery by Metlox." $200.00+

*Granada Cookie Canister,* "Made in Poppytrail Calif." Snyder. $30.00-40.00

*Cow*, "Made in Poppytrail Calif." $225.00-250.00

**Below:** *Cow with Bell*, no flowers, "Made in Poppytrail Calif." Clyde and Takasugi. $300.00+

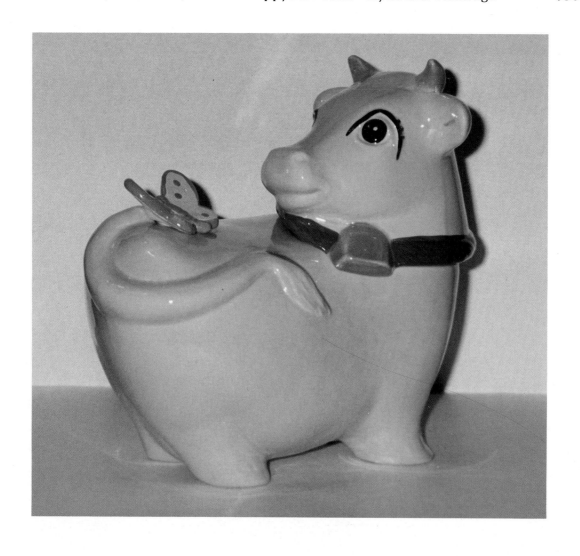

"TERRA MADRE"
for Metlox
Hecho en Mexico

*Metlox Catalog Sheets, 1988-1989.*

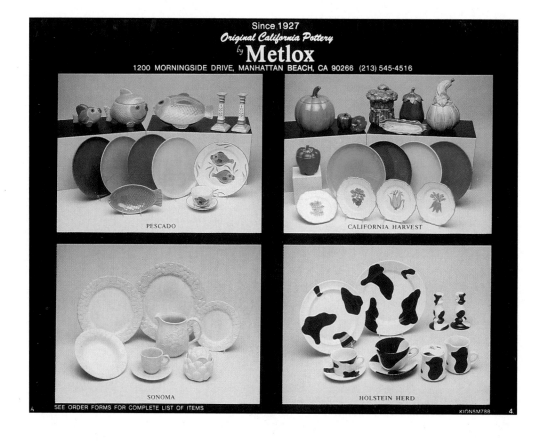

Metlox Catalog Sheet.

Poppytrail Art Ware Catalog Sheet By Metlox.

**OWL LINE**

| | | | RETAIL LIST |
|---|---|---|---|
| 1. | 120 330 | Salt Shaker · 5 ¼" H. | 5.50 |
| 2. | 120 340 | Pepper Shaker · 4 7/8" H. | 5.50 |
| | 120 450/470 | Owl Canister Set, 6 pcs. complete | 39.95 |
| 3. | 120 450 | Owl Canister · L., 2½ Qt. | 16.95 |
| 4. | 120 460 | Owl Canister · M., 2 Qt. | 12.50 |
| 5. | 120 470 | Owl Canister · S., 1½ Qt. | 10.50 |
| 6. | 120 580 | Owl Planter · 5¾" H. | 17.95 |
| 7. | 120 890 | Ashtray · 6" | 3.95 |
| 8. | 120 900 | Ashtray · 7" | 5.95 |
| 9. | 120 910 | Ashtray · 8" | 6.95 |
| 10. | 121 450 | Blue Owl Cookie Jar, 2½ Qt. | 16.95 |
| 11. | 122 450 | White Owl Cookie Jar, 2½ Qt. | 16.95 |
| 12. | 120 450 | Owl Cookie Jar, 2½ Qt. | 16.95 |

**DAISY ACCESSORIES**

| | | | RETAIL LIST |
|---|---|---|---|
| 13. | 050 280 | Daisy Twin Server · 9 7/8" L. | 13.95 |
| 14. | 050 310 | Cake Plate · 13" | 19.95 |
| | 450 470 | Daisy Canister Set, 6 pcs. complete | 44.95 |
| 15. | 050 450 | Daisy Canister, 3½ Qt. · L. | 17.95 |
| 16. | 050 460 | Daisy Canister, 3 Qt. · M. | 14.50 |
| 17. | 050 470 | Daisy Canister, 2½ Qt. · S. | 12.50 |
| 18. | 050 550 | Topiary Cookie Jar, 2¾ Qt. | 17.95 |
| 19. | 050 750 | Chip & Dip, 12¼" | 17.95 |
| 20. | 050 830 | Footed Bowl, 6½" | 10.75 |
| 21. | 050 840 | Footed Compote, 8 3/8" | 14.75 |
| 22. | 050 870 | Soap Dish, 5½" | 3.95 |
| 23. | 050 890 | Ashtray · Square, 4¼" | 3.95 |
| 24. | 050 900 | Ashtray · Square, 5" | 4.95 |
| 25. | 050 910 | Ashtray · Square, 6½" | 5.95 |
| 26. | 051 310 | Cake Plate, White, 13" | 14.95 |

*Poppytrail Art Ware Catalog Sheet by Metlox.*

*Poppytrail Art Ware Catalog Sheet by Metlox.*

**COOKIE JARS**

| | | | RETAIL LIST |
|---|---|---|---|
| 1. | 522 550 | Wheat Shock Cookie Jar - 4 Qt. | 15.95 |
| 2. | 523 550 | Grapefruit Cookie Jar - 3 Qt. | 15.95 |
| 3. | 524 550 | Clown - White Cookie Jar - 3 Qt. | 17.95 |
| 4. | 525 550 | Pretty Anne Cookie Jar - 2½ Qt. | 16.95 |
| 5. | 526 550 | Yellow Cow Cookie Jar - 2½ Qt. | 19.95 |
| 6. | 527 550 | Teddy Bear Cookie Jar - 3 Qt. | 16.95 |
| 7. | 528 550 | Gingerbread Cookie Jar - 3½ Qt. | 19.95 |
| 8. | 531 550 | Little Piggy Cookie Jar - 3 Qt. | 16.95 |
| 9. | 532 550 | Cookie Bandit Cookie Jar - 2¾ Qt. | 17.95 |
| 10. | 534 550 | Noah's Ark Cookie Jar - 2½ Qt. | 18.95 |
| 11. | 535 550 | Owls On Stump Cookie Jar - 2½ Qt. | 18.95 |
| 12. | 537 550 | Cookie Girl Cookie Jar - 2½ Qt. | 12.95 |
| 13. | 538 550 | Teddy Bear White Cookie Jar - 3 Qt. | 16.95 |
| 14. | 548 550 | Mouse Mobile Cookie Jar | 19.95 |
| 15. | 549 550 | Koala Bear Cookie Jar | 17.95 |
| 16. | 550 550 | Mushroom Cottage Cookie Jar | 18.95 |
| 17. | 551 550 | Miller's Sack Cookie Jar | 15.95 |
| 18. | 552 550 | Walrus Cookie Jar | 24.95 |
| 19. | 553 550 | Dog Cookie Jar | 19.95 |
| 20. | 554 550 | Whale Cookie Jar | 24.95 |
| 21. | 555 550 | Parrot Cookie Jar | 24.95 |
| 22. | 556 550 | Calico Cat Cookie Jar | 22.95 |
| 23. | 557 550 | Gingham Dog Cookie Jar | 22.95 |

# Miscellaneous

This miscellaneous section covers a broad spectrum of jars. Some are imports, some are studio ceramics, some are unidentified, and some were identified after our photography session. Too many wonderful jars would be omitted if a miscellaneous section were not included in this book.

**Row 1:**    *Mark IV*, "Classic I" on license plate.                                              $125.00-150.00

               *Cadillac Convertible*, "Classic I."                  $90.00-110.00

**Row 2:**    *Cadillac*, unmarked.                                  $90.00-110.00

               *Volkswagen*, "Classic I" on front license plate. Paper label, "Copyright 1986, Expressive Designs, Florida 33314." Braly.      $125.00-150.00

**Row 3:**    *Deserted Jalopy*, unmarked. This car could easily pass for Sierra Vista, but we have never heard of anyone finding it marked.    $50.00-60.00

               *Checkered Cab*, "Classic I" license plate.            $90.00-110.00

**Below:**    *Golfer*, Paper label "Ceramica, Artistica, San Miguel Mod. No., Made in Mexico." Braly.                              $40.00-50.00

               *Angel,* "YOU'RE AN ANGEL! –HAVE ONE" around top of base, otherwise unmarked. Snyder.                          $30.00-40.00

**Row 1:**  *Mercedes*, "Copyright 1986 EXPRESSIVE DESIGNS FLORIDA 33314" on paper label on the bottom. "THIS PRODUCT IS HAND PAINTED AND FINISH MAY VARY SLIGHTLY, MADE IN TAIWAN." License plate, "Classic I." Snyder.                                                                                   $150.00-175.00

**Row 2:**  *56 T-Bird*, unmarked. "Classic I" on license plate. Expressive Designs Inc. Made in Taiwan. Snyder.                                                                                   $70.00-90.00

 *Corvette*, unmarked. Licensed plate, "Classic I."                                        $70.00-90.00

**Row 3:**  *Buick*, unmarked. "Cookie" on license plate. Snyder.                   $90.00-110.00

 *Cadillac*, unmarked.                                                                                 $75.00-100.00

**Below:**  *Hedi Schoop King.* DiRenzo.                                                        $250.00+

 *Darner Doll,* by Hedi Schoop for L.A. Pottery. DiRenzo.              $75.00-100.00

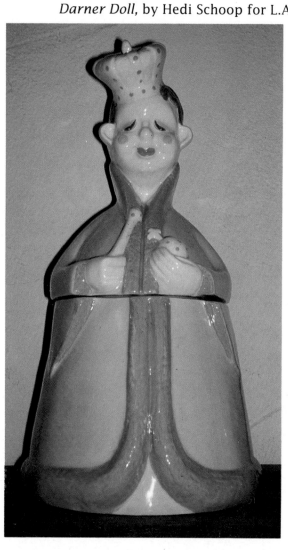

**Row 1:**   *Hawaiian Spook House,* "Hand-crafted Huia Clay Works, Hawaii. LaRue." Braly.                                     $40.00-45.00

*Devil with the Root of all Evil,* "EVR." Braly.                                     $45.00-55.00

*Raccoon in Stump,* "Made in Taiwan" paper label. Braly.                                     $20.00-25.00

**Row 2:**   *Market Lady,* "Leslie Cope" on bottom. "Leslie Cope 67" on side. Signed "Betty Ford." Braly.                                     $175.00-185.00

*Cross-Eyed Bird,* "C J 6 USA." Braly.                                     $150.00-175.00

*Lioness and Cub,* by California Originals. "739 USA" on bottom, "739" on lid. Braly.                                     $125.00-150.00

**Row 3:**   *Three-Faces of Indian,* (tobacco jar), unmarked. Braly.                                     $30.00-40.00

*Dinosaur,* On paper label. "Home Concepts, Japan." Braly.                                     $30.00-35.00

*Lion,* unmarked. Braly.                                     $35.00-40.00

**Below:**   *Toilet,* unmarked. This jar placed third in "The Ugliest Cookie Jar Contest" held by C. Keith and Judy A. Lytle in *Cookie Jarrin'.*                                     $35.00-40.00

**Row 1:**     *Boy Chef*, "ACUARIO" incised into bottom of base. Snyder.      $65.00-75.00

                *De-Lee Child Chef*, "...Lee, Hollywood, CA ©...1950" incised into bottom
of base. Snyder.      $70.00-90.00

Jack Chipman expands further on De-Lee Art: De-Lee was located in Los Angeles at 5413 West Washington Blvd. from about 1939 until its demise sometime in the fifties or early sixties. Delores and Lee (hence "De-Lee") Mitchel were the owners. Delores was designer-modeler of the majority of the ware, although free-lance and other designers were used at the height of production in the late forties.

                *Bear*, "...FRANKLIN PORCELAIN © FP 81" incised into the bottom. Snyder.      $40.00-50.00

**Row 2:**     *Clown*, "Kooky Klown © By Newhauser, Pat. Pending Green Products, Cleveland."    $100.00-125.00

                *Rooster*, "Martston." Snyder.      $30.00-40.00

                *Royal Haeger Cylinder*, "Royal Haeger USA."      $35.00-45.00

**Row 3:**     *Elephant with Sailor Hat and Heart*, unmarked. Snyder.      $35.00-45.00

                *Bananas*, unmarked Red Wing. Snyder.      $60.00-70.00

                *Elephant*, unmarked. Wells.      $200.00-225.00

**Below:**     *Pine Cones*, "Caty Crafts, Custer, SD." Wilson.      $30.00-40.00

                *Scottish Terrier*, "Made in Portugal." Clyde and Takasugi.      $65.00-75.00

**Row 1:**   *Whale*, unmarked.                                                                          $40.00-50.00

*Carrot*, "5558...."                                                                      $25.00-35.00

**Row 2:**   *Cookie Hour Clock*, unmarked plastic. Wooldridge.                           $20.00-25.00

*Rag Doll*, unmarked. This jar has been found with a "Starnes" paper label. Starnes was never a producer, so it is uncertain who actually made this jar.                                                    $70.00-80.00

*Lion and Lamb*, unmarked.                                                                $30.00-40.00

**Row 3:**   *School Bus with Frustrated Driver*, unmarked.                                $40.00-50.00

*Froggie Goes A-Courtin'*, unmarked. This jar has been guessed to be Brayton and Sierra Vista. The facts are not yet known. Perhaps someone has found *Froggie* with a paper label and will enlighten us.        $225.00-250.00

*Duck with Shawl*, unmarked.                                                              $30.00-35.00

**Below:**   *Donut Chef*, chocolate, unmarked.                                            $275.00-325.00

*Donut Chef*, vanilla, unmarked. Snyder.                                                  $275.00-325.00

The *Donut Chefs* remain a mystery. We do feel two different companies were involved in the manufacture. The underside of the bases are below. What do you think?

280

**Row 1:**    *Dutch Kids*, stamped "J 702."        $20.00-25.00

          *Play House,* unmarked.        $15.00-18.00

          *Baseball Player,* unmarked.        $20.00-25.00

**Row 2:**    *Clown* biscuit jar, "10025."        $15.00-20.00

          *Cylinder with Glove, Bat, and Ball Finial,* impressed "E-9224 ©1977, Suzy's Zoo." Braly.        $30.00-35.00

          *Topo Gigio,* "©MARIA PEREGO DISTRIBUTED BY ROSS PRODUCTS, INC. NY." Supnick.        $175.00-225.00

**Row 3:**    *Dragon,* "Puff."        $30.00-40.00

          *Cow with Flowers,* unmarked.        $25.00-35.00

          *Chuck Wagon,* turned around, "Cookie Wagon" on front, unmarked.        $65.00-75.00

**Below:**    *Noah's Ark,* unmarked, but believed to have been produced by the same company that produced the *Chuck Wagon* on Row 3. This would be evident if the *Chuck Wagon* was turned around. Devine.        $65.00-75.00

**Row 1:**    *Pumpkin with Black Cat*, unmarked.    $65.00-75.00

*Ceramichrome Skeleton Pumpkin* designed by Jean Williams. "Hand Painted, Made in USA."    $80.00-90.00

**Row 2:**    *Curly*, Gare, unmarked.    $20.00-30.00

*Pumpkin*, with light-sensitive noisemaker from Wal-Mart.    $30.00-40.00

*Skull with Spider*, Ceramichrome, "Hand Painted, Made in USA."    $55.00-65.00

**Row 3:**    *Santa*, reproduction of plastic *Santa*.    $15.00-20.00

*Christmas Grandma*, Alberta's Molds.    $40.00-45.00

*Rudolph*, Clay Magic, unmarked.    $65.00-75.00

**Below:**    *The Whistler,* from "The Collection of Rose. #28"    $95.00-110.00

*Indian* (well disguised McCoy reproduction), stamped "SE MN POTTERY, KELLOGG, MN. 55945."    $60.00-80.00

*Pinocchio* (Metlox reproduction), "Hand painted, Made in USA."    $60.00-80.00

# North American Ceramics

The Los Angeles, California-based North American Ceramics is no longer in business. They ceased production of cookie jars a few years ago, thinking everyone was too cholesterol conscious to want cookie jars, and began specializing in Mexican glass.

| | | |
|---|---|---|
| **Row1:** | *Cadillac*, "ACCJ - 3 ©1987 NAC USA." | $100.00-125.00 |
| | *Crown Victoria*, "ACCJ 8 ©1986 NAC USA." | $150.00-175.00 |
| **Row 2:** | *Airplane*, "DCJ 34, 1987 NAC USA." | $100.00-125.00 |
| | *Woody Wagon*, "ACCJ 6 1987 NAC USA." | $55.00-65.00 |
| **Row 3:** | *Porsche*, "ACCJ 13 ©1987 Car and Driver NAC USA." | $175.00-200.00 |
| | *Porsche*, "ACCJ 13 © 1987 Car and Driver NAC USA." | $175.00-200.00 |
| **Below:** | *Beachbound Woody*, (Fred's 1992 Christmas present) "ACC -6 ©1986 NAC USA." | $250.00-350.00 |

**Row 1:**  *Fire Truck,* "CJ 31 1986 NAC USA."                                                           $100.00-125.00

*Andretti Race Car,* "ACCJ 10© NAC USA." Signed, "Michael Andretti."
Decal, "Limited Edition #259 of 10,000."                                                                      $200.00-225.00

**Row 2:**  *Softie Cat,* unmarked.                                                                              $30.00-40.00

*Dinosaur,* "CJ 50 ©1986 - NAC USA."                                                                            $30.00-40.00

**Row 3:**  *Moose,* "DCJ-19 ©1985 NAC."                                                                          $20.00-30.00

*Santa Claus,* "CJ-20 © 1985© NAC U.S.A."                                                                      $125.00-175.00

*Peter Panda,* "DCJ-24 © 1985© 1985© NAC."                                                                      $30.00-40.00

# Parawan Pottery

Amos C. Hatch was principal of Parawan High School in Parawan, UT. The high school was interested in including a pottery class in their curriculum but could not find an experienced, qualified teacher. Amos Hatch went to the University of Utah to expand his knowledge and enable himself to teach the class.

Parawan Pottery was founded in 1946, and remained open through 1978. Everything was produced in a shed behind the Hatch home. Amos made his molds, did the pouring, cleaning, and firing in intervals of spare time he found between taking care of his invalid son.

The pitchers were given as wedding gifts by Amos Hatch and seem to be the most plentiful pieces of Parawan found today. The pottery was sold mostly through a local dime store and Big Rock Candy Mountain located in the Utah National Park. The price structure was simple and standard: $1.50 for small pieces, $2.00 for large pieces, and $3.00-4.00 for the sour dough and cookie jars. The lids for the sour dough and cookie jars were hand-carved from cross sections of trees. Local businessmen contracted Amos to make banks for the town's yearly picnic where they were given as gifts.

The colors exhibited are natural clay colors from clay found in a secret spot in the Utah mountains. The only exception is the *Liberty Bell* produced in 1976. Clay was brought back from South America by Hatch specifically for the bells. Amos Hatch died at the age of 92 on Febuary 19, 1985.

| | | |
|---|---|---|
| **Row 1:** | *Coffee Mug*, "Hatch Parawan UT." | $25.00-35.00 |
| | *Chocolate Mug*, "Hatch Parawan UT." | $45.00-55.00 |
| | *Cookie Jar*, "AC Hatch Parawan UT." | $125.00-150.00 |
| | *Liberty Bell*, unmarked. | $75.00-85.00 |
| | *Cow Creamer*, unmarked. | $40.00-50.00 |
| **Row 2:** | *Nut Bowl*, unmarked. | $20.00-25.00 |
| | *Pitcher*, "Hatch Parawan UT." | $25.00-30.00 |
| | *Honey Pot*, "Hatch Parawan UT." | $25.00-35.00 |
| | *Pitcher*, "Hatch Parawan UT." | $25.00-30.00 |
| | *Egg Cup*, unmarked. | $18.00-22.00 |

Additional pieces of Parawan pottery include sour dough jars, banks, salt and pepper shakers, bud vases, and egg cups.

# Pottery Guild

It is believed Pottery Guild cookie jars were manufactured by the Cronin China Company, circa 1930's through early 1940's. Additional examples may be found in *The Collector's Encyclopedia of Cookie Jars, Book I*.

| | | |
|---|---|---|
| **Bottom left:** | *Boy with Fruit*, unmarked. Snyder. | $100.00-125.00 |

# Purinton

Purinton Pottery was founded in Wellsville, OH by Bernard Purinton in 1936. Purinton was moved to Shippenville, PA in 1941, where it remained until production ceased in 1959.

| | | |
|---|---|---|
| **Bottom right:** | *Humpty Dumpty*, unmarked. | $175.00-200.00 |
| | *Rooster,* "Purinton Slip Ware." Snyder. | $60.00-75.00 |

# PeeDee or Pitman-Dreitzer

**Row 1:**    *Billy Banana* (large figurine), "©1942 Pee Dee." Snyder.                          $20.00-25.00

*Albert Apple,* apple butter condiment, "FKR 1942 © Pee Dee." Snyder.          $20.00-30.00

*Stella Strawberry* (small figurine), "©1942 Pee Dee FKR." Snyder.              $12.00-15.00

*Pumpkin Bowl*, covered, "USA Pee Dee." Snyder.                                $12.00-18.00

*Billy Banana* (small figurine), "©1942 Pee Dee FKR." Snyder.                  $10.00-12.00

*Lee Lemon* (small figurine), "©1942 Pee Dee FKR." Snyder.                     $10.00-12.00

*Stella Strawberry*, condiment (for jam), unmarked. Snyder.                    $20.00-30.00

# Pfaltzgraff

Pfaltzgraff made the *Muggsy* line from 1948 to 1960. This line was designed by Norman and Dorothy Jessop, both art directors from Baltimore, MD. Norman was ill and confined to his home when he began designing and modeling character mugs. In search of someone to produce their line, they contacted Pfaltzgraff of York, PA. Production soon began.

The best known in the *Muggsy* line are six character mugs, *Jerry the Jerk, Handsome Herman, Sleepy Sam, Flirty Gertie, Pickled Pete,* and *Cockeyed Charlie*. These mugs are available in old and new styles. On the old style, the facial features protrude from the mug. On the new style, the hair, lips, and eyebrows have been painted on a smooth surface. The bottom of the old style says "Pfaltzgraff" in a curved shape, followed by the character's name. The newer version lists the character first.

Pfaltzgraff also produced a set of sportsman mugs: *Pigskin Pete, Diamond Dick, Rodney Reel, Muscles Moe, Fairway Freddie, Brawny Bertram*. These mugs are the same size as the character mugs. There are three cigarette servers, *Nick, Jigger,* and an unnamed third. *Burnie* is the ashtray. There are six Hi-Ball beakers that look like the character mugs with *Rugged Richard* taking the place of *Flirty Gertie*. The utility jars were named *Handy Harry, Pretzel Pete,* and *Herky Jerky. Derby Dan* is actually a pretzel jar, according to a 1954 catalog. *Myrtle* is the sprinkle bottle. She is available with white or black skin. There is a set of four bottle stoppers. For children, there are *Ko-Ko the Clown* mug, *Ho-Ho the Elephant* cereal dish, and *Yo-Yo the Giraffe* plate. In addition, there are several unmarked cookie jars, *Old Lady in the Shoe, Cookie Cop, Cookie Time, Floral Jar, Cookie Flyer Train, Clown, Merry-Go-Round, French Chef, Cookie Bag, Cookie House,* and an hors d'oeuvre dish called *Canapé Carrie*. Items that look like *Muggsy,* but are not marked, were not designed by the Jessops and cannot be called *Muggsy*.

Lonnie A. Haley, Evening Shade, AK

**Row 2:**    *Ko-Ko Mug*, unmarked. Snyder                                                   $30.00-40.00

*Sleepy Sam*, stamped "SLEEPY SAM, *Muggsy*, THE PFALTZGRAFF POTTERY CO. York, Penna. Designed by JESSOP." Snyder.          $25.00-30.00

*Handy Harry* utility jar, stamped "HANDY HARRY, *Muggsy*, The PFALTZ-GRAFF POTTERY CO. York, Penna. Designed by JESSOP." Snyder.     $150.00-175.00

*Pickled Pete*, stamped "PICKLED PETE, *Muggsy*, THE PFALTZGRAFF POTTERY CO. York, Penna. Designed by JESSOP." Snyder.          $25.00-30.00

**Row 3:**    *Old Lady in Shoe*, unmarked. Snyder.                                           $150.00-175.00

*Chef*, unmarked. Snyder.                                                      $175.00-225.00

*Stagecoach*, "CJ-4 PFALTZGRAFF USA©" in raised lettering on the bottom of jar. Snyder.          $175.00-200.00

# Regal China

Regal China Corporation of Antioch, IL, ceased operations on June 30, 1992, due to declining decanter sales and the inability to find a buyer for the company. The company had been in business for more than fifty years manufacturing china, decanters, lamp bases, vases, and specialty products such as cookie jars and salt and pepper shakers.

The Novelty Salt and Pepper Shakers Club commissioned Regal China to design and produce their convention shakers for the 1991 and 1992 conventions. These sets were sold on a limited basis to the current membership only.

**Left:** *Advertising Plaque*, mark visible. Firestone.          $350.00+

**Row 1:** *Cookie Jarrin's Little Angel*, "Handcrafted in the U.S.A., Designed by Regal China Corporation 1992, Cookie Jarrin' ©." This is the only black jar ever done by Regal China. It is also the last cookie jar modeled and designed at Regal before their closing. Each jar was numbered and available to *Cookie Jarrin'* subscribers for the issue price of $150.00 plus shipping.

*Cookie Jarrin's Little Angel*, one of six samples done at Regal China. Marked in mold, "Handcrafted in the U.S.A. by Regal China Corporation 1992." Sample only, not valued.

*Cookie Jarrin's Little Angel*, color sample. #1 Prototype, Handcrafted in the U.S.A., Designed by Regal China Corporation 1992, Cookie Jarrin' ©."          $150.00+

**Row 2:** *Potato Chip* canister (large). "Pat. Pending 387" on base. Snyder.          $275.00-325.00

*Soap* canister (large). "Pat. Pending 387" on base. Snyder.          $275.00-325.00

**Row 1:**   *A Nod to Abe*, "6th S and P Convention, 1991 Chicago, Illinois, designed by Regal China © U.S.A."                                    $40.00-50.00

*Humpty Dumpty* salt or pepper shaker, unmarked.                    Set, $125.00-175.00

*Humpty Dumpty* cookie jar (also in yellow) marked in mold, "Humpty Dumpty 707."                                                         $275.00-325.00

*Humpty Dumpty* salt or pepper shaker, mate above.              Set, $125.00-175.00

*The Leaf People,* "7th Annual Salt and Pepper Novelty Shakers Club Convention, Burlington, Vermont 1992, Mfg. by Regal China Corp." Only 400 convention sets were produced by Regal China for the 1992 convention. This is the last set of shakers ever designed and/or produced by Regal China.

**Row 2:**   *Snuggle-Hug Bunnies*, "Copr. 1958 R. Bendel."                    $125.00-150.00

*Cat*, unmarked. Braly.                                                       $350.00-375.00

*Snuggle-Hug Bears*, "Copr. 1958 R. Bendel."                         $125.00-150.00

**Row 3:**   *Monkey* bank, "© C Miller."                                            $40.00-60.00

*San Joaquin Snack Jar*, "© Creation of James B. Beam Distilling Co. Genuine Regal China 1977, C. Miller Regal China Corporation." 1500 of the colorful snack jars were made for the San Joaquin Valley Jim Beam Bottle & Specialties for a fund raising project. The cornucopia represents the fruits of the prolific San Joaquin Valley, and the unique fox head on the cover represents the mascot of the Beam clubs. The height is 12".                          $75.00-100.00

*Oriental Lady with Baskets*, unmarked. Braly.                      $350.00-400.00

# Shawnee

Shawnee did not produce a large number of cookie jar examples. Shawnee collectors search for each and every decal and color variation they can possibly find, just to expand their collections.

**Row 1:** *Mugnificent Muggsy* (reproduction), limited edition commemorative. Incised into bottom of base, "MARK SUPNICK's COMMEMORATIVE EDITION, 1992 MUGGSY, USA" Decal signature of Mark Supnick, series number, and signature of decorator, "SA Corl."                                   $150.00+

*Jo-Jo Clown*, gold-trimmed, "Shawnee U.S.A. 12."                                   $500.00+

*Puss 'n Boots*, tail over foot, "Patented Puss 'n Boots USA." Supnick.                                   $130.00-140.00

**Row 2:** *Jack Tar* (reproduction), limited edition commemorative, "Celebrating 50 Years of Service" on ribbon, "50" on medal, "GOB" to right. Incised into bottom of base, "MARK SUPNICK'S COMMEMORATIVE EDTION, 1992, SAILOR BOY, USA." Decal signature of Mark Supnick, serial number, and signature of decorator, "SA Corl."                                   $150.00+

*Happy 50th Birthday Smiley* (reproduction) limited edition commemorative, "MARK SUPNICK'S COMMEMORATIVE EDITION, 1992, SMILEY, USA." Decal on bottom, signature of Mark Supnick, and signed by decorator SA Corl with the series number.                                   $150.00+

*Jack Tar* (reproduction), limited edition commemorative, "Celebrating 50 Years of Service" on ribbon, "50" on medal, "GOB" to right. Incised into bottom of base, "MARK SUPNICK'S COMMEMORATIVE EDITION, 1992, SAILOR BOY, USA." Decal signature of Mark Supnick, serial number, and signature of decorator, "SA Corl."                                   $150.00+

**Row 3:** *Drum Major*, gold trimmed. "USA 10."                                   $500.00+

*Smiley with Hair*, "USA." Braly.                                   $500.00+

*Drum Major*, "USA 10."                                   $350.00+

**Below:** *Little Chef,* "USA."                                   $60.00-70.00

*Wonderful Winnie* (reproduction), limited edition commemorative, "MARK SUPNICK'S COMMEMORATIVE  EDITION, 1993 "WINNIE PIG, USA." Decal on bottom, signature of Mark Supnick and signed by decorator "SA Corl" with the series number.                                   $175.00+

# Sierra Vista Ceramics

Sierra Vista began as a family venture in Pasadena, CA, in 1944. Reinhold Lenaburg and his son William were co-owners of Sierra Vista. Leonard, another son of Reinhold, stepped into the already established business and replaced his brother William. William Lenaburg eventually established Hondo Ceramics. Sierra Vista was one of the major suppliers for Walter Starnes, jobber.

**Row 1:** *Space Ship*, (finial missing) unmarked. Snyder.     If mint, $175.00-200.00

*Space Ship*, "Sierra Vista, California" in bottom of base. Bass.     $200.00-225.00

*Pig*, "Sierra Vista California" in mold. Snyder.     $50.00-60.00

**Row 2:** *Owl*, "Sierra Vista California, 60..." in /mold. Snyder.     $35.00-45.00

*Round House*, "Sierra Vista Ceramics, Pasadena, CA. Made in USA © 56" on the bottom of the base. Snyder.     $40.00-45.00

*ABC Bear*, "Sierra Vista Ceramics, Calif., USA" on bottom of the base. Snyder.     $50.00-60.00

**Row 3:** *Shoe House*, "Sierra Vista Ceramics ©1957 Pasadena, Calif." on bottom of base. Snyder.     $50.00-60.00

*Mushrooms*, "Sierra Vista Ceramics, Pasadena, CA USA ©1957" on bottom of base. Snyder.     $40.00-45.00

*Cottage*, "Sierra Vista ©53, California ©1953 USA" on bottom of base. Snyder.     $35.00-45.00

**Below:** *Clown Jack-in-the-Box*, "Sierra Vista Ceramics." Honchar.     $100.00-125.00

*Flower Pot*, "Genuine Hand Made Starnes California U.S.A." on paper label. Though this jar is included in the Sierra Vista section, it is unknown who actually made it. There are matching salt and pepper shakers available. The jar can also be found in yellow. Duke.     $25.00-35.00

**Row 1:**   *Dog House* with paper label, "Genuine Hand Made Starnes, California U.S.A."
Snyder.                                                                                    $100.00-125.00

*Clown* bank, unmarked. Snyder.                                                            $10.00-12.00

*Clown* bank, wedges, unmarked. Snyder.                                                    $10.00-15.00

*Clown*, "Sierra Vista, California" on bottom of base. Although the Clowns re-
semble each other, it is not proven that Sierra Vista made the banks. We
have never seen a Sierra Vista item with wedges. Snyder.                                    $35.00-45.00

**Row 2:**   *Humpty Dumpty*, "Sierra Vista Ceramics © 57 Pasadena Cal. USA" on base.
Snyder.                                                                                    $125.00-150.00

*Mammy* spoon holder, "Starnes 904 California" on paper label, manufac-
turer unknown. Snyder.                                                                      $50.00-60.00

*Circus Wagon*, "Sierra Vista Ceramics, Pasadena Cal" on base.                             $40.00-50.00

*Magic Maid* (magnetic bobby pin holder), "Patent Pending Starnes, Inc.
L.A. Calif...," manufacturer unknown. Snyder.                                               $15.00-20.00

*Clown*, "Sierra Vista California USA" on bottom of base. Snyder.                           $30.00-35.00

**Row 3:**   *Rooster*, "Sierra Vista California" on bottom of base. Note the Rooster
on page 237 of *Book I* has bars and is not marked. Snyder.                                 $40.00-50.00

*Rooster* egg cup, unmarked. Snyder.                                                        $5.00-8.00

*Rooster* egg plate, unmarked. Snyder.                                                      $10.00-12.00

*Rooster* hors d'oeuvre, unmarked. Snyder.                                                  $10.00-12.00

*Rooster* hors d'oeuvre, unmarked. Snyder.                                                  $10.00-12.00

*Rooster* spoon holder, or ashtray, unmarked. Snyder.                                       $5.00-8.00

*Noah's Ark*, "Pat Pend. Starnes Calif. ©" on base. Snyder.                                $125.00-150.00

# Sigma

No amount of inquiries could dredge up any information on Sigma other than it was an import business and is no longer in operation.

**Row 1:**    *Planetary Pal* (round head), "Planetary Pals by David Hyman for Sigma the Tastesetter®, ©MCMLXXXIV."    $80.00-90.00

*Hot Air Balloon*, "Sigma © The Tastesetter Victorian Ascensions 1956, Los Angeles, Cal." marked in the mold. "Sigma" paper label. Kaulbach.    $40.00-50.00

*Planetary Pal* (square head), "Planetary Pals by David Hyman for Sigma the Tastesetter®, ©MCMLXXXIV." Wooldridge.    $80.00-90.00

**Row 2:**    *Victoria*, "VICTORIA, Tastesetter by Sigma, designed by David Straus."    $65.00-75.00

*Peter Max*, stamped."© Peter Max 1989. Made in Japan." on paper label.    $175.00-225.00

*Circus Lady*, "CIRCUS David Straus" in mold. "Tastesetter © Sigma, PLEASE NOTE THAT ALL PIECES ARE HAND DECORATED, SO COLOR VARIANCE COULD OCCUR. LABORATORY TESTED TO COMPLY WITH FDA GUIDELINES, Made in Japan."    $65.00-75.00

**Row 3:**    *The Last Elegant Bear*, "The Last Elegant Bear, Dennis Kyte for Sigma the Tastesetter®, ©MCMLXXXIV."    $55.00-60.00

*Fireman Dog*, "Sigma the Tastesetter®, ©MCMLXXXIV."    $75.00-95.00

*Star Wars*, "© Lucas Film Ltd., designed by Sigma the Tastesetter™."    $100.00-125.00

**Below:**    *Pig Chef*, "Sigma the Tastesetter MCMLXXIC." Honchar.    $60.00-80.00

*Pix Theater*, "AMERICAN ROADSIDE John Beeder for Sigma the Tastesetter" incised into mold. Snyder.    $40.00-50.00

*Penguin*, "Krazy Kids and Kritters™ David Hyman For Sigma The Tastesetter, Made in Japan" on paper label. Snyder.    $55.00-60.00

# Studio Ceramists

## Corl's Kiln

Shirley Corl lives in rural Caro, MI. Shirley is a talented ceramist who designs and produces limited edition cookie jars, both privately and commercially. Shirley and her husband, Bill, are avid antiquers who spend most of their free time from April through November attending auctions, flea markets, estate sales, and garage sales, constantly adding to their antique furnishings, collectibles, and cookie jar collection.

**Row 1:**  *Ugly Pumpkin Witch*, "11/50, S Corl."                              $50.00-60.00

   *Victorian Santa*, "S Corl, 25/75."                              $150.00-165.00

**Row 2:**  *Witch with Pumpkin*, "5/50 S Corl."                              $90.00-100.00

   *Skull with Spider,* "40/50 S Corl."                              $60.00-70.00

Addtional items for Corl's Kiln can be found in Black Americana, Characters, and Shawnee.

# K. Wolfe Studio

Kathy Wolfe lives in West Bloomfield, MI. She attended commercial art classes throughout high school and college. She and her husband, Doug, belong to the Siberian Husky Club of greater Detroit, and raise Huskies. Kathy developed a line of Siberian Husky items for the Husky Club to sell at dog shows. She also designed a line of all-breed dog wreaths and necklaces that are sold at California dog shows.

When her crafts started to take over the house, they built a studio to accommodate the growing business and to allow Kathy to produce more products in less time. Clients contact Kathy for specialty items they want in ceramic, wood, or plastic. One client in forensic pathology has Kathy molding skulls and bones of humans and animals for use by medical students and doctors. This is unusual, but interesting.

Kathy produced commemorative shakers for the Michigan chapter of the Novelty Salt and Pepper Shakers Club. In 1991, Kathy was commissioned to produce the trademark Big Boy and hamburger salt and pepper shakers (see advertising), and the *Bob's Big Boy* cookie jar, 1992, each in limited editions and available only through Elias Brothers of Warren, MI. Kathy created the Jazz'e Junque cookie jar for Mercedes DiRenzo, of Chicago, IL, and is currently working with General Motors Procuring licensing for its new electric car.

| | | |
|---|---|---|
| **Row 1:** | *Cola Santa*, "AP 1992 Kathy Wolfe." | $150.00-200.00 |
| | *Wolfe*, with "Paw Print, Wolfe Original, Limited Edition." | $100.00-125.00 |
| **Row 2:** | *Electric Car* (General Motors), "9/100 KW." | $150.00-200.00 |
| | *Skull*, modeled from an actual human, unmarked. | $90.00-100.00 |

Additional jars from K. Wolfe studio are featured in the Black Americana and Advertising sections.

# Linda Kulhanek

Linda Kulhanek of Burt, MI is not a studio ceramist by trade. She and her husband own Tri-Star Mold Company. The *Tri Star Mammy* and *Acoma Indian Storyteller* are originals, both created by Linda as mold models for their Tri Star Line. After an Ohio dealer elaborated at length about how he had found an old Mammy mold and planned to produce a limited run for collectors, we felt it was important to reveal the true origin.

**Below:**   *Tri Star Mammy*, "Limited Edition, Hand painted and sculpted by Linda Kulhanek, #008 1992 © 1987." Another version of the Tri-Star Mammy can be seen in Black Americana.                                                    $100.00-125.00

*Acoma Storyteller*, "Acoma Storyteller." This Linda Kulhanek original was painted by Kathy Wolfe.                                                    $150.00-175.00

## Clay Works

The owners of Clay Works previously owned Clay Magic, a commercial mold company. Working closely with Shirley Corl, Lynn Amiot also became interested in producing limited editions.

**Left:**   *Flirt-ie Floss-ie*, "Clay Works, Made in U.S.A., Limited Edition, Flirt-ie Floss-ie LA, L. Amiot 5/60."                    $100.00-125.00

# The New Rose Collection

The Black Americana section covers several examples from The New Rose Collection. *The Whistler* (both the black and white versions) is from The Collection of Rose, a trade name of Rose Saxby.

**Below:**    *Pastel Cow*, "Pastel Cow, No. 6, The New Rose Collection."                  $45.00-50.00

                *Mallard Duck*, "Mallard, Mallard, Mallard, No. 2, The New Rose Collection."    $45.00-50.00

                *Cow Head*, "By the New Rose Collection, No. 1."                    $40.00-50.00

                *Count*, "Replica By the New Rose Collection, No. 12."            $130.00-140.00

                *Parlor Car Tours*, "By the New Rose Collection, No. 1."           $70.00-75.00

# Treasure Craft

Treasure Craft of Crompton, CA continues to play an important role in the collectibles market. A plant in Mexico has opened and will be producing part of its line. It is now an importer, technically, as well as a US-based manufacturer.

**Row 1:**    *House*, "Treasure Craft 19©60 Compton, Calif." on base.    $30.00-35.00

    *Mexican Bandito*, "Treasure Craft © Made in USA" on base.    $40.00-50.00

    *Van*, "Treasure Craft © Made in USA" on lid.    $50.00-60.00

**Row 2:**    *Football with Coach*, "Treasure Craft, Made in USA" in lid. "© 1983 David Kirschner Production, All Rights Reserved."    $100.00-125.00

    *Tiki* salt or pepper shaker, "Treasure Craft © USA."    Set, $8.00-10.00

    *Tiki* cookie jar, "Treasure Craft © Made in USA" on base.    $40.00-50.00

    *Tiki* salt or pepper shaker, mate above.    Set, $8.00-10.00

    *Rose Petal Place* (without decal), "Treasure Craft © Made in USA" on lid. "© 1983 David Kirschner Production, All Rights Reserved." Braly.    $80.00-90.00

**Row 3:**    *Jukebox* (original release, ¼" taller and ¼" larger in girth than the 1992 release), "Treasure Craft © Made in USA."    $100.00-125.00

    *Chef*, "Treasure Craft © Made in USA" in lid.    $35.00-45.00

    *Monk*, "Treasure Craft © Made in USA."    $30.00-40.00

**Below:**    *Nanna*, "Test Glaze C, Collector Series, Supnick, 1/23/92."

    *Nanna*, "Test Glaze E, Collector Series, Supnick, 1/23/93."

    *Nanna*, "Test Glaze A, Collector Series, Supnick, 1/23/93."

No pricing is available on the test glaze Nannas. They are samples of glaze color, used to aid in determining color choice.

**Row 1:**   *Palomino Cookies* cylinder, "Pottery Craft #509 © Made in USA" on lid, paper label inside base. Snyder.                                    $30.00-35.00

*Pig Chef,* "Treasure Craft © Made in USA."                                    $35.00-45.00

*Hen,* "Treasure Craft, ©Made in USA" in lid. Snyder.                          $40.00-45.00

**Row 2:**   *Circus Bear,* "Treasure Craft © Made in USA."                     $40.00-45.00

*Toucan,* "© Treasure Craft USA." Discontinued.                                $40.00-45.00

*Cylinder* or *Canister,* "Treasure Craft © Made in USA" in lid, and paper label inside base. Snyder.                                            $15.00-20.00

**Row 3:**   *Castle,* reissue for 1992, "© Treasure Craft."                    $40.00-45.00

*Cookiesaurus,* "© Treasure Craft" in lid.                                     $35.00-40.00

*Katrina,* "© Treasure Craft, Made in USA" in rim of lid. Only 40 Katrinas were produced due to production problems no doubt, the red paint!              $400.00+

*Treasure Craft Catalog Sheet, 1990.*

**Row 1:**     *Pick-Up Truck* (original issue), "Treasure Craft © Made in USA" in lid.       $275.00+

**Row 2:**     *Tabby with Fish Bowl*, "© Treasure Craft, Made in USA" in lid.       $35.00-45.00

            *Panda*, "© Treasure Craft, Made in ©USA" in lid.       $35.00-45.00

            *Mushroom House,* "Treasure Craft © Made in USA" in lid.       $35.00-45.00

**Row 3:**     *Jukebox* (re-issue, 1992), "Treasure Craft, Made in USA."       $35.00-45.00

            *Gumball Machine* (re-issue 1992), "Treasure Craft, Made in USA." in lid. Snyder.       $35.00-45.00

            *Old-fashioned Radio*, "Treasure Craft © Made in USA" in lid.       $35.00-45.00

**Below:**     *Hedgehog with Grappling Hook*, unmarked. This jar appears to be a character from *Rose Petal Place.*       $100.00-125.00

            *Pick-Up Truck*, re-issue, "Treasure Craft Collector Series, 1992, OLD RED TRUCK, Series #041, Made in U.S.A." Treasure Craft did a special limited edition run of one hundred pieces for Mark and Ellen Supnick.       $175.00+

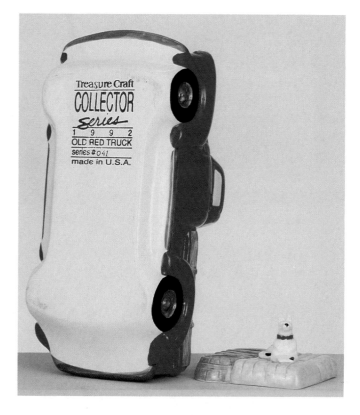

*Treasure Craft Catalog Sheet 1984.*

*Treasure Craft Catalog Sheet 1986.*

*Treasure Craft Catalog Sheet 1986.*

**COUNTRY CRITTERS™**

**PET SHOP™**

*Treasure Craft Catalog Sheet 1986.*

*Treasure Craft Catalog Sheet 1986.*

## Sculptured Cookie Jars

Treasure Craft

366-81
366-80
348-81
348-80
369-80
369-81
364-81
364-80
357-81
357-80
371-81
371-80

*Treasure Craft Catalog Sheet 1986.*

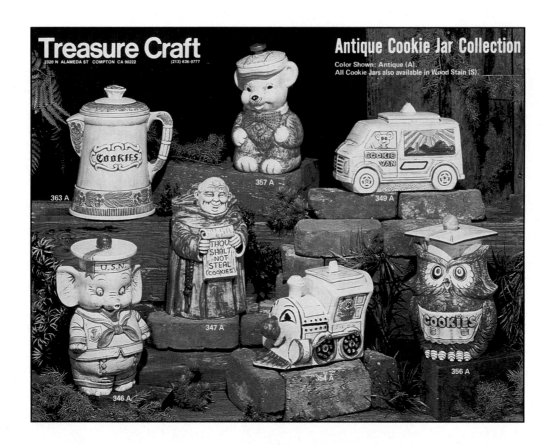

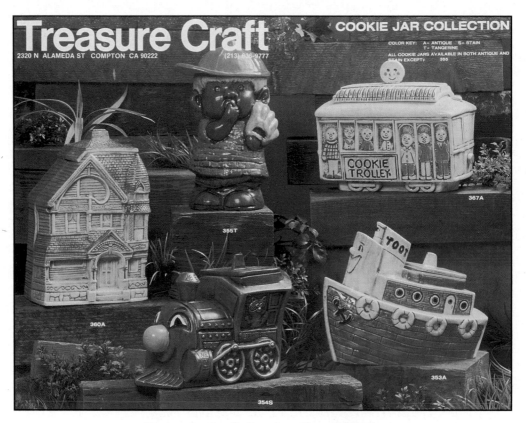

*Treasure Craft Catalog Sheets 1979.*

*Above: Treasure Craft Catalog Sheet 1977.*
*Below: Treasure Craft Catalog Sheet 1985.*

*Above: Treasure Craft Catalog Sheet 1984.*
*Below: Treasure Craft Catalog Sheet 1987.*

*Above: Treasure Craft Catalog Sheet 1975.*
*Below: Treasure Craft Catalog Sheet 1979.*

# Twin Winton

Twin Winton creations can be described as cute, whimsical, cuddly, life-like, almost "Disney-ish" with hand-painted eyes lending animation to the characters. Loving and happy are also very appropriate adjectives to describe Winton designs.

We continue to gather facts slowly on Twin Winton. The following is taken from personal correspondence with Don Winton. The Wintons formed a business partnership with Helen Burke in 1936 at Busch Gardens, Pasadena, CA. Don Winton is and always was the designer. Helen Burke did sales and hand decorating. Ross was moldman and business manager for Burke-Winton through 1940, at which time the partnership was dissolved.

Don began creating three-dimensional characters for Disney licensees in 1954. He designed tub and float toys for manufacturers of plastic squeeze and pull toys. Later, he designed a series of anniversary coins for Disney. More recently came Roly from the Disney movie, *101 Dalmatians,* for Treasure Craft.

In the 1980's Don Winton designed several cookie jars for Al Levin of Treasure Craft.

The Winton *Santa* featured on page 196, *Book I* was designed by Don Winton for Scioto in the mid-70's. He sculptured this jar to achieve the ultimate in a cookie jar and considers it his best. The small *Angel with Lollipop* candy jar, bearing so much likeness to the Brush *Angel,* was designed by Don Winton for Alberta's Molds.

We have just begun to "sample the diggings" where Winton is concerned. Candid memories continue to surface of companies and individuals for which Don Winton has designed. We love Winton-design cookie jars, and remember fondly the day we picked up our first jar in a Joplin, MO flea market. We had no idea that the Collector's Series was desirable. We gathered up the *Sheriff Bear* and took him home to become the foundation on which to build. We are still gathering. When all the nominees are in and the votes tallied, Don Winton will win hands down for creativity and originality. How can anyone that loves Brush cookie jars not love Winton? Brush is Winton with little exception.

| | | |
|---|---|---|
| **Row 1:** | *Cookie Coach*, unmarked. Snyder. | $75.00-85.00 |
| | *Sailor Elephant*, in Collector's Series, unmarked. | $100.00-125.00 |
| | *Sailor Elephant*, reproduction with the original marks left on, "Twin Winton © '60, Made in USA." Snyder. | $20.00-25.00 |
| **Row 2:** | *Squirrel* planter, "Twin Winton © Calif. U.S.A." Snyder. | $18.00-22.00 |
| | *Barrel* salt or pepper shaker, Twin Winton © Calif. U.S.A." Snyder. | Set, $20.00-30.00 |
| | *Barrel* cookie jar, "Twin Winton © Calif. USA." | $45.00-60.00 |
| | *Barrel* salt or pepper shaker, mate above. | Set, $20.00-30.00 |
| | *Poodle* napkin holder, "Twin Winton © San Juan Capistrano." Snyder. | $20.00-30.00 |
| **Row 3:** | *Owl* stamped "Twin Winton Collector's Series © California USA." Incised into pottery. "Twin Winton © Calif. USA" | $100.00-125.00 |
| | *Barn*, Collector's Series, stamped "Twin Winton © San Juan Capistrano, Calif. U.S.A." | $100.00-125.00 |
| | *Lamb*, stamped "Twin Winton © San Juan Capistrano, Calif. Collector's Series." | $100.00-125.00 |

**Row 1:**  *Hotei*, stamped "Twin Winton © San Juan Capistrano, Calif. U.S.A."                    $65.00-75.00

*Hobby Horse*, stamped "Twin Winton Collector's Series." Rose.                    $150.00-175.00

*Donkey*, incised "Twin Winton © Calif. USA." Stamped "Twin Winton
Collector's Series © California USA." Snyder.                    $100.00-125.00

**Row 2:**  *Stove*, unmarked.                    $50.00-55.00

*Pirate Fox*, Collector's Series, "Twin Winton, Made in Calif. USA © 63"
incised. Stamped, "Twin Winton © San Juan Capistrano, Calif. U.S.A."                    $100.00-125.00

**Row 3:**  *Mother Goose* salt or pepper shaker. Bass.                    Set, $50.00-75.00

*Mother Goose*, "1961 © Twin Winton, Made in Calif." incised into pottery. Stamped "Twin Winton Collector's Series © California  USA." Snyder.    $100.00-125.00

*Mother Goose* salt or pepper shaker, mate above. Bass.                    Set, $50.00-75.00

*Mother Goose*, "Twin Winton, Made in Calif. USA © 1962." on bottom of
base. Snyder.                    $55.00-65.00

**Below:**  *Howard Johnson's Restaurant*, "Twin Winton USA."                    $750.00+

**Row 1:**    *Modern Head*, "Twin Winton © Calif. USA."                                    $250.00+

*Pot o' Candy*, "Twin Winton © Pasadena USA." Snyder.                    $25.00-35.00

*Two-Story House* salt or pepper shaker.                                Set, $35.00-45.00

*Two-Story House* cookie jar, unmarked.                                $125.00-150.00

*Two-Story House* salt or pepper shaker, mate above.                Set, $25.00-35.00

**Row 2:**    *Pot o' Cookies*, "Twin Winton" paper label on bottom. Snyder.        $25.00-30.00

*Pot* salt or pepper shaker, unmarked.                                Set, $18.00-22.00

*Pot o' Cookies*, unmarked.                                            $25.00-35.00

*Pot* salt and pepper shaker, mate above.                            Set, $18.00-22.00

*Pot o' Cookies*, unmarked. Snyder.                                    $20.00-25.00

There is also a canister set available in addition to the cookie jar, candy dish, and shakers. They are *Pot o' Flour, Pot o' Sugar, Pot o' Coffee, and Pot o' Tea.*

**Row 3:**    *Grandma,* stamped "Twin Winton El Monte, Calif."                    $75.00-95.00

The *Grandma,* marked "El Monte," can also be found marked "William H. Hirsch." Winton modeled this same *Grandma* for Alberta's Molds, and she can be found across the country in all types of finishes. The wood finish is the guide in separating the old from the new. No studio ceramist can effectively duplicate it.

*Grandma,* "Twin Winton Calif. – U.S.A. © 1962" on the bottom. Snyder.    $85.00-95.00

*Grandma's Cookies,* unmarked.                                        $45.00-55.00

**Below:**    *Wheelbarrow,* "Twin Winton © Calif. USA."                            $50.00-60.00

| | | |
|---|---|---:|
| **Row 2:** | *Potbellied Stove* salt or pepper shaker, unmarked. Snyder. | Set, $20.00-25.00 |
| | *Potbellied Stove* cookie jar, "Twin Winton Calif. USA." Wells. | $35.00-45.00 |
| | *Potbellied Stove* salt or pepper shaker, mate above. Snyder. | Set, $20.00-25.00 |
| | *Cop* salt or pepper shaker. "Winton Calif." on bottom. | Set, $25.00-35.00 |
| | *Cop* cookie jar, "Twin Winton © U.S.A." | $85.00-95.00 |
| | *Cop* salt or pepper shaker, mate above. | Set, $25.00-35.00 |
| **Row 2:** | *Elf* bank, "Twin Winton © Calif. USA." | $25.00-35.00 |
| | *Snail*, "Designed by Twin Winton Calif." | $125.00-150.00 |
| | *Child in Shoe* bank, unmarked. Snyder. | $25.00-35.00 |
| **Row 3:** | *Elf* salt or pepper shaker, "© Twin Winton © Calif. USA." | Set, $20.00-25.00 |
| | *Cookie Elf*, "Twin Winton © Calif. U.S.A." Snyder. | $35.00-45.00 |
| | *Elf* salt or pepper shaker, mate above. | Set, $20.00-25.00 |
| | *Elf* salt or pepper shaker, reproduction. "©Twin Winton Calif. U.S.A." The original mark can carry over onto a reproduction. Even if these shakers are not reproductions, the paint does not appear to be authentic. Snyder. | Set, $10.00-15.00 |
| | *Cookie Elf*, "Twin Winton © Calif. U.S.A." Snyder. | $30.00-40.00 |
| | *Elf* salt or pepper shaker, mate above. Snyder. | Set, $10.00-15.00 |
| **Below:** | *Cookie Time Clock*, unmarked, verified by Don Winton. | $55.00-65.00 |

**Row 1:**   *Fire Engine*, "Twin Winton © Calif. U.S.A." Snyder.            $50.00-60.00

               *Fire Engine*, "Twin Winton © Calif. U.S.A."            $40.00-50.00

**Row 2:**   *Cookie Cable Car*, unmarked. Snyder.            $55.00-65.00

               *Cook Stove*, unmarked. Snyder.            $35.00-45.00

**Row 3:**   *Barn*, unmarked. Snyder.            $50.00-60.00

               *Barn*, unmarked.            $30.00-40.00

               *Barn*, "Twin Winton" label. Snyder.            $40.00-50.00

**Below:**   *Dobbin* salt or pepper shaker, "Twin Winton Calif. USA."            Set, $35.00-45.00

               *Dobbin* bank, "Twin Winton © Calif. USA."            $25.00-35.00

               *Dobbin* salt or pepper shaker, mate above.            Set, $35.00-45.00

**Row 1:**   *Cookie Catcher*, unmarked. Snyder.                                   $45.00-55.00

*Child in Shoe*, "Twin Winton © Calif. U.S.A." Snyder.                 $35.00-45.00

**Row 2:**   *Barn* salt and pepper shakers, "Twin Winton." Snyder.        Set, $20.00-30.00

*Tea Sty*, "Twin Winton California USA."                                       $12.00-15.00

*Shack* napkin holder, unmarked. Snyder.                                  $15.00-20.00

*Persian Cat* ashtray, unmarked. Snyder.                                   $12.00-15.00

**Row 3:**   *Cookie Barn*, "Twin Winton California USA."                         $35.00-45.00

*Flour Stable*, "Twin Winton California USA."                             $25.00-35.00

*Sugar Dairy*, "Twin Winton California USA."                             $20.00-25.00

*Coffee Coop*, "Twin Winton California USA."                            $15.00-20.00

CAREFUL! There is a ceramic mold on the *Barn* canister set.

**Below:**   *Cereal Bowl*, "Twin Winton Pasadena" and "W."               $25.00-35.00

*Mug*, "Twin Winton" and "D."                                                  $15.00-25.00

**Row 1:**    *Ye Old Tea Bucket*, "©Twin Winton Calif" on back of band.     $15.00-20.00

           *Ye Old Salt Bucket* (Canister, not shaker), "Twin Winton Calif."     $10.00-15.00

           *Ye Old Cookie Bucket*, "Twin Winton © 59."     $30.00-35.00

           *Ye Old Salt and Pepper Buckets*, "Twin Winton, Calif."     Set, $18.00-22.00

           *Ye Old Salt and Pepper Buckets*, "Twin Winton, Calif."     Set, $18.00-22.00

**Row 2:**    *Ye Old Cookie Bucket*, "Twin Winton © 59."     $35.00-40.00

           *Ye Old Flour Bucket*, unmarked.     $30.00-35.00

           *Ye Old Sugar Bucket*, "Twin Winton Calif." on back of band.     $25.00-30.00

           *Ye Old Coffee Bucket* "Twin Winton Calif." on back of band.     $20.00-25.00

**Row 3:**    *Elf* candy jar, "Twin Winton © 63, Made in Calif. USA."     $25.00-35.00

           *Dog in Basket*, circular stamp "Twin Winton © El Monte, Calif."     $40.00-50.00

           *Kitten in Basket*, circular stamp "Twin Winton © El Monte, Calif.     $40.00-50.00

**Below:**    *Hillbilly Bank*, circular stamp "Twin Winton © 38, Made in USA."     $60.00-80.00

CAREFUL! There is a ceramic mold on the *Hillybilly Bank.*

**Row 1:**    *Frog* salt and pepper shakers, unmarked.          Set, $35.00-45.00

             *Turtle* candy jar, "Twin Winton Calif. USA © 63."         $40.00-50.00

             *Chipmunk* salt and pepper shakers, "Twin Winton Calif."    Set, $20.00-30.00

**Row 2:**    *Frog*, unmarked.          $65.00-75.00

             *Chipmunk* cookie jar, "Twin Winton Calif. USA."    $35.00-45.00

             *Elephant* candy jar, "Twin Winton Calif. USA."    $35.00-45.00

**Row 3:**    *Light House*, unmarked.          $200.00+

             *Ole King Cole*, "Twin Winton © Calif. USA."    $200.00-225.00

             *Magilla Gorilla*, "Twin Winton © San Juan Capistrano, Calif."    $300.00+

**Below:**    *Cookie Chef*, "Twin Winton © Calif. USA."    $150.00-175.00

**Row 1:**    *Ranger Bear* salt or pepper shaker, unmarked.    Set, $25.00-30.00

*Ranger Bear* bank, "Twin Winton Calif. U.S.A."    $35.00-45.00

*Ranger Bear* bank, "Twin Winton Calif. U.S.A." Snyder.    $35.00-45.00

*Ranger Bear* bank, "Twin Winton Calif. U.S.A."    $40.00-50.00

*Ranger Bear* salt or pepper shaker, mate above.    Set, $25.00-30.00

**Row 2:**    *Ranger Bear* wall pocket, unmarked.    $20.00-25.00

*Teddy Bear Talking Picture*, unmarked. Snyder.    $65.00-75.00

*Ranger Bear* spoon rest, unmarked.    $10.00-15.00

*Teddy Bear* salt and pepper shakers, unmarked.    Set, $35.00-45.00

**Row 3:**    *Teddy Bear*, unmarked.    $40.00-50.00

*Ranger Bear with Badge*, stamped "Twin Winton San Juan Capistrano." Snyder. $40.00-50.00

*Ranger Bear* planter, "Twin Winton © Calif. USA."    $15.00-20.00

**Below:**    *Hotei* salt or pepper shaker, unmarked. Darrow.    Set, $30.00-40.00

*Hotei* bank, "© Twin Winton Calif. USA." Darrow.    $40.00-50.00

*Hotei* cookie jar, "©Twin Winton Calif USa" Darrow.    $90.00-120.00

342

**Row 1:**  *Porky Pig*, "Twin Winton © Calif. USA."                                             $65.00-75.00

*Ranger Bear*, "Twin Winton © San Juan Capistrano Calif. USA."      $35.00-45.00

*Porky Pig*, "Twin Winton © Calif. USA."                                             $45.00-55.00

**Row 2:**  *Hotei* bank, "© Twin Winton Calif. USA."                                      $35.00-45.00

*Sailor Elephant*, "Twin Winton © Made in USA" impressed. Stamped
"Twin Winton San Juan Capistrano Calif. USA."                              $30.00-40.00

*Hotei* napkin holder, unmarked. Snyder.                                           $25.00-30.00

**Row 3:**  *Owl*, "Twin Winton © Calif. USA."                                                  $35.00-45.00

*Owl* salt or pepper shaker, "Twin Winton Calif."                      Set, $20.00-25.00

*Owl*, "Twin Winton © Calif. USA."                                                  $35.00-45.00

*Owl* salt or pepper shaker, mate above.                                   Set, $20.00-25.00

*Owl,* "Twin Winton © Calif. USA" incised into bottom of base. Stamped
"Twin Winton San Juan Capistrano."                                               $35.00-45.00

**Below:**  *Owl*, "Twin Winton © Calif. USA."                                                  $35.00-45.00

Cookie jars sold for $3.00 wholesale in the 1965-66 catalogs.

**Row 1:**    *Gun Fighter Rabbit* salt or pepper shaker, single, "Twin Winton Calif."    Each, $10.00-15.00

*Sailor Mouse* salt or pepper shaker, single, unmarked.    Each, $10.00-15.00

*Cop*, collector's series, "Twin Winton Calif. USA."    $100.00-125.00

*Owl* salt or pepper shaker, single, "Twin Winton Calif."    Each, $10.00-15.00

*Teddy Bear* salt or pepper shaker, single, unmarked.    Each, $10.00-15.00

**Row 2:**    *Elephant* planter, "Twin Winton © Calif. USA."    $20.00-25.00

*Squirrel* salt and pepper shakers, unmarked.    Set, $20.00-30.00

*Turtle* candy jar, "Twin Winton © Calif. USA."    $40.00-50.00

**Row 3:**    *Nut* salt and pepper shakers, "Twin Winton © Calif. USA."    Set, $20.00-30.00

*Raccoon* lamp, "Twin Winton © Calif. USA."    $100.00-125.00

*Pirate Fox* salt or pepper shaker, single. "Twin Winton Calif USA." Snyder.    Each, $10.00-15.00

*Dobbin* napkin holder, unmarked. Snyder.    $25.00-35.00

**Below:**    Display plaque that was included in all original shipments.    $125.00-150.00

**Row 1:**  *Lamb* salt and pepper shaker, unmarked.                                    Set, $20.00-30.00

*Lamb* napkin holder, unmarked.                                          $20.00-30.00

*Lamb* spoon rest, unmarked. Snyder.                                     $15.00-20.00

*Lamb* bank, "Twin Winton Calif."                                        $20.00-25.00

**Row 2:**  *Hen on Nest*, "Twin Winton © Calif. USA."                           $45.00-55.00

*Cookie Guard*, unmarked, but verified by Don Winton.                    $65.00-75.00

*Hen on Basket* salt and pepper shakers, "Twin Winton © Calif. USA."    Set, $20.00-30.00

**Row 3:**  *Coffee Grinder,* unmarked.                                          $100.00-125.00

*Pirate Fox*, "Twin Winton © Calif. USA."                                $45.00-55.00

*Bambi* napkin holder, unmarked.                                         $20.00-25.00

**Below:**  *Ma* and *Pa* mugs, Stamped "Twin Winton © Ceramics, Pasadena Calif."
Duke.                                                                    Each, $35.00-45.00

**Row 1:**     *Cow* napkin holder, unmarked.       $35.00-45.00

                *Cow* creamer, unmarked.       $35.00-45.00

                *Tommy Turtle*, stamped "Twin Winton © San Juan Capistrano Calif. USA."       $65.00-75.00

                *Happy Bull* salt and pepper shakers.       Set, $20.00-30.00

**Row 2:**     *Cow* salt or pepper shaker, unmarked.       Set, $30.00-35.00

                *Dog* salt and pepper shaker, "Twin Winton © Calif. USA."       Set, $35.00-45.00

                *Dog* wall pocket, "Twin Winton © California USA."       $35.00-45.00

                *Kitten* salt and pepper shakers, unmarked.       Set, $20.00-30.00

                *Cow* salt or pepper shaker, mate above.       Set, $30.00-35.00

**Row 3:**     *Churn* salt or pepper shaker, unmarked.       Set, $25.00-35.00

                *Cookie Churn*, "Twin Winton Calif. USA."       $65.00-75.00

                *Churn* salt or pepper shaker, mate above.       Set, $25.00-35.00

                *Dog with Bow*, "Twin Winton © San Juan Capistrano Calif. USA."       $100.00-125.00

**Below:**     *Hillbilly Lamp*, "Twin Winton Pasadena, Calif – M." Snyder.       $125.00-150.00

**Row 1:**     *Mouse* salt and pepper shakers, "Twin Winton Calif. USA."     Set, $35.00-45.00

*Hen on Basket* salt and pepper shakers (The red trim has probably been added to match someone's kitchen.), "Twin Winton Calif. USA."     Set, $30.00-35.00

*Ranger Bear* salt and pepper shakers, "Twin Winton Calif. USA."     Set, $20.00-30.00

*Butler* salt and pepper shakers, unmarked.     Set, $35.00-45.00

**Row 2:**     *Indian* salt and pepper shakers, (We do not feel these shakers have original paint.) "Twin Winton Calif. U.S.A." Snyder.     Set, $20.00-30.00

*Lamb* salt and pepper shakers, unmarked.     Set, $20.00-30.00

*Noah's Ark*, "Twin Winton © Calif. USA."     $35.00-45.00

CAREFUL! There is a ceramic mold of *Noah's Ark*; we question the authenticity of this jar.

*Donkey* salt and pepper shakers, "Twin Winton Calif. USA."     Set, $30.00-35.00

*Indian* salt and pepper shakers (original wood-finish), "Twin Winton Calif. USA."     Set, $30.00-35.00

**Row 3:**     *Friar Tuck* salt and pepper shakers, "Twin Winton © Calif. USA."     Set, $20.00-30.00

*Porky Pig* napkin holder, unmarked. Snyder.     $35.00-45.00

*Porky Pig* bank, "Twin Winton © Calif USA."     $35.00-45.00

*Sailor Elephant* bank, "Twin Winton © Pasadena."     $35.00-45.00

*Sailor Elephant* dime bank (same size as shaker), "Twin Winton Calif." Snyder.     $20.00-25.00

*Sailor Elephant* salt or pepper shaker, single, "Twin Winton Calif." Snyder.     Each, $10.00-15.00

Salt and pepper shakers sold wholesale for $1.50 per pair in the 1965-66 catalogs.

**Row 1:**  *Dutch Girl* spoon rest, unmarked. Snyder.  $20.00-25.00

*Dutch Girl* napkin holder, "A.D." Snyder.  $20.00-25.00

*Dutch Girl* bank, "Twin Winton © Calif. USA."  $35.00-45.00

**Row 2:**  *Sailor Elephant* spoon rest, unmarked. Snyder.  $20.00-25.00

*Sailor Elephant* talking picture, unmarked.  $65.00-75.00

*Sailor Elephant* napkin holder, unmarked.  $20.00-25.00

**Row 3:**  *Kitten* salt or pepper shaker, single, unmarked.  Each, $10.00-15.00

*Kitten* bank, "Twin Winton Calif. USA."  $35.00-45.00

*Kitten* spoon rest, unmarked.  $20.00-25.00

*Kitten* bank, "Twin Winton Calif. USA."  $35.00-45.00

*Lion* salt and pepper shakers, unmarked.  Set, $25.00-35.00

**Below:**  *Hillbilly Lamp*, "Twin Winton Pasadena, Calif. – M" Bass.  $100.00-125.00

355

The Hillbilly line was produced from 1946 through 1950 (apparently this was the glazed line, not the wood-finish).

**Row 1:**  *Hillbilly* tankard, "TW Pasadena."  $30.00-40.00

*Hillbilly* pitcher, "TW Pasadena."  $50.00-65.00

*Hillbilly* pitcher, "TW Pasadena."  $50.00-65.00

*Hillbilly* tankard, "TW Pasadena."  $30.00-40.00

**Row 2:**  *Hillbilly* mug, "TW Pasadena."  $15.00-20.00

*Hillbilly* mug, "TW Pasadena."  $15.00-20.00

*Rail Fence for Pouring Spouts,* obvious markings.  $100.00-125.00

*Hillbilly Pouring Spouts* four, unmarked. Bass.  Each, $10.00-15.00

*Hillbilly* mug, "TW Pasadena."  $15.00-20.00

*Hillbilly Punch Cup,* "TW Pasadena."  $8.00-10.00

**Row 3:**  *Hillbilly Outhouse,* unmarked.  $300.00+

The wood-finish Hillbilly ice buckets are featured in the 1965 and 1966 catalogs.

*With Jug,* Hillbilly ice bucket, "Twin Winton Made in Calif. USA © 1962."  $100.00-125.00

*Suspenders,* Hillbilly ice bucket, "Twin Winton © Calif. USA."  $100.00-125.00

**Below:**  *Bottoms Up,* Hillbilly ice bucket, "Twin Winton © Calif. USA."  $100.00-125.00

*Bathing,* Hillbilly ice bucket, "Twin Winton, Made in Calif. USA © 1962."  $100.00-125.00

Hillbilly ice buckets were $5.00 each in the 1965-66 catalogs with the exception of *Bathing,* which was $6.00.

**Row 1:**   *Walrus,* "Twin Winton © Calif. USA."        $150.00-175.00

           *Duck* salt or pepper shaker, "Twin Winton Calif."        Set, $35.00-45.00

           *Rubber Ducky,* "Twin Winton, San Juan Capistrano, Calif. USA." Braly.        $100.00-125.00

           *Duck* salt or pepper shaker, mate above.        Set, $20.00-30.00

           *Smiling Bear with Badge,* unmarked. Braly.        $40.00-50.00

**Row 2:**   *Barn,* unmarked. Braly.        $35.00-45.00

           *Apple,* unmarked. Braly.        $65.00-75.00

           *Hotei,* unmarked. Braly.        $65.00-75.00

**Row 3:**   *Tug Boat,* unmarked.        $85.00-95.00

           *Bambi,* "Twin Winton © Calif. USA."        $65.00-75.00

           *Cookie Catcher,* "Twin Winton, Pasadena, Calif." Bass.        $85.00-95.00

**Below:**   *Hillbilly Lamp,* "Twin Winton, Pasadena." Bass.        $100.00-125.00

**Row 1:**   *Cowboy* ashtray, "Open Range, Twin Winton, Pasadena, with a *T* over *W* brand, *B*." Snyder.                                                                    $40.00-45.00

*Cowboy* ashtray, "Open Range, Twin Winton, Pasadena, with a *T* over *W* brand, *B*." Snyder.                                                                    $40.00-45.00

*Saddle* salt or pepper shaker, "Twin Winton Pasadena." Snyder.                   Set, $20.00-25.00

*Steer* coaster, "Twin Winton Pasadena."                                                           $10.00-15.00

*Saddle* salt or pepper shaker, mate above.                                                    Set, $20.00-25.00

**Row 2:**   *Cigarette Box with Match Barrel*, "TW Pasadena."                                    $50.00-60.00

*Bathing Hillbilly* container, "Twin Winton Ceramics Pasadena, Calif." Snyder.   $20.00-25.00

*Hillbilly* salt or pepper shaker, unmarked. Snyder.                                      Set, $20.00-25.00

*Hillbilly* pretzel bowl, "B."                                                                         $30.00-40.00

*Hillbilly* salt or pepper shaker, mate above.                                               Set, $20.00-25.00

*Hillbilly* ashtray, "Clem." Snyder.                                                                  $40.00-45.00

**Row 3:**   *School Boy*, stamped "Twin Winton © Ceramics, Made in Pasadena, Calif."   $25.00-35.00

*Fishing Boy*, stamped "Twin Winton © Ceramics, Made in Pasadena, Calif."     $30.00-40.00

*Figurine Display Plaque*, "TWINTON © 1972- T-21." Snyder.                            $75.00-95.00

*Maid Marian* salt or pepper shaker from *Famous Lovers Series*, "Don Winton, R."                                                                                            Set, $75.00-95.00

*Robin Hood* salt or pepper shaker, mate to *Maid Marian* above.                 Set, $75.00-95.00

# Ungemach

Ungemach Pottery was located in Roseville, OH, from 1937 through 1984. There was a close association between the Ungemach family and A.N. Allen of American Bisque. Their work is similar, close enough for cookie jar collectors to mistakenly identify Ungemach jars as American Bisque. On page 215 of *Book I* is a jar commonly referred to as *Candy Baby*. We now know this jar is actually called *Puppet* and was produced by Ungemach rather than American Bisque.

Two of the jars on the bottom row of page 213 have also been positively identified as Ungemach. The *Deer* is called *Fawn*. The *Clown Head* is not *Pinky Lee*, as we suspected, but Ungemach's *Happy Clown*. We feel sure the *Poodle* in the center of the row is also Ungemach's, but it was not included in the 1958 catalog sheet discovered by Harvey Duke. There is a *Cat* with tail curled over the lid, similar in looks to the *Poodle*, which was also believed to be American Bisque. It, too, is Ungemach.

# Vandor

Vandor is an importer/distributor, based in Salt Lake City, UT. Vandor was 35 years old in 1992.

**Row 1:**   *Mona Lisa* bank, stamped "Vandor 1992 Pelzman Designs, Made in Sri Lanka." Snyder.                                           $20.00-25.00

*Mona Lisa* salt and pepper shaker, stamped "1992 Pelzman Designs, Made in Sri Lanka."                                             Set, $16.00-20.00

*Mona Lisa* cookie jar, "Vandor 1992 Pelzman Designs, Made in Sri Lanka."     $50.00-55.00

*Mona Lisa* teapot, stamped "Vandor 1992 Pelzman Designs, Made in Sri Lanka." Snyder.                                                      $36.00-40.00

**Row 2:**   *Baseball* bank, unmarked, paper label missing. Snyder.                        $25.00-30.00

*Ball and Bat* salt and pepper shakers, "Vandor © 1991, Made in Taiwan on paper label. Snyder.                                               Set, $16.00-20.00

*Baseball* cookie jar, "The Great American Game © 1991 Pelzman Designs, Taiwan, Vandor."                                                  $50.00-55.00

*Cowboy* salt and pepper shakers, "Vandor © 1991 Made in Taiwan" on paper label. Snyder.                                                       Set, $16.00-20.00

*Cowboy* cookie jar, stamped "American Frontier © 1991 Pelzman Designs, Taiwan, Vandor."                                                   $55.00-60.00

The entire Crocagator line has been discontinued.

**Row 3:**   *Crocagator with Parasol* salt and pepper shaker, "Vandor" in mold, "Made in Korea" paper label. Snyder.                                    Set, $16.00-20.00

*Crocagator* teapot, "Vandor" in mold, "Made in Korea" paper label. Snyder.   $30.00-35.00

*Crocagator Shoes* salt and pepper shakers, "Vandor" in mold, "Made in Korea" on paper label. Snyder.                                              Set, $15.00-20.00

*Crocagator* cookie jar.                                                                  $35.00-40.00

*Crocagator* bank, "Vandor in mold, "Made in Korea" paper label. Snyder.      $16.00-20.00

*Bellhop* salt and pepper shakers. "Vandor" in mold, "Made in Korea" paper label. Snyder.                                                       Set, $16.00-20.00

*Swamp* soap dish, "Vandor" in mold, "Made in Korea" paper label. Snyder.     $16.00-20.00

*Pages 364 and 365 show 1989 Vandor Catalog sheets.*

*50's*

**COOKIES**

1307
10" x 12"

1386
8½" x 8"

1315

1311

1310

1316

1387

# Cowmen Mooranda

1852

1853

1856

1851
S & P

1858

1850

CHA CHA CHA

MUG

COWMEN MOORANDA

1859

1069

1860

1854

# Vallona Starr

The Peter Pumpkin Eater in *Book I* has been found marked two ways, Vallona Starr and Gilner. Lois Lehner lists Triangle Studios/Vallona Starr first in Los Angeles, then in El Monte, CA through 1951. We now know Gilner burned in 1957, so it is likely Gilner either purchased some molds or was a part of Triangle Studios/ Vallona Starr.

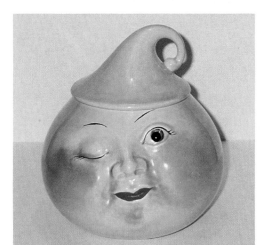

**Left:** *Winky* (name assigned by Vallona Starr), "Vallona Starr 302 © 51." Clyde and Takasugi.    $150.00-175.00

# Walt Disney

Walt Disney jars remain among the top three all-time favorites with cookie jar collectors. They actually wield a double whammy because they are characters and they bear the Disney name. Who could resist? The demand for Disney jars does not wane. In fact they appear to be even more popular among collectors. If a jar appears marked "Walt Disney," it automatically becomes a must for any collection. They simply do not decline in value.

**Row 1:** *Winnie the Pooh's Treats*, "©MCMLXIV Walt Disney Productions" on the bottom of the jar. Snyder.    $85.00-95.00

*Winnie the Pooh*, "© Disney, Mexico" on bottom of the base. Snyder.    $50.00-60.00

*Pinocchio* bank, stamped "Walt Disney © Productions, DERECHOS RESERVADOS, CERAMIC DE CUERNAVACA, MEXICO." Paper label above coin slot, "AHORO CONSTANCIA BIENESTAR, SISTEMA BANCOS DE COMERCIO."    $500.00+

**Row 2:** *Mickey's Wonderful Time for Cookies*, California Originals, "© 1980 505 Walt Disney Productions." Snyder.    $70.00-90.00

*Down on the Farm Mickey*, California Originals, "Walt Disney Productions 860."    $70.00-90.00

*Mickey Makes Music*, "© Walt Disney Productions." Snyder.    $50.00-60.00

**Row 3:** *Bambi*, antiqued version, "© Walt Disney Prod. USA 868."    $275.00-300.00

*Aladdin*, Burger King premium, "©Disney, Mfg. for Burger King Corp."    $3.00-5.00

*Genie with Lamp*, in mold "© Disney, Treasure Craft"    $50.00-60.00

*3 – D Mickey* salt or pepper shaker, "© Walt Disney Productions."    Set, $15.00-18.00

*3 – D Mickey* cookie jar, "Treasure Craft, Made in USA" inside lid, stamped "© Walt Disney Productions" on unglazed bottom of base.    $40.00-50.00

**Row 1:**  *Roly Dalmatian* salt or pepper shaker, "TIC © Disney USA."  Set, $15.00-18.00

*Roly Dalmatian* water pitcher, "Treasure Craft © Disney, Made in USA" on bottom.  $35.00-40.00

*Roly Dalmatian* teapot, "Treasure Craft © Disney, Made in USA" on bottom.  $25.00-35.00

*Roly Dalmatian* salt or pepper shaker, mate above.  Set, $15.00-18.00

**Row 2:**  *Gourmet Mickey*, "© Disney, Treasure Craft, Made in USA."  $30.00-40.00

*Mrs. Potts*, "© Disney, Treasure Craft, Made in USA."  $50.00-60.00

*Mrs. Potts* teapot, "Treasure Craft © Disney, Made in USA" embossed lettering. Snyder.  $40.00-45.00

**Row 3:**  *Bull Dog Café*, "Treasure Craft © Disney, Made in USA"  $65.00-75.00

*Pinocchio*, "© Disney, Treasure Craft, Made in USA" inside lid. "© Disney, Treasure Craft, Made in USA" on base.  $50.00-60.00

**Below:**  *Snow White*, California Originals (Fred's 1993 birthday gift), "© Walt Disney Prod. 866 USA."  $500.00+

**Row 1:** *Alice in Wonderland* salt or pepper shaker, undecorated blank by Regal China, "© Walt Disney Productions" across back of skirt. "Alice in Wonderland" on the bottom. Each, $150.00-175.00

*Dopey* lamp, paper label "© Walt Disney, Dopey, Bailey Corporation, Cleveland, Ohio." $200.00-225.00

*Tweedle Dee-Dum* salt or pepper shaker, undecorated blank by Regal China, "Walt Disney Productions ©" on back. "Tweedle Dee-Dum" on bottom. Single, $175.00-200.00

**Row 2:** *King of Hearts* pitcher by Regal China, "Walt Disney © Productions, King of Hearts." $325.00-375.00

*Mad Hatter* teapot (minus lid) by Regal China, "© Walt Disney Productions, Mad Hatter." With lid, $600.00-750.00

*White Rabbit* covered sugar by Regal China, "Walt Disney © Productions, White Rabbit" on bottom. $350.00-375.00

*Alice in Wonderland* planter, "Alice in Wonderland © Walt Disney Productions." $100.00-125.00

**Row 3:** *Big Al* bank, "Walt Disney Productions" on back. Snyder. $25.00-35.00

*Big Al* cookie jar, "© Disney" on back. $50.00-60.00

*Big Al* bank, stamped "© Walt Disney Productions." On paper label. "Made in Taiwan" $20.00-25.00

**Below:** *Dumbo*, "© Disney, Mexico." Was sold in Disney theme parks. $65.00-75.00

*Mickey Mouse in Car* bank, "Walt Disney Productions." $20.00-25.00

# Wisecarver Originals

The artistic skills of Rick Wisecarver continue to grow in his Roseville, OH studio. Rick is probably best known in the cookie jar community for his Black Americana jars. In 1992 he branched out, to bring life to classic fairy tale characters.

**Row 1:**  *Indian Maiden*, "Wihoa's Limited No. 10, 1989, Rick Wisecarver." Discontinued. $125.00-150.00

*Geronimo*, "Chiricahua Warrior, Old Age 1905, Wihoa's Original Cookie Classic, Roseville, Ohio No-1-89, Rick Wisecarver, 1989 R Sims" on back of base. $125.00-150.00

*Swan*, "©, ® G931-0999" on bottom. "Wihoa's Cookie Classic by Rick Wisecarver 1983 RS" on back of base. Discontinued. Rare, less than 50 ever produced. $150.00-175.00

**Row 2:**  *Indian Chief*, standing, "RS Original Wihoa's Limited 1985, Color Test No. 3, Rick Wisecarver." Discontinued. First Indian jar done, less than 50 ever produced. Braly. $200.00-250.00

*Jer-see II & Jer-see IV*, "Jer-see II and IV, Wihoa's Original Cookie Classic by Rick Wisecarver, Special No. 1, Sept. 1990, R Sims" on back of base, "©, ® G-931-0999" on bottom of base. *Only* Jersey cow ever produced. $175.00-200.00

*Indian Chief*, standing, "Roseville, Ohio, Wihoa's Original Cookie Classic." Discontinued. $200.00-250.00

**Row 3:**  *Indian Chief*, sitting, "Roseville, Ohio, Wihoa's Original Cookie Classic 1989." Discontinued. $125.00-150.00

*Tepee*, "Wihoa's Cookie Classic by Rick Wisecarver, Roseville, Oh, No 1 89, Richard Sims." Discontinued. $150.00-175.00

*Raccoon*, "© Wihoa's Original Cookie Classic by Rick Wisecarver, Richard Sims 10/89, Roseville, O 43777" on bottom of base. $100.00-125.00

**Below:**  *Display Plaque*, "Rick Wisecarver Original Cookie Classics Hand Sculptured - Handpainted Quality NOT Quantity. $40.00-50.00

**Row 1:**  *Hill Folk*, "© 89, Wihoa's Original Cookie Classic by Rick Wisecarver, Rosevill O 43777, R Sims" on bottom of the base. "Wihoa's Cookie Classic by Rick Wisecarver, Original" on the back of the base.  $150.00-175.00

*Cow and Calf*, "Wihoa's Cookie Classic by Rick Wisecarver #31, 1991, RS."  $125.00-150.00

**Row 2:**  *Beauty and the Beast*, "Wihoa's Cookie Classic by Rick Wisecarver, R Sims, No 14, 1992."  $150.00-175.00

*Covered Bridge*, "Wihoa's Cookie Classic © by Rick Wisecarver, R Sims, Roseville, O 43777" on the back of the base. Discontinued. Rare.  $200.00-225.00

*Red Riding Hood*, "Wihoa's Cookie Classic by Rick Wisecarver, No. 1, 1991 RS Color Test ® G-931-0999." Limited edition of 150.  $250.00+

**Row 3:**  *Mill*, "Rick Wisecarver, Wihoa's Original, #1, 1990 © Cookie Classic by Rick Wisecarver, R Sims, Roseville, Oh" on the back of the vase. Discontinued. Rare, less than ten ever produced.  $150.00-200.00

*Miss America* (originally designed to be a Black Miss America), "© ®G931-0999" on bottom of base. "Special one-of-a-kind, Wihoa's Cookie Classic by Rick Wisecarver" on the back of the lid. Libby Roerig.  $200.00-225.00

*Rumpelstiltskin*, "Rumpelstiltskin, Rick Wisecarver #20 1992RS" on the back of the lid.  $150.00-175.00

**Below:**  *Little Red Riding Hood*, "Rick Wisecarver Cookie Classic R Sims, September 1, 92, 'One of a Kind,' Happy Birthday to Joyce Roerig."  $350.00+

# Contributing Collectors, Consultants, and Dealers

**A Company of 2 (David Brdecko)**
P O Box 35851
Albuquerque, NM 87176

**Adrian Pottery (Randy and Stephanie Adrian)**
2219 Oakview Dr
Jefferson City, MO 65109

**Alfano Art Pottery (Sam and Denise Alfano)**
36180 Henry Gaines Road
Pearl River, LA 70452

**A Little Company (Michael Buonaiuto & Shelley Tincher Buonaiuto)**
131 Sam Street
Santa Fe, NM 87501

**Appleman, Glenn**
188 17th Street
Brooklyn, NY 11215

**Banuelos, Helen**
204 Palmyra
Houston, TX 77022

**Beggs, Richard (Master of Restoration)**
9553 White Tail Trail
Kernersville, NC 27284

**Bell Captain (Gerald Meyer)**
3428 Leora St.
Simi Valley, CA 93062

**Berry, Carol**
South Carolina

**Burnette, Carolyn**
Georgia

**Carol's Collectibles (Doug & Carol Irwin)**
47 S Lake Drive
Antioch, CA 94509

**Cauwells, Dianne (Black Americana)**
Tennessee

**Cavanagh, Henry**
679 Lapla Road
Kingston, NY 12401

**Charlie's Collectibles (Charlie and Rose Snyder)**
Rt. 4, Box 79
Independence, KS 67301

**Clyde and Takasugi**
2947 Hollyridge Drive
Los Angeles, CA 90068

**Cookie Jar Antiques (Keith and Judy Lytle)**
99 Greensboro Way
Antioch, CA 94509

**Corl's Kiln (Shirley Corl)**
2978 W Deckerville
Caro, MI 48723

**Darrow, Diana**
RR 1, 1726 Rt. 13
DeRuyter, NY 13052

**Desert Notions**
832 N Main Drive
Apache Junction, AZ 85220

**Devine, Joe (Royal Copley)**
P O Box 883
Council Bluffs, IA 51502

**Dorian, Mark J. (Master of Restoration)**
101 W. Olive
Fresno, CA 93728

**Duke, Harvey (Pottery Expert, Consultant)**
115 Montague St
Brooklyn, NY 11201

**Essentially Cookie Jars-n-Stuff (Nancy Spruill)**
P O Box 8742
Virginia Beach, VA 23450

**Erwin Pottery (Negatha Peterson)**
1219 N Main
Erwin, TN 37650

**Firestone, Glenn & Sherry**
10106 SW 126th Street
Miami, FL 33176

**Giles, Robert and Linda**
3530 Autumn Walk Drive
Riverside, California 92503

**Grace, Shirley**
46835 Auberry Rd
Auberry, CA 93602

**Guffey, Rich and Linda**
2004 Fiat Court
El Cajon, CA 92019

**Honchar, George and Barbara**
P O Box 1800
Greenwood Lake, NY 10925

**James, JD and Pat**
P O Box 1005
Buckeye Lake, OH 43008

**Janet's Jars (Janet Wilson)**
518 West Overland
Scottsdale, NE 69361

**Jazz'e Junque (Mercedes DiRenzo)**
3831 N Lincoln Ave
Chicago, IL 60613

**Jean's House of Cookie Jars (Bob & Jean Kaulbach)**
Rt. 8 Box 320
Joplin, MO 64804

**J.C. Miller (Jerry and Clarice Miller)**
244 S Athenian
Wichita, KS 67213

**Jessen, Jack and Carol (Dealers)**
215 Dorseyville Road
Pittsburgh, PA 15215

**Johnson, Steve (Little Red Riding Hood)**
4003 Jefferson Street
Sioux City, IA 51108

**Judy Posner Collectibles (Judy Posner)**
RD 1, Box 273
Effort, PA 18330

**Keefauver Pat**
939 W. Badger Pass Lane
Orange, California 92665

**K. Wolfe Studio (Kathy Wolfe)**
3351 Walnut Lake Road
West Bloomfield, MI 48232

**Lichtenstein, Dr. Bruce (Brayton Laguna)**
53 Daffodil Lane
Wantagh, NY 11793

**Lindberg, Glen and Joanne (McCoy)**
79 Lexington Drive
Metuchen, NJ 08840

**Mangus, Jim and Bev (Shawnee authors)**
5147 Broadway NE
Louisville, OH 44641

**McCoy Pottery (Roger Jensen)**
212 S Gateway
Rockwood, TN 37854

**Memories of Mama® (Bill and Diane Goodin)**
910 W 6th Street, Dept. R
Sand Springs, OK 74063

**Mincks, Lavonna**
South Carolina

**The New Collection of Rose (Gary and Rose Saxby)**
512 W Washington
Warren, IL 61087

**Not Just Cookie Jars (Don and Katherine Braly)**
18210 Bamwood
Houston, TX 77090

**Okamoto, Michele**
1301 Bent Trail Circle
Southlake, TX 76092

**Patton, Brenda L.**
1525 N Wycoff Avenue
Bremerton, WA 98312-2805

**Potter, Mary**
19669 Sequoia
Cerritos, CA 90701

**Pottery Plus (David Shupp)**
2266 W Giles Road
N Mushegon, MI 49445

**Prestwood, Dewey and Chiquita (McCoy)**
120 Echo Drive
Lenoir, NC 28645

**Rose, Jack and Karen**
10200 E 87th Street
Raytown, MO 64138

**Shawnee Pottery Collector's Club (Pamela Curran)**
P O Box 713
New Smyrna Beach, FL 32170-0713

**Supnick, Mark and Ellen**
8524 NW 2nd Street
Coral Springs, FL 33071

**Timmerman, Herb and Donna**
475 Meadowbrook Dr, Apt. 104
West Bend, WI 53095-2470

**Tomorrow's Antiques Today (Sylvia Tompkins – Novelty Salt and Pepper Shakers Club)**
25-C Center Drive
Lancaster, PA 17601

**The Twins Antiques & Collectibles (Doris McClanahan and Phyllis Hefley)**
P O Box 425
Wayne City, IL 62895

**Vanderbilt, Duane and Janice (Shawnee Authors)**
4040 Westover Drive
Indianapolis, IN 46268

**Walker, Bunny**
P O Box 502
Bucyrus, OH 44820

**Wallick, Corrine**
5060 Via de Amalfi
Boca Raton, FL 33496

**Wayne's Collectibles (Wayne Bass)**
12452 E 224 Street
Hawaiian Garden, CA 90716-1718

**Wells, Lee Roy and Shirley**
RR 1 Box 170
Exeter, Mo 65647

**Williams, George D, III**
2000 Regency Pky, Suite 281
Cary, NC 27511

**Wise, Janice (Collector/dealer)**
415 W. Walnut
El Segundo, CA 90245

**Wisecarver Cookie Classics (Rick Wisecarver)**
42 Maple Street
Roseville, OH 43777

**Wooldridge, Juarine**
RR 1, Box 1304
Cassville, MO 65625

# Bibliography

Chipman, Jack, *Collector's Encyclopedia of California Pottery*. Collector Books, Paducah, Kentucky.

Curran, Pam, *Shawnee Pottery Collector's Club*, New Smyrna Beach, Florida.

Huxford, Sharon and Bob, *The Collector's Encyclopedia of McCoy Pottery*. Collector Books, Paducah, Kentucky.

Lehner, Lois, *Lehner's Encyclopedia of U.S. Marks on Pottery, Porcelain & Clay*. Collector Books, Paducah, Kentucky.

Nichols, Harold, *McCoy Cookie Jars, From the First to the Last*. Nichols Enterprises, Ames, Iowa.

Roerig, Joyce Herndon, *Cookie Jarrin'*, **The** *Cookie Jar Newsletter*. Walterboro, South Carolina.

Webster, Roy, *Under A Buttermilk Moon*. August House, Little Rock, Arkansas.

Westfall, Ermagene. *An Illustrated Value Guide to Cookie Jars, Books I and II*. Collector Books, Paducah, Kentucky.

# Additional Sources

Curran, Pam. *Shawnee Pottery Collector's Club*, P.O. Box 173, New Smyrna Beach, Florida 93728.

Duke, Harvey. *Hall China Current Price Guide Update*, $8.50; *Superior Quality Hall China*, $16.45; *Hall Two*, $16.45, *Stangl Pottery*, $22.45. ELO Books, Box 020627, Brooklyn, New York 11202. *The Official Price Guide to Pottery and Porcelain*, $12.95 + shipping, call 1-800-733-3000.

Hull, Joan Gray. *HULL The Heavenly Pottery*. 1376 Nevada SW, Huron, South Dakota 57350.

Lynch, Kathy. *Our McCoy Matters*, P O Box 14255, Parkville, Missouri 64152.

Mangus, Jim and Bev. *Shawnee Pottery, An Identification & Value Guide*, Collector Books, Paducah, Kentucky. Call 1-800-626-5420.

Sanford, Steve and Martha. *The Guide to Brush-McCoy Pottery*, 230 Harrison Avenue, Campbell, California 95008.

Thornburg, Irene. Novelty Salt and Pepper Shakers Club, 581 Joy Road, Battle Creek, Michigan 49017.

Vanderbilt, Duane and Janice. *The Collector's Guide to Shawnee Pottery*. Collector Books, Paducah, Kentucky. Call 1-800-626-5420.

# Pottery Restoration

Beggs, Richard 9553 White Tail Trail, Kernersville, North Carolina 27284.

Dorian, Mark J. 101 W. Olive, Fresno, California 93728.

## M

# Schroeder's
# ANTIQUES
## Price Guide

. . . is the #1 best-selling antiques &
collectibles value guide on the market
today, and here's why . . .

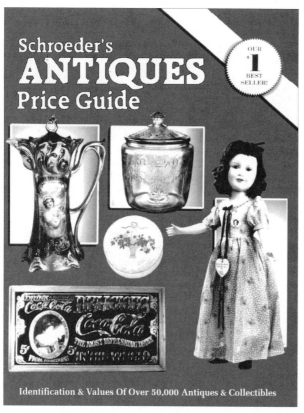

**8½ x 11, 608 Pages, $12.95**

- *More than 300 advisors, well-known dealers, and top-notch collectors work together with our editors to bring you accurate information regarding pricing and identification.*

- *More than 45,000 items in almost 500 categories are listed along with hundreds of sharp original photos that illustrate not only the rare and unusual, but the common, popular collectibles as well.*

- *Each large close-up shot shows important details clearly. Every subject is represented with histories and background information, a feature not found in any of our competitors' publications.*

- *Our editors keep abreast of newly-developing trends, often adding several new categories a year as the need arises.*

---

If it merits the interest of today's collector, you'll find it in *Schroeder's*. And you can feel confident that the information we publish is up to date and accurate. Our advisors thoroughly check each category to spot inconsistencies, listings that may not be entirely reflective of market dealings, and lines too vague to be of merit. Only the best of the lot remains for publication.

Without doubt, you'll find
**SCHROEDER'S ANTIQUES PRICE GUIDE**
the only one to buy for
reliable information and values.

**COLLECTOR BOOKS**
*A Division of Schroeder Publishing Co., Inc.*